# School governors: leaders or followers?

Edited by
Angela Thody

LONGMAN

*Published by* Longman Information and Reference,
Longman Group Limited, 6th Floor, Westgate House, The High,
Harlow, Essex CM20 1YR, England and Associated Companies
throughout the world.



A catalogue record for this book is available from The British Library

ISBN 0-582-25329-2



Typeset by Fakenham Photosetting Ltd, Fakenham, Norfolk
Printed by Redwood Books, Trowbridge, Wilts.

# Contents

# Contributors

**Angela Thody** is Reader in Management at the University of Luton. She has been involved in training school governors since 1984, has researched and lectured nationally and internationally in school governance and has published numerous articles and books including *Moving to Management: School Governors in the 1990s* (Fulton, 1992). She was a school governor for seven years (until 1993) when she decided that writing about governance was marginally easier than being a governor. She is currently researching governors from the business community.

**Charles Batteson** lectures on initial and in-service teacher education programmes at Lancaster University. He previously taught in South London.

**Kevin Brehony** is Senior Lecturer in Education at the University of Reading where he teaches Qualitative Research Methods on the Faculty of Education's Research Student Training Programme, convenes an Early Years Research Group and is director of the Education and Society MA programme. Prior to entering academic life he was a primary school teacher in the West Midlands and then a research student at the Open University. He was awarded his doctorate in historical sociology in 1987. From 1988 until 1993 he was co-director, with Professor Rosemary Deem from Lancaster University, of the ESRC funded 'Reforming School Governing Bodies' project. He has been a school governor and chair of governors in a primary school and is currently Treasurer of the British Sociological Association.

**Stephen Brigley** is research officer in the School of Management at Bath University and a member of the National Executive of the Campaign for State Education. He has previously taught in schools, colleges and university education departments. He has researched school governance for his doctoral thesis and for the Leverhulme project, 'Parents as School Governors'. His recent publications cover topics related to the government and management of schools, social and moral education and issues of research methodology.

**Denise Syndercombe-Court** is a university lecturer who lives and works in East London where she is also a school governor.

**Anne Curtis** is a researcher and governor trainer in Oxfordshire. She has been a teacher in primary, secondary and adult schools since 1968 and has also spent five years at Rank Xerox (UK) Ltd. She has recently gained her MEd and her research has been concerned with governors and their training and development. She has been a governor for eight years and is a governor representative on Oxfordshire's working parties on school governor training.

**Brian Cusack** is a New Zealander who regularly contributes to national and international conferences and publications in educational administration. He specialises in public policy analysis and has an active interest in the changes which are reshaping the way people govern themselves and others. He has wide ranging experience in New Zealand education and is currently an executive officer with the New Zealand Educational Administration Society.

**David Gamage** is a Senior Lecturer in Educational Administration at the University of Newcastle, Australia and recently Visiting Associate Professor at the University of Manitoba, Canada. He was formerly Registrar at the Open University of Sri Lanka and has also served at La Trobe University and at the Phillip Institute of Technology, Melbourne, Australia. His research interests are school-based management, institutional amalgamation, comparative education, higher education and Asian studies.

**Richard Hatcher** is Senior Lecturer in Educational Studies at the University of Central England in Birmingham. He has recently completed a research study of the effects of LMS on issues of racial equality, focusing on the implications for school governing bodies (with Barry Troyna and Deborah Gewitz). His current concerns are with policy processes in education.

**Lynda Huckman** is research fellow at the University of Wales, Cardiff. Her research interests include financial and resource management and school governance. She is currently studying the support and curriculum needs of secondary schools.

**Alastair Macbeth** is Senior Research Fellow in the Department of Education at the University of Glasgow. His background includes being a pilot in the RAF, an organisation and methods officer for ICI and teaching in primary and secondary schools. He has worked on four continents and has been a secondary headteacher. His specialist field is educational administration and he has written extensively on parental involvement in schools and in school management about which he has directed national and international studies. He is currently adviser to the European Parents' Association.

**Terry Mahoney** has taught at primary, secondary, further and adult education levels. His interest in school governors began in 1977 when his own children started school. He is the author of *Governing Schools: Powers, Issues and Practice* (Macmillan, 1988) and numerous articles and he has been a school governor. He has been working in governor training since 1981: whilst working for the Workers' Educational Association he was responsible for training programmes in Leicestershire and Derbyshire. In 1989 he moved to Hertfordshire where he is Head of the Governor and Local Management Service. Amongst other duties, he is responsible for arranging the training needs of 7,000 governors in 500 governing bodies. He is writing here in a personal capacity.

**Jane Martin** is Research Fellow in the School of Education, the University of Birmingham, currently working on the *New Forms of Education Management* project for the ESRC Local Governance Programme with particular research interests in the role of governors and parents in school management. Recent work has included projects for the Department of Education and for the Organisation for Economic Co-operation and Development.

**Stewart Ranson** is Professor of Education in the School of Education, the University of Birmingham. He has written extensively on the politics of public participation in schools as part of a learning society and is leading a major UK study of school and college management, *New Forms of Education Management*, as part of the ESRC Local Governance Programme.

# 1 Telling it how it was — and is?

Angela Thody

Listen to the voices that speak about governorship past and present.

## Governors talking

It's interesting — puts me in touch with what my own children are doing and — yes — I feel it might give them a bit of an edge — my being a governor. I think, if I'm honest that's why I first got into it, but since I've found out it's not so easy, I needed more to keep me in than just interest in my children. You get to feel it's your school — that's why I stayed on and got co-opted after my children moved on to college.

. . .

I was so tired; it was about 10.30p.m. at night before we finished the meeting and it had been such hassle — all those arguments about teachers' pay — and some of the governors felt we ought to know what each teacher earns — and then we had to decide about the redundancy. It was cold, dark and wet going home and I asked myself what on earth I was doing this for — it's voluntary and unpaid and I want to enjoy my voluntary activities. I have hassle at work — I don't want it in my leisure time.

. . .

I regret the day I ever read that pamphlet 'Why don't you become a school governor?' which the government put out to persuade us to take on this job. I finished up taking holiday time to be at a pupil exclusion committee — it's laughable really — fancy spending a holiday doing that. On the other hand, I suppose I must enjoy it or I wouldn't have stood for election again. I think it must be having chances to do things I wouldn't otherwise do — like deciding a budget and making the big plans.

. . .

Oh yes — I've heard about governing bodies that are always arguing with their headteachers but here we get on fine — can't remember even a difference of opinion — I think she likes our advice — and I still think that's mainly what we're here for. I've been governing for fifteen years and I don't think it's changed much in its essence — Yes we meet more often and sometimes I worry that I've maybe forgotten to produce some plan or document the government wants but the head seems to know what she's doing.

. . .

(Comments from governors at a training day, led by the author, in Powys, 1993).

## Researchers reflecting

In order to help governors cope with the workload, they must make choices. First, they must decide at which *stage* of management they are going to be involved. For example, in the sequence of activity for any initiative, governors are best involved in the planning and reviewing stages, leaving the implementation and review to school staff. Secondly, they must decide the *aspects* of management in which they can be most profitably involved. Governors' expertise and efforts can be effectively deployed in any of six aspects: product management (i.e. the curriculum), strategic planning, financial management, human resource management, public relations or quality assurance. Thirdly, governors have to define what is the best individual contribution they can make. This could be as a director (business guide, planner, overviewer) or as a consultant (using their expert knowledge for the benefit of the school) or as a representative (a channel to the outside and from the outside) (Thody, 1992).

. . .

Governor influence was found to have minimal impact on the

curriculum in two thirds of the primary schools surveyed and in sixty per cent of the secondary schools. Governors reported their uncertainty and lack of confidence concerning curriculum issues. They felt that they had too much responsibility and that their training did not adequately prepare them for curriculum responsibilities. When senior staff rated factors conducive to whole curriculum management, active and supportive governors were considered to be the least important factor (Weston, P. et al. 1992, pp.30, 40–43).

. . .

The hypothesis . . . suggests that governing bodies have developed a 'hidden curriculum' of covert roles which have predisposed governing bodies towards being supportive and protective of the principals and staffs of their schools. These existing elites have absorbed governors and prevented them from becoming contenders for power in schools. The 'public curriculum' of governing bodies is their overt functions i.e. those that are codified in the laws. These would seem to place upon governors the expectations that they would control and direct their schools' managers.

(These) overt functions (are) intentions and (governors') covert functions are their activities. The intentions . . . are those functions which the participants think are the objectives of their organisations. Activities are those functions which the participants are observed to be performing (Gross, 1969, p.284). Covert functions can also be thought of as unintended outcomes of activities or as the usually subconscious operations of the participants. Covert functions can arise simply from being a governor, not necessarily from doing anything. Passive governors can be as functional as active ones.

The covert functions are those of consent, protection, educational protectionism and provision of illusory democracy. Governors . . . have shown . . . consent to headteachers and (have) thereby legitimated principals' power to direct their schools. (They also provide) protection for headteachers from the stresses of school management. Heads can gain such protection . . . by using governors for referral of decisions, for deflecting criticism from themselves and for avoiding stress through an emphasis on collective forms of management . . . Governors' consent and protection are particularly evident . . . in matters relating to the curriculum . . . governors support professional interpretation of the curriculum and of methods of pedagogy.

The provision of illusory democracy is the last covert function of governors. One of the reasons for the changes in the power and composition of governing bodies was to extend democracy but no real extension has occurred. Only those classes and types of people already well served by our democratic organs have taken office as school governors. In addition, any new groups enfranchised by the system have, like those already well represented, become assimilated into supporting existing rulers. Such mechanisms as the Annual Parents' Meeting and the Report serve only to emphasise the unreality of school level democracy.

> Governors have acquired covert roles because they do not have the resources, nor the will, to develop their overt powers . . . (they lack control of) resources critical to the survival of (their) organisations . . . i.e. finance, community power, knowledge and personality power (Thody, 1990, pp.4–5, 10, 11, 12, 13).

. . .

> The major roles played by Scottish School Boards were to support their schools, to express parents' viewpoints and to help refurbish their schools. Governors recorded considerable frustration because they felt they had achieved nothing. They were likely to become 'disillusioned and disheartened' (Munn and Holroyd, 1989, pp.27, 29, 35).

. . .

> School governing bodies vary greatly in interpreting their roles and exhibit uncertainty about whether or not they are behaving in appropriate ways. 'Our studies of governing bodies enable us to suggest different models, each based on a different conception of what a governing body has as its purpose . . . The *accountable* governing body centres its efforts on the school . . . (and) . . . the school's abilities to meet the needs of the community it serves . . . (It) exists to control the activities of the school . . . The governing body could, itself, be called to account for the way in which the school was performing . . . The *advisory* governing body provides a forum in which school activities are reported to the laity and tested against their ideas of what a school should be doing . . . it provides some safeguard against professional malfunction . . . The *supportive* governing body . . . (looks) outwards to influence the activities of other bodies . . . Its purpose is to provide support for the school in its relationship with other institutions . . . The *mediating* governing body . . . (expresses) the interests of the various parties and promote(s) a consensus' (Kogan, 1984, pp.144–159).

. . .

Those fulfilling governorship roles in other European states see their roles variously as trustees, delegates, stakeholders, representatives or participants with their participation classified as deciding, ensuring, advising or informing (Macbeth et al, 1984).

Scottish school boards lack involvement in issues of major educational concern (Macbeth et al, 1980).

. . .

School boards emerge in four typologies. The first is the *dominated* board whose 'members are chosen on the assumption that since they share the ideology of the dominant group, they will take the advice of community leaders . . . they represent the community elite . . . there is no organised opposition'. The second type is that of the *factional* board where 'voting is more important than discussion . . . the majority faction always wins . . . Board members represent . . . factions and . . . act according to the ideology of the group they represent'. Thirdly, there is the *status congruent* board in which members 'are equal in status and . . . act as individuals . . . there is full discussion and arrival at consensus in an atmosphere of detachment from the interests of any particular segment of the community'. Finally there is the *sanctioning* board which 'does little but exercise its right to approve or reject proposals from the community or the administration . . . it tends to perform perfunctorily' (McCarty and Ramsey, 1971, pp.19–20).[1]

. . .

The powers of governing bodies should not be increased because they are a: 'potentially disruptive and unpredictable element' (Baron and Howell, 1968, p.194).

## Governors' training manuals' advising

. . . the changes brought about by the Education Acts of 1986 and 1988 involve a movement of actual power to governors . . . These powers may appear quite small, as in some respects they are (Leonard, 1989, p.136).

At the end (of governors' meetings), members, their brains corroded beyond redemption, resolve to go home and do something really exciting, like counting the pages of the telephone directory (Wragg and Partington, 1989, pp.2–3).

Books written for school governors are not often explicit on the roles expected of a governor. The reader must usually infer from the contents what is the role envisaged by an author. Most either offer very short discussion of the role (Bullivant, 1988; Baker, 1990) or tend to assume that role is the same as legal functions (Leonard, 1989; Burgess and Sofer, 1986).

Under the heading, 'What do governors do?', Bullivant lists governors' legal powers but elsewhere, stresses the oversight role of governors and their part in deciding levels of service and general policies (Bullivant, 1988). Burgess and Sofer eschew role descriptions emphasising that governors' 'functions are rooted in the law' (1986, p.15).

Baker does not introduce a role definition until half way through his book. He defines the role as 'to support, inform and influence the school' (Baker, 1990, p.55). To be effective, governors are advised to be sure to attend meetings, do their background reading about the school and the curriculum, visit the school, learn staff names and responsibilities, attend school functions. All this advice could have been written prior to all the legislation of the 1980s. Baker's elaboration of the role continues his supportive theme. Governors are advised to 'Ask questions and seek full and accurate answers', and 'Governors are expected, but not required, to give the Head a written statement of the basic framework for discipline in the school and *to offer guidance and support* (my italics) on exceptional discipline problems' (Baker, 1990, p.35).

Harding (1987) stresses that the role of governors is to bring in the outsiders' views but he admits there is 'no easy answer' to the question, 'Just what are governors supposed to do?' (Harding, 1987, p.4) The job is 'ill defined and obscure' (Harding, 1987, pp.4, 88), enjoyable but 'likely to be time consuming and often difficult' (Harding, 1987, p.5). The role will vary, Harding considers, according to circumstances (1987, p.89) a view supported by Mahoney in his listing of possible descriptors for a governor as 'adviser, supporter, watchdog, moderator, facilitator, guardian, manager, director, trustee' (Mahoney, 1988, p.4). Which of these becomes operative at particular times, will depend on the circumstances.

The governors' dilemma in selecting the appropriate behaviour for particular times, has been accurately described as 'something of a balancing act between stamping a certain amount of individuality on school decision-making, and taking full account of the headteacher's role as manager and the ultimate responsibility of the LEA for schools in its area' (Harding, 1987, p.84). The changed role of the

LEA since this was written alter the details of the quotation, but not its spirit. The author stresses that such power sharing is a distinguishing attribute of British politics which 'weaves its way through the education system like a spider's web' (Harding, 1987, p.85), a view with which Wragg and Partington concur (1989, Chapter 1).

The format of this power sharing between headteachers and governors is largely to be decided by headteachers although these should consult with their governors (Leonard, 1989, p.43); if this does not happen then 'the chairman (*sic*) . . . is best placed to exercise gentle pressure in private' (Leonard, 1989, p.43). Wragg and Partington consider that the nomenclature 'governor' is unhelpful in sorting out the power sharing. Governing, they claim, implies giving 'orders to subordinates . . . (but) their function is less to control the school than to help sort out problems' (Wragg and Partington, 1989, p.3). They stress that headteachers and their staff should make the decisions about day-to-day running of the school. This emphasis is repeated in the advice that governors should oversee the school's 'policies and its use of resources but not in tiresome detail' (BBC Governor Training Project, quoted in Sallis, 1991, p.12).

## Officials' describing

> At first sight, the range of responsibilities described in this guide may seem daunting. But governors do not have to be experts in order to tackle them . . . governors (are encouraged) . . . to work closely with each other and with the head . . . employers must give employees who are school governors 'reasonable time off' to perform their duties . . . An employer may, if he (*sic*) chooses, give time off with pay, but he does not have to do so . . . governors may be able to claim help (for travel and subsistence for attending meetings) . . . the LEA must offer (governor) training . . . free of charge . . . individual governors will bear no personal financial liability as long as they act in good faith . . . in a well-managed school, the head and governing body will work in close partnership . . . Governors have a general responsibility for the effective management of the school . . . But they are not expected to take detailed decisions about the day-to-day running of the school — that is the role of the head . . . Governors have an important role in deciding how . . . money is to be spent to the best possible advantage of the pupils (DfE, 1988, Sections 1.1, 1.2, 2.2, 2.3, 2.5, 2.6, 2.9, 3.1, 3.2, 13.1).

## National Commission on Education, 1993, recommending

> The governing bodies of schools have considerable powers. They are responsible for the appointment of headteachers. They help establish, with the head, the aims and policies of schools. They are also responsible with the head for deciding how to spend a school's budget; in this they are accountable both in narrow financial terms and also in terms of getting best value out of the money spent. Their accountability is to the school and the community and also to the LEA, or, in the case of grant-maintained schools, to the Secretary of State. . . . We have no doubt that governing bodies vary greatly in effectiveness . . . The powers of governors were much increased in 1986 and 1988, and adjustment to this both by governors and heads takes time. Many . . . are deterred from serving by the difficulty of giving enough time to the task . . . the task of ensuring that every governor has sufficient training is immense . . . turnover among governors . . . can be high. . . . It is not . . . easy for governors to keep in touch with current feelings . . . No precise definition of where the role of the governing body ends and that of the head begins is laid down in legislation . . . Though we point out the problems confronting governing bodies, we do not wish in any way to suggest that they should not exist or should not be encouraged and helped to carry out their responsibilities . . . It is, however, clearly unrealistic to assume that every school will have a governing body which can be relied on to perform to the standards which would be expected, say, of the governing council of a university or the board of a large public company' (NCE, 1993, pp.355–356).

## Towards consensus or individualism?

Different views, different voices, different experiences. Has school governing developed differentially or are there commonalities emerging now that the changes of the 1980s have had time to mature a little? How have school governors responded to the demands placed on them? Is there a case for reviewing school governorship or is it too early for that?

This book brings together the views of researchers, governors and governor trainers — and some who are all three combined. It provides studies of what has happened in the nations of the United Kingdom and examples of similar systems elsewhere in the world.

Each enables us to reflect on how different configurations of powers, appointments, roles and responsibilities may influence how governors behave but equally on how different contexts may not be such a dominant influence as expected.

Each system, and the schools within that system, is facing the same issue of responding to felt need to involve the 'community' in participating in decisions on schooling. All those who are part of the management of schooling have to resolve the same dilemma, i.e. how to make community involvement a reality while balancing it with professional interests and with those of the national political systems. How might these issues of balance be resolved?

It is, perhaps, a sign of the maturity of school governance, that this question is being asked and attempts made to answer it. A 1992 DfE/HMI conference for school governors was entitled 'Drawing the line'. Contributors considered whether or not it would be possible to provide guidelines (possibly legal ones) for delineating those responsibilities which should be primarily governors' and those which should be primarily the responsibilities of headteachers and their senior staff. The conference delegates concluded that it was not yet possible to do so but the raising of the issue demonstrated that governors are moving on beyond immediate practicalities and could be said to be seeking role, rather than task, definition.

In the early and middle 1980s, there was euphoria as the Taylor Report's recommendations (1977) resulted in the extension of the tasks of governors and of their representative base. The euphoria somewhat disappeared under the deluge of detailed legislatory requirements which followed. Governors felt that their job was to become fully conversant with every aspect of education and with every particular of management.

Progressing towards the mid 1990s, it might be said that governors are now reasonably conversant with the legal requirements. It may be time, therefore, to reconsider the role for which the legal requirements are just the underpinnings, not the whole. The aim of this book is to assess where we have reached in the developing role of school government and to provide information on which may be based the next moves for school governorship.

Perhaps those future moves might begin with looking at the past for guidance:

> In a governor . . . the fountain of all excellent manners is Majesty; which is the whole proportion and figure of noble estate, and is properly a beauty or comeliness in his countenance, language and gesture apt to his dignity and accommodate to time, place and company; which, like as the sun doth its beams, so does it cast on the beholders . . . a

pleasant and terrible reverence (Elyot, 1531, *The Governor*, II ii).

## Note

1. American school boards, which are the subject of this extract, are not strictly comparable with those of English school governing bodies but there are some similarities in responsibilities and powers and both groups can be described as outsiders to their organisations. Clearly, however, there are some distinctions in methods of appointment, powers, specialist knowledge and remuneration while it could also be claimed that USA assumptions cannot be applied in our context. Nonetheless, the parallels offered are at least worth investigating. English school governorship must either be treated as a unique case, which is a possible but limiting interpretation, or as one having some parallels with similar institutions which can lead us to question our assumptions and to guide our thoughts to new explanations for our own phenomena. For that reason, this book contains other international examples.

## Bibliography

Baker, L. (1990) *The School Governor's and Parent's Handbook*, Slough: Foulsham.
Baron, G. and Howell, D. A. (1968) *School Management and Government*, Royal Commission on Local Government, Research Studies 6, London: HMSO.
Bullivant, B. (1988) *You Are the Governor*, London: Bedford Square Press.
Burgess, T. and Sofer, A. (1986) *The School Governor's Handbook and Training Guide*, 2nd edn. London: Kogan Page.
DfE (1988) *School Governors: A Guide to the Law*, London: Department for Education (The Guide is regularly updated with replacement sections sent to governors rather than a whole new Guide being issued annually. Hence the most current copies will contain pages dated 1988, from which these extracts are written).
Gross, E. (1969) 'The definition of organisational goals', *British Journal of Sociology*, **20**, 3, pp.277–294.
Harding, P. (1987) *A Guide to Governing Schools*, London: Harper and Row.
Kogan, M. (Ed) (1984) *School Governing Bodies*, London: Heinemann.
Leonard, M. (1989) *The School Governors' Handbook*, Oxford: Blackwell.
Macbeth, A. M., Mackenzie, M. and Breckeridge, I. (1980) *Scottish School Councils: Policy Making, Participation or Irrelevance?* Edinburgh: HMSO.
Macbeth, A. M., Corner, I., Nisbet, S., Nisbet, A., Ryan, D. and Strachan, D. (1984) *The Child Between*, Studies Collection, Education Series No 13, Brussels: Commission of the European Community.
McCarty, D. J. and Ramsey, C. E. (1971) *The School Managers: Power and Conflict in American Public Education*, Westport, Connecticut: Greenwood Publishing.
Mahoney, T. (1988) *Governing Schools: Powers, Issues and Practice*, London: Macmillan.
Munn, P. and Holroyd, C. (1989) *Pilot School Boards: Experiences and Achievements*, Edinburgh: Scottish Council for Research in Education.
NCE (National Commission on Education) (1993) *Learning to Succeed*, London: Hamlyn.
Sallis, J. (1991) *School Governors: Your Questions Answered*, London: Hodder and Stoughton.

Taylor Report (1977) *A new partnership for our schools*, London, HMSO.
Thody, A. M. (1990) *Towards a New Interpretation of Governors' Roles in the 1980s*, Unpublished PhD, University of Leicester.
Thody, A. M. (1992) *Moving to Management: School Governors in the 1990s*, London: Fulton.
Weston, P. et al. (1992) *The Quest for Coherence*, Slough: NFER.
Wragg, E. C. and Partington, J. A. (1989) *A Handbook for School Governors*, 2nd edn. London, Routledge.

# 2 The starting point

Angela Thody

The voices of Chapter 1 are not singing the same words but they appear to be singing the same tune. The school governance tune could be described as having within it, two major themes. The first is that of governing bodies within the polity. The second is that of governing bodies within the management of schools. This chapter discusses these two themes, describing both the overt and the covert functions of governors. Subsequent chapters elaborate on the themes, providng evidence from different aspects of governance and from different countries.[1]

Within the polity, governing bodies can be analysed in terms of their contributions to democracy. How have their election and selection mechanisms operated? Who composes governing bodies? How effective have governing bodies been as channels for representation and as means of ensuring accountability to stakeholders' wishes?

Within the management of schools, governing bodies can be assessed for their contributions to the efficiency of the operation of their organisations. How are powers being divided between school leaders and school governors? Is there overlap or clear separation? Do particular configurations of power sharing make for efficient school management? In what ways are governing bodies organising their work? To which areas of management are they most contributing; is it to education, pedagogy, finance, marketing, personnel or quality control?

## Democracy: the *overt* response of governing bodies

Within the context of national political systems, school governorship seems an issue of little importance yet it could be seen as of major significance for the development of democratic polities in the twenty-first century. The model of school government may have to be the solution to finding the resources to manage public services when there is no longer the money to provide them as has been done in the past. Governments everywhere are reducing their central and regional bureaucracies which have previously administered public services. What is to replace them as the state 'withers away'? Could it be the notion of 'volunteer, part time, unpaid' public servants?

This is the model that has been adopted in the British education system through the induced rebirth of the concept of powerful school governors. The manner in which it has operated may indicate a possible system of managing the incorporation of democracy in other state provision. Alternatively, it might indicate a need for reform or abolition of school governance.

Community representation in school governance is part of the wider Anglo-American traditions of democracy; 'the people' should, in some way, be involved in the government of the people's schools. This is partly in pursuit of public involvement in policy making and partly in response to the need to make effective, the contextual issues outlined above which have latterly been much vaunted by governments (Wagner, 1989; Burgess, 1992; Choice and Diversity, 1992). School governing bodies are intended as means of facilitating responsiveness to citizens as consumers (consumers defined as parents, employers and community) in a free market. The practical limitations on allowing a free market to operate in education need the addition of other mechanisms to ensure accountability to what the community wants, hence the invention of school governance (or rather the re-invention, since powerful governance was used for some state schools between 1870 and 1902). School governors can help perform the function of making schools market, or citizen, responsive (or consumer–citizen responsive, to use the terminology devised by Woods, 1994).

## Overt Democracy: selection of governors

In the United Kingdom, democratic accountability has taken the form of direction and control of the education system by central and local governments (which are subject to the checks of the electoral system). During the late nineteenth century and again in the late twentieth century, this has been reinforced at institutional level, through the granting of extensive powers to boards of school governors who direct each school. The governors' own accountability is mediated through their election or selection mechanisms and through the requirement that they meet with, and report to, parents annually.

Each school's governing board consists mainly of non-educationalists all but one of whom are part-time volunteers. The headteacher, who is a paid, full-time employee of the school, may chose whether or not to be a voting governor although headteachers will usually be present at governors' meetings. Collectively, each governing body is responsible for staffing, budget, planning, curriculum, admissions and exclusions, buildings and salaries. The powers, composition and names of these boards have varied since their inception in the nineteenth century (Gordon, 1974) but underpinning them has been our political system's belief in the efficacy of incorporating active citizens in the first line government of the state.

This belief in the efficacy of democracy is partly reflected in the way in which English and Welsh school governors are selected. Some governors are directly elected as teacher or parent governors. Some are nominated by people who have been directly elected; this group are the local authority nominees chosen by the local political parties. Some are selected by the elected and nominated groups combined; this group are the co-opted governors. Elected governors, local authority governors and co-opted governors together make up over 75 per cent of the governing body. The remainder are other nominees such as those representing lower tier local government bodies, charitable trusts (which founded schools that have since become publicly maintained) and the principal.

The mixture of appointing systems appears to be a breech in democracy but underlying the electoral system is less the aim of having elections as a symbol of democracy and more the objective of ensuring that school government is not dominated by teaching staff. Collectively, the outsiders should outweigh the educationalists. There is, in addition, the democratic protection that in no way can headteachers themselves appoint or dismiss governors (though there is anecdotal evidence that school principals often approach parents or other contacts to ask them to stand for election or co-option).

## Overt democracy: policy making by governors

One of the objectives of democracy is to involve citizens in making policies and governing bodies reflect this. The role of the governor has been defined as to 'take part in important decision making' (Baker, 1990, p.55) although this must be 'with the advice of the head and other professionals' (ibid.) and the role in policy making is mainly to be advisory. In contrast, 'the main function of governing bodies is to make policy decisions and recommendations . . . One of the essential roles . . . is to determine the main lines of development of the school' (Harding, 1987, p.87). The differences between these two authors may be a matter of personal attitudes but they may be influenced by the dates of writing. Harding's views emerged as governors first essayed their new powers; Baker's views came after some experience when perhaps, more realistic counsels prevailed about what governors *can* do, as opposed to what the law implies they *should* do.

**Overt democracy: representation**

The democratic functions of governors, in addition to those of policy making, centre around those of representation. Most governors' manuals stress the representative role in which governors are seen as a vital link between the school, the community and the LEA (Baker, 1990, p.55; Harding, 1987, pp.4, 5; Mahoney, 1988, p. 223; Bullivant, 1988, p.23). Such general statements are amplified with specific advice, for example, 'Find out if parents are generally satisfied with your school and if local residents think well of it.' (Baker, 1990, p.56).

It is stressed that this representation is part of the public duty of democracy. 'To be a school governor is to fulfil a public duty or service and is part of the tradition of British public administration' (Harding, 1987, p.3). Governors are described as ordinary members of the public (Bullivant, 1988, p.7), 'from all walks of life, who reflect all manner of opinions and values and represent a broad range of political opinion' (Harding, 1987, p.4). 'They should represent different elements in the community' (Burgess and Sofer, 1986, p.11) bringing the outside view into schools from their own outside experience and reflecting 'the ways in which the local community views the school' (Bullivant, 1988, p.26). Governors are also deemed to represent parents for whom governors can raise difficult issues with the school since governors should remember that their aim is 'not to be popular' (Bullivant, 1988, p.31) (hardly the advice which one would give to democratic representatives in other bodies).

This representative role appears to be gaining in importance because it politicises parental influence. Munn stresses how governorship is challenging traditional views of parent–school interaction because it directs parents to consider the 'collective well-being of the school, rather than an individual parent's private interest . . . (and) they go beyond parent or parent teacher associations in having clearly defined statutory responsibilities . . . In the long run they may be a more important vehicle for parents to exert influence than school choice' (Munn, 1993, p.8). In England and Wales, the requirement that all schools should have an Annual Parents' Meeting, at which governors could be questioned about their management of the school, is a major means through which parental influence might operate. While it is easy to denigrate these meetings because of the low numbers attending, nonetheless, some parents do attend and these meetings could be viewed as pilots for a new form of public democracy which will take time to develop. The improvement in the

Annual Reports to Parents over the six years since the requirement for these was introduced demonstrate how such development can occur (stimulated by governor training courses and the *Times Educational Supplement* annual competition to find the best reports).

**Overt democracy: political education**

School governing bodies may prove to be an important vehicle for extending experience of political system involvement to groups not previously able or willing to participate. About 40 per cent of governing bodies' members are female, a higher percentage of representation than is found amongst local government councillors or MPs. Those whose occupations and career interests preclude their taking on the extensive roles of local or central government politicians, can find a more manageable commitment in school governance. About 80 per cent of school governors are in full-time employment. A slightly wider social class representation appears to have occurred through school government than appears to exist in other representative organs. The middle classes, arguably those who most need to maintain a meritocratic society, are well represented.

**Overt democracy: monitoring the policy makers**

The people's representatives, in any democracy, have a further role, i.e. that of monitoring the policy makers. Governors, therefore, have to check the actions of the staff, especially those of the headteacher and of other leaders in the school. This includes both a generalist function, (e.g. satisfying themselves that the National Curriculum is being delivered and that a development plan has been produced) and a specialist one (e.g. ensuring that pupils with special educational needs receive appropriate education, that the needs of pupils with special educational needs are made known to all staff and that teachers are aware of the importance of identifying and teaching appropriately children with special needs). This monitoring role has been referred to as assessment (Bullivant, 1988) and as accountability (Burgess and Sofer, 1986) although many writers are at pains to point out that this function must not be confused with inspection and that it is monitoring with a gentle face. 'It is for the governors to represent the public interest by receiving reports, by asking questions and making comments and suggestions' (Burgess and Sofer, 1986, p.16). This differentiation between governors' monitoring and inspection has been underlined by the requirements of OFSTED inspections, introduced for England and Wales from 1993. Governors' themselves have to be assessed by the OFSTED inspectorate for their contributions to the school and it is the governors' responsibility to ensure that any requirements made of schools following an OFSTED inspection are put into effect.

## Illusory democracy: the *covert* response of governing bodies

School governance could be described as providing an illusion of democracy. It is a way of demonstrating that democracy has been achieved; the structures of democracy exist but the reality is not as the legal form implies it might be.

Illusory democracy could be described as a feature common to all our democratic arrangements. 'Modern democracy ceases to be a form of delegated rule by the people and becomes instead a form of rule by professional politicians and government officials over people' (Hirst, 1988, p.195). School governors are neither professional politicians nor government officials but it could be argued that they have become, or are intended to become, a 'front' for the former and a substitute for the latter. School governors, as conductors for professional politicians, are, for example, charged with ensuring that the government's National Curriculum is put into effect. School governors, as replacement public servants, must undertake such detailed administrative tasks as ensuring that copies of a school's action plan for correcting deficiencies noted by OFSTED, must be sent within five working days of completion, to parents, the local education authority, school employees, the local TEC (if the school concerned is a secondary school) and to appointees of foundation governors (if the school is voluntary aided or controlled) (Inspection of Schools, 1993: Annex A1).

The use of the word 'illusory' may give rise to negative reactions. This is reflected in discussions related to our political system as a whole; Whitehead and Aggleton (1986, p.443), for example, regard its existence as the result of conspiracy theory but Grant and Angus dispute this (Grant in Spence and Borthwick, 1984; Angus, 1989, p.21). Illusory democracy should, however, be regarded as neither good nor bad per se but as a necessary function of a political system:

- It exists to make democracy function at all, however imperfectly
- It provides channels which might become conduits for 'real' democracy should need arise (The Annual Parents' Meeting, for example)
- It legitimates the rulers (of increasing importance in view of the current political vilification of schools which can be

balanced by governors who support their headteachers and staff).

Its origins could be said to lie in the 'illusion' that was used to justify the extension of govenors' powers. It might be inferred from the rapid redevelopment of governing bodies in the 1980s, that there had been a strong demand from the public, to be involved in governing schools but there is no evidence that there was ever an overwhelming insistence on such participation. At the time when the initiation of the current policies for school government began to be discussed in England and Wales, from the late 1970s, there were a few vociferous, mainly middle-class individuals and organisations, who were suggesting greater parental involvement, but nothing that could be termed a massive demand for participation nor for the extensive powers that school governors have since acquired.[2] A similar lack of interest in managing schools has been apparent in New South Wales where school councils were offered as an option for schools provided that parental communities choose to have them. The government found it necessary, however, to apply pressure to school principals to ensure that most schools opted for councils since the communities concerned did not seem sufficiently keen to adopt them.

## Covert democracy: the illusion of accountability

Governors are outsiders to a school. Decisions they take will not have to be put into effect by themselves but instead, by the school's full-time managers. They will have to live with the consequences of governors' decisions on a day-to-day basis which governors will not. Thus governors might be described as having power without accountability. The arrangements (or lack of arrangements) for collective, factional or individual dismissal of governors also demonstrate this lack of accountability.

### *Collective dismissal*

Should there be failings in schools, governors are unlikely to feel greatly affected. If, for example, a governing body fails to achieve OFSTED requirements for improving their schools, the governors could then be dismissed. The Annual Parents' Meeting could pass a resolution of No Confidence in a governing body, but few such meetings have been quorate to do this, reports of such votes have not been discovered (though it is not possible to be certain that this means that none have occurred) and it is unclear whether or not such a vote would lead to the governing body having to resign. One must also ask how effective is the possibility of dismissal of the whole governing body as a mechanism for ensuring responsiveness when governorship is onerous, unpaid and of interest for the limited period when governors' children are at the school?

### *Factional dismissal*

The only provision for dismissal of faction of a governing body arises when the political control of a local education authority changes. In this circumstance, all the governors of the same political persuasion as the minority party can be replaced by those of the new majority party and this has happened in many local authorities. This could be viewed as democratic since the new governors will have a clear mandate from all the local electorate. Equally, it could be questioned because it is not a democracy directly related to the school and not one that permits governors to be dismissed for reasons directly connected to issues at the individual schools which they govern.

### *Individual dismissal*

Should those who elect, appoint or co-opt governors become dissatisfied with a governors' performance, there are no means of dismissing individuals. The electoral mechanism does not operate as a control instrument. The prospect of loss of a governorship at the next election is unlikely to worry a significant number of governors; some will have no further interest in the school as their children will have left before the next elections; others will have found the job sufficiently onerous not to want re-election. None has any financial reason for continuing to be a governor since, for most, governance will have been a cost not a gain. Those who are interested in continuing to serve as governors have often been co-opted after either failing to be elected or when they have ceased to be eligible for the elected categories. Only for teacher–governors might the electoral system operate as an effective control on their activities as governors; teachers continue to be eligible for election for their whole time in a school (which is likely to be longer than that of pupils' parents) and teachers are in daily contact with their electorate which can 'call them to account' over a cup of coffee in the staff room. Governors appointed by the local authority might have the party whip withdrawn should they fail to represent party views or otherwise perform unsatisfactorily, but this need not force a resignation. There appear to be no methods by which a co-opted governor might be dismissed. It is feasible that those appointed by, for example, diocesan authorities might be asked to resign by those authorities, but there does not appear to be a legal mechanism for this.

Annual Parents' Meetings were introduced to help make school governors accountable to parents but these meetings have not developed as an effective means of ensuring accountability. Not only have there been low turnouts but it appears that the parents who attend are often themselves teachers, thus restricting the meeting to being largely a dialogue for professionals (Thody, 1990; Hinds, 1993). It is more difficult to estimate the democratic impact of the written Annual Reports to Parents but the language in which they are written can deter all but those with reading skills much beyond those of even Key Stage 4 of the National Curriculum (Thody, 1990).

**Covert democracy: limited representation**

Despite the extensions in representation outlined above, school governance still remains largely the province of the upper socio-economic groups and there appear to be very few representatives of ethnic minority groups even in schools with a majority of such groups amongst the pupils. The numbers of female governors has declined since the 1988 Education Act. (Thody, 1990, Chapter 10; Jefferies and Streatfield, 1989; Buckby, 1992a.) The franchise is restricted to parents and teachers. There is anecdotal evidence that interest in contesting elections has declined as have the numbers voting, especially in inner city schools where there have also been difficulties in maintaining active membership of governing bodies after elections. Such difficulties are reflected in the description of governors as 'ordinary folk who find themselves elected, coerced, co-opted or even, for all we know, tricked by their crafty fellows into becoming school governors' (Wragg and Partington, 1989, p.1).

Those who could be deemed to be the most closely affected by schools, i.e. the pupils, are excluded from representation unless they are over 18 years of age. In this case they might serve as co-opted or LEA governors although this is unlikely to happen. In contrast, secondary schools piloting school governance in Norway in 1992–3 voted to include pupils as governors but to exclude parents.

Governors from the business community might be said to have preferential status since there is a 'reserved category' for them. In co-opting governors, governing bodies should take account of the extent to which 'they and the other governors are members of the local business community' (1986 Education Act, Clause 6 (a) (i). It is expected that at least one governor will be from the business community (grant-maintained and voluntary-aided schools may also have governors sponsored by companies, 1993 Education Act). It is interesting to note that New Zealand also has reserved categories in case of under-representation of particular groups but that their reservations are for Maori, women and working-class representatives.

The practical outcome of the election and selection system is to reproduce the same exclusivity that occurs in our other representative organs — a 'demos (which) will fail to protect the interests of those who are excluded' (Dahl in Laslett and Fishkin, 1979, p.127). It appears that parents of children disadvantaged by the system tend not to be represented (Angus, 1989, p.22; Hatcher, 1993).

**Covert democracy: immaturity**

School government has not yet developed party and pressure group arrangements. The party mechanism has been much criticised at a national level (Rose, 1974, 1980; Mackenzie, 1963; Crossman, 1972; Bogdanor, 1983) but it does offer at least the possibility of collating some views and of providing a means whereby promises made at elections can be translated into policies. School governance lacks this mechanism and elections for parent and teacher governors do not seem to have been concerned with policy promises. Election manifestos tend to stress rather vague characteristics, such as 'commitment to the school' and evidence of committee service as proof of potential as a governor. The small group of appointed party representatives within each governing body do not dominate numerically.

Sectional interests have yet to emerge as pressure groups within governing bodies. All the requirements for factional operation are present in embryo (Thody, 1989; Thody and Wilson, 1988). What may be preventing their development could be the lack of political sophistication of governors (most of whom will be relatively new to political negotiation), the lack of time governors have for factional meetings and the few occasions on which governors meet. Perhaps they do not know each other well enough to learn how to operate factionally. Perhaps they are constrained by feelings that the interests of the school should transcend factionalism. Whatever the reasons, it is likely that the lack of maturity in pressure group activity could restrict governors' ability to balance the power of professionals in education decision-making.

Governors' bargaining strength is similarly restricted nationally. Until 1994, there was no national governing bodies' association to represent their interests. The three groups who were (and continued to be) operative nationally, represented either individual governors (National Association of Governors and Managers which has around 6,000 members, a tiny part of the approximately 960,000 governors) or LEAs and governor training providers (Association for Governor Information and Training) or a mixture of these (Independent Centre for School and College Governors). The three associations did not operate collectively. There appeared to be a need for a unified body (Morrish, 1993), perhaps similar to the New Zealand School Trustees' Association, whose members comprise 95 per cent of New Zealand's governing bodies and which is a nationally recognised negotiator (Styles, 1993).

## Management: the *overt* response of governing bodies

In re-introducing extensive powers for school governing bodies, the British government was, no doubt, subscribing to the popular view that educationalists need help in creating efficient organisations as schools have had to adapt to the demands of commercial activity. This was deemed to be especially necessary as English and Welsh schools moved to site-based management between 1988 and 1993. This entails control of virtually all their funds and the concomitant responsibilities of staffing, marketing, finance, buildings, student admissions, grounds and equipment. Who better, politicians might have asked, to advise on this than those from outside professions who are used to having such responsibilities? Such questioning is reflected in an advice book for business community governors that 'schools now need to be run like companies with the governing bodies being boards of directors and the headteachers the managing directors' (Moreland and Opie, 1988, p.3).

Academic research, in the USA is beginning to produce evidence that, to some extent, supports these opinions. Composition of both boards of directors of companies and of school boards, is deemed to have great significance in producing effective decision-taking which provides organisational leadership (Pearce, 1992; Pearce and Patrick, 1993).[3] This impact is considered to be at its greatest when boards include strong outsiders (i.e. those not employed by the host company) with expertise and who represent the community's needs. This current research builds on earlier work which sought to demonstrate correlations between the characteristics of directors and their power (Zald, 1969). 1992 investigations in England point to the same recommendations for English companies (Cadbury, 1992). There is, however, very little empirical evidence 'aimed at the level of analysis of organisational governing bodies . . . more detailed data are needed . . . It is through the processes and mechanisms of corporate governing bodies that leaders themselves establish organisational direction by forming strategic choices amongst their peers' (Leavy and Wilson, 1994, p.192). This extract relates to company boards, not to those of schools but the conclusions from each sector could have implications for the other. School government research to establish the data that Leavy and Wilson think necessary for business, is well advanced, as this book demonstrates, and could be an example for researchers in corporate governance. Conversely, there is evidence from research into business boards of directors that their control increases 'as the wider context becomes more turbulent and unpredictable' (ibid.), a conclusion that could have significance in the turbulent context of education.

The powers given to school governors could also be seen as linked to the need to find ways of solving Britain's economic difficulties in the late 1980s. There was concern amongst politicians and industrialists that the recession in the British economy was partly due to the failings of the education system to prepare workers adequately for the economic needs of the country. There were criticisms of the standards achieved by British schools in international comparisons and anecdotal accounts of employers disturbed by the literacy and numeracy standards of applicants for jobs. One of the solutions to this has been to find ways of integrating schools and the economy. One means of integration could be seen as that achieved through school governing bodies from whence it was believed that they could directly influence school curriculum choices and teaching methods hence increasing the effectiveness of schools' contributions to the state of the nation's economic health.

This could help ensure that the Conservative economic thinking, which had been democratically endorsed through the national electoral process, was brought to bear upon current concerns for schools to be run as businesses and for the curriculum to reflect the state's move to a more market-oriented economic system so that students would be better prepared for the enterprise culture.

It is difficult to decide the extent to which governors may have contributed overtly to the effectiveness of school management. There are studies of the effectiveness of governing bodies (NFER, forthcoming; Esp and Saran, forthcoming). There are studies of effective schools (Mortimore, et al., 1988) and of particular elements which can create effective schools (Southworth, 1990). There are OFSTED reports evaluating the effectiveness of individual schools. None of these attempt to make connections between governance and effectiveness and those not specifically relating to governing bodies make very little, if any, reference to their existence, much less to their relevance to effectiveness.

A pilot study of governors from the business community in 1993, attempted some simplistic correlations between governors' activities and possible contributions to school effectiveness (Thody, 1994). 'The central issue ... appear(ed) to be the extent to which business governors (could) retain sufficient of their outsider linkages to bring pressure to bear on schools to adopt the [arguably] more efficient ways of business' (ibid.). The chances of their doing so appeared to be limited because it 'appeared that a majority of these governors were operating at higher levels of management in schools than in their business occupations ... (although) ... A great variety of practical assistance in small ways from business to ... schools (had been made available) and ... business governors have contributed to the curriculum in many ways through facilitating industrial contacts ... through participating in education industry links ... (and through) assistance with school project work' (ibid.). Many governors thought that they contributed their management skills and specialist knowledge although it was found that they did not appear to serve on the sub-committees appropriate to their specialisms at work (ibid., Tables IX and X).

Apart from such limited studies, one has to make the assumption that a happy, supportive and effectively operating governing body must make some difference, at least to staff morale and it is from that assumption that reflections arise on the covert contributions of governance to efficiency.

## Management: the *covert* response of governing bodies

The covert contributions of governors to school efficiency could be defined as those of *consent* and *protection*.

Governors' *consent* is here defined as the function of legitimating the pivotal position of principals in the determination of policy for their schools. This consent also appears to operate for the purpose of confirming the rightness of any policies determined by headteachers. Politically, consent establishes the basis of the micro-polity of the school because consent supports, and thereby legitimates the head. Managerially, it provides a means of avoiding problems which might have arisen had governors fully adopted the questioning, critical role implied in the legislation of the 1980s.

The governors' role of *protection* arises from the function of consent but extends beyond it. Again it helps ensure the efficiency of governing body operation and thereby, one assumes, the effective management of the school. Legitimation by governors' consent lends support to principals and can help to protect them from some of the stresses of school management. Heads can gain protection from governors providing a forum to which heads can refer decisions. This can permit heads to arrange deferment or amendment of decisions about which they themselves feel unhappy. Heads can tell staff and parents that decisions have to be referred to governors for decision. Heads then do not have to appear to be refusing ideas from staff and parents themselves since the collectivity of the governors can 'take the blame'. School principals are still largely the gatekeepers of what is presented to the governors since the headteachers must decide where the line is drawn between day-to-day manage-

ist knowledge. The nature of the school also encourages deference to the professionals. It can continue the staff pupil relationship into adulthood (Wilson, 1972) and adults are constrained by expectations about 'the entrenched roles of education participants' (Angus, 1989, p.24). Headteachers privately concur with this, stating 'off the record' that they feel their governors do not understand educational issues. Governors who are also parents fear arguing with professionals for fear of repercussions for their own children. Supporting professionals could also have been inadvertently reinforced by central government; governors, asked at short notice for consultative reports for government and requested to implement frequent changes of policy with little money and little warning have felt increased empathy with teachers. The whole consent and protection function is also reinforced by the colonisation of governing bodies by educationalists. Most surveys show that about one third of governing body members have education linked occupations.

## Conc[illegible]sions

In the [illegible]ve typology of the overt and covert functions of governing bodies, [illegible]ders will recognise echoes of the descriptors of McCarty and Ra[illegible] (1971) and of Kogan (1984) both of which were outlined in Cha[illegible]One; there are shades of Bacon's co-optation (1978)[3] and of the [illegible]of MacBeth (1980). They were my starting points, since develo[illegible]th my own experience as a governor, a governor trainer and as [illegible]rcher in school government to produce this analysis of where [illegible]orship stands in the early 1990s. How will my views matur[illegible]ruse the other contributions to this book? Each comes from [illegible]t vantage point but each has been asked to consider how t[illegible]nce can contribute to the themes of democracy and of mana[illegible]ach has been asked to reflect on how they see the ples [illegible]s developing during the 1990s.

## [illegible]ot[illegible]

[illegible]hese themes to the other states whose examples are presented [illegible] emphasised in several sources (see, for example, Ellison et [illegible] in Education, 7, 3, September 1993; International Directions

[illegible]ssions, 1977. Organisations active at the time included the [illegible]ducation, the National Association for Governors and [illegible]ign for the Advancement of State Education. Individuals, [illegible]ty Taylor and Ann Holt, now noted national experts on [illegible]were just beginning to gain national recognition — Joan [illegible]ember of the Taylor Committee.



ment and general conduct of the school. This protection is a useful device where heads feel uncertain or where decisions are likely to be controversial. Governors also deflect criticism from heads. Governors' protectionism applies also to curriculum issues. Governors are generally likely to be supporters of the professionals' views on the curriculum.

### Covert management: how and why consent and protection operate

Anecdotal evidence suggests that some governors participate very little at governors' meetings but this is still deemed to be consent since it has been accepted that in political systems, 'Signes of consent are either Espress, or by inference . . . (the latter are) sometimes the consequence of words, sometimes the consequences of Silence; sometimes the consequences of Actions, sometimes the consequences of Forbearing an Action' (Hobbes, 1651, p.69). Consent can be indicated by inaction, by silent acquiescence, by a small sign (such as nodding the head) or by a written confirmation (Plamenatz, 1968, pp.7–8). Even non-participation must itself be recognised as a form of participation (Srivastva and Cooperrider, quoted in Angus, 1989, p.24). The only time that inaction does not count as consent appears to be when governors are asleep (Simmons, 1976).

Demonstrating consent contributes to effectiveness because it helps smooth the path of decision taking and implementation. Governors subconsciously recognise the importance of supporting their schools because consent is in the interests of all. Therefore governors frequently express support for their schools both privately and publicly (e.g. Munn and Holroyd, 1989, p.25; Munn and Brown, 1989, p.8).

It is also in the particular interests of the elite that governors consent. Governors interpret 'the interests of all' as meaning acceptance of the guidance of heads because head's government has been validated by what Tussman terms, 'the aware elite' (quoted in Pitkin, 1972, p.61). Headteachers could be considered to be members of such of an elite because of their social standing. Those within governing bodies who consider themselves to be in the elite with the headteacher (because of equivalent economic or educational status) consent because the heads domination gives them the outcomes that they want.

The likelihood of consent operating and ensuring the smooth running of governing bodies becomes apparent when it is realised how difficult it is to break the habits of consent. Governors have to be very disturbed to do this since consent is the natural response to those in authority (Pateman, 1979, pp.251–253). Friendship and personal knowledge reinforce the likelihood of consent (ibid., p.254). Governors also consent because they have a choice whether or not to do so and because 'It is a psychological fact ... that men reconcile themselves more easily to obeying persons whose power to give orders is dependent on their wishes' (Plamenatz, 1968, p.147). The few major battles between governors and heads which have become *cause célèbres* demonstrate how strongly governors have to feel before they will take action opposing their headteachers (e.g. William Tyndale School, reported in Auld, 1976; Roehampton Church of England Primary School 1988, the *Telegraph*, 11 July 1988; Carhill School, 1989 in Galton and Patrick, 1989, Chapter 7; Culloden School (Batteson herein Chapter III).

**Covert management: the practice of consent and protection**

Guidance provided for governors stresses the supportive roles which will provide consent and protection. 'Support the school particularly if you feel it is not getting a fair deal. Defend the school against unwarranted criticism' (Baker, 1990, p.55). These are sample statements from a book which also advises governors to write letters of praise or other comment since schools welcome feedback (ibid., p.57). Bullivant is less accepting of this protection role: 'Don't just adopt the attitude, "my school right or wrong".' (Bullivant, 1988, p.31) but she notes the difficulty of doing this. 'Try not to be so close to the school that you are blind to its defects. It may sometimes be difficult to maintain a balance between total support for the school and being critical of everything it does, but, as a governor, you must try' (ibid., p.31). Governors should act together as 'a support to the school' (Burgess and Sofer, 1986, p.11), 'standing up for it when it is in trouble' (ibid., p.16). This advice is strengthened in discussions of why governors should visit their schools: 'to find out how you can help the school ... to be supportive to the head teacher in his (*sic*) need to have a concerned outsider with whom to discuss problems' (Burgess and Sofer, 1986, p.63). Overall, this role is aptly summarised as demonstrating 'enthusiasm and commitment' (Mahoney, 1988, p.5) through governors' promotion and protection of their schools (ibid., p.223).

The importance of consent in the legitimation of school principals is stressed by Leonard who believes that governors should be publicly supportive of their headteachers. He suggests that disagreements should be privately resolved between the headteacher and the chairperson, hence 'allowing the head to respond without loss of face' (Leonard, 1989, p.43). Generally, though, Leonard feels that governors should be pro-active leaders since he rather denigrates those governing bodies which chose to delegate most of their



decision-taking to the headteachers (ibid., p.135). Teacher governors are expressly reminded to ensure public consent in governors' meetings and to keep disputes with their headteachers to the privacy of staff meetings (Wragg and Partington, 1989, p.63).

Governors' guidebooks anticipate governors' consent in decision-making: 'Most governing bodies look to the head for a clear lead on almost every issue' (Wragg and Partington, 1989, p.65). 'Take part in important decision making with the advice of the head and other professionals' (Baker, 1990, p.55). Such advice appears to have been taken by governors and their provision of consent can be apparent a
governing bodies' meetings which provide a termly forum at whic
consent for the principal's rule can be re-affirmed. Heads can
governors' meetings to certify the rightness of their decisions and
meetings become, in effect, a supporters' club. The chairpers
who usually visit their schools weekly, re-enforce this func
There will often be questioning of headteachers at meeting
usually the outcome is reaffirmation of consent.

Acceptance of the idea that governors do consent takes le
form in the powers that governors have to delegate to head
and the general authorisation for heads to act on behalf of
in day-to-day management of the school. There will als
consent point when a new head is appointed, a new scho
school changes its status.

Governors also protect heads by offering shared d
which can relieve heads of the stress of solo decisio
school principal expressed this as follows: 'My job i
journey ... (but) judging the pace (of this) is
governors (view) the same journey from a different
will enable them ... to offer advice from the
interested but impartial adviser. I can't get that a
and I value it enormously. It helps me sleep
Middleton, 1989, p.11).

Educational protectiveness was early no
governors. A headteacher reported that
report on curriculum policy within the sc
and immediately went on to discuss som
just don't want to appear critical' (Mun
Governors appear to support professio
deferring to the head and staff when c
(Golby and Brigley, 1988; Coryton,
similar 'ideology of professionalism
effective abrogation of the role of
happening within company board
when the non-executives 'go n
happens because the non-profes

3. This is defined as the process of incorporation whereby potential contenders for power are converted to supporters by existing leaders in order to avoid themselves being ousted or the organisation destabilised. Bacon (1978, p.182) first adopted the use of this term in the context of school governorship in his seminal work arising from his research on Sheffield's school governorship. He adapted it from Philip Selznick's 1949 study, *TVA and the Grassroots: A Study in the Sociology of Formal Organisations*, University of California Press.

## Bibliography


Angus, L. B. (1989) 'Democratic participation and administrative control'. *International Journal of Education Management*, **3**, 2, pp.20–26.

Auld, R. (1976) *The William Tyndale Junior and Infant School*, London: ILEA.

Bacon, W. (1978) *Public Accountability and the School System*, London: Harper and Row.

Baker, L. (1990) *The School Governor's and Parent's Handbook*, Slough: Foulsham.

Baron, G. and Howell, D. A. (1968) *School Management and Government*, Royal Commission on Local Government, Research Studies 6, London: HMSO.

Bogdanor, V. (1983) *The People and the Party System*, Cambridge University Press.

Buckby, R. (1992a) 'Governing bodies 1988–1992', *Management in Education*, **6**, 4, pp.5–6.

Buckby, R. (1992b) *Perceptions of the Governing Body*, Unpublished MA thesis, University of Leicester, England.

Bullivant, B. (1988) *You Are the Governor*, London: Bedford Square Press.

Burgess, T. (1992) *Accountability in Schools*, Harlow: Longmans.

Burgess, T. and Sofer, A. (1986) *The School Governor's Handbook and Training Guide*, 2nd edn. London: Kogan Page.

Cadbury Report (1992) *Committee on The Financial Aspects of Corporate Government*, Draft Report. PO Box 433, Moorgate Place, London.

*Choice and Diversity* (1992) London: HMSO.

Coryton, D. (1987) 'Parents vote for teacher power', *Education*, 20 November, **170**, 21, p.436.

Crossman, R. H. S. (1972) *Inside View*, London: Cape.

Dahl, R. A. (1979) 'Procedural democracy' in Laslett, P. and Fishkin, J. (Eds) (1979) *Philosophy, Politics and Society*, Oxford: Blackwell.

Ellison, L., Garrett, V. and Simpkins, T. (Eds) (1992) *Implementing Educational Reform: the Early Lessons*, Harlow: Longmans.

Esp, D. and Saran, R. (1995) *Effective Governors for Effective Schools*, Harlow: Longmans.

Galton, M. and Patrick, H. (1989) *Curriculum Provision in Small Schools*, London: Routledge and Kegan Paul.

Golby, M. and Brigley, S. (1988) *Parents as School Governors*, Exeter: Fairway Publications.

Gordon, P. (1974) *The Victorian School Manager*, London: Woburn.

Grant, W. (1984) 'The role and power of pressure groups' in Borthwick, R. C. and Spence, J. E. (Eds) *British Politics in Perspective*, University of Leicester Press.

Harding, P. (1987) *A Guide to Governing Schools*, London: Harper and Row.

Hatcher (1993) School Governors as a Hegemonic Process, British Sociological Association Research Seminar, Reading University.

Hinds, T. (1993) 'Annual governors' meetings — is it worth the effort?' *Management in Education*, **7**, 1, pp.29–30.

Hirst, P. (1988) 'Representative democracy and its limits, *Political Quarterly*, **59**, 2, pp.190–205.

Hobbes, T. (1615, 1914) *Leviathan*, Everyman Edn, London: Dent.

*Inspection of Schools* (Revised Ed. 1993) London: HMSO.
*International Directions in Education.* This broadsheet, published three times per year by the Commonwealth Council for Educational Administration since 1993, provides regular summaries of developments in the systems and schools of many countries. These summaries clearly demonstrate similarities amongst states contextual themes and school developments in both management and curriculum (with the possible exception of Canada).
Jefferies, G. and Streatfield, D. (1989) *The Reconstitution of School Governing Bodies*, Slough: NFER.
Leavy, B. and Wilson, D. (1994) *Strategy and Leadership*, London: Routledge.
Leonard, M. (1989) *The School Governors Handbook*, Oxford: Blackwell.
MacKenzie, R. T. (1963) *British Political Parties*, London: Heinemann Mercury Books.
Mahoney, T. (1988) *Governing Schools: Powers, Issues and Practice*, London: Macmillan.
Martin, Y. (1993) BEMAS paper.
Moreland, D. and Opie, R. (1988) *School Governors from the Business Community*, London: The Industrial Society.
Mortimore, P. et al. (1988) *School Matters*, London: ILEA Open Books.
Morrish, J. (1993) 'Governors need governors', *Management in Education*, **7**, 4, pp.23–24.
Munn, P. (1993) (Ed.) *Parents and Schools*, London: Routledge.
Munn, P. and Brown S. (1989) *Pilot School Boards: First Impressions*, Edinburgh: Scottish Council for Research in Education.
Munn, P. and Holroyd C. (1989) *Pilot School Boards: Experiences and Achievements*, Edinburgh: Scottish Council for Research in Education.
Parker, H. (1989) 'Outsiders come inside', *Management Today*, October, pp.131–138.
Pateman, C. (1979) 'Political obligation and conceptual analysis' in Laslett, P. and Fishkin, J. (1979) (Eds) *Philosophy, Politics and Society*, Oxford: Blackwell.
Pearce, J. A. (1992) 'Board composition from a strategic contingency perspective', *Journal of Management Studies*, **29** (4), pp.412–438.
Pearce, J. A. and Patrick, S. K. (1993) 'School board composition and performance: lessons from corporate America', *Management in Education*, **7**, 3, pp.31–32.
Pitkin, H. (1972) 'Obligation and consent' in Laslett, P., Runciman, W. G., Skinner, Q. (Eds) *Philosophy, Politics and Society*, Oxford: Blackwell.
Plamenatz, J. P. (1968) *Consent, Freedom and Political Organisation*, Oxford University Press.
Rose, R. (1974) *The Problem of Party Government*, London: Macmillan.
Rose, R. (1980) *Do Parties Make a Difference?* London: Macmillan.
Simmons, A. J. (1976) 'Tacit consent and political obligation', *Philosophy and Public Affairs*, **5**, pp.274–291.
Southworth, G. (1990) 'Leadership, headship and effective primary schools', *School Organisation*, **10**, 1, pp.3–16.
Styles, M. (1993) 'An umbrella is vital', *Management in Education*, **7**, 4, pp.25–26.
Thody, A. M. (1989) 'School governors revisited', in *Local Government Policy Making*, **16**, 3, December, pp.27–36.
Thody, A. M. (1989b) 'Who are the governors?' in *Education Management and Administration*, **17**, 3, Summer 1989, pp.139–146.
Thody, A. M. (1990) *Towards a New Interpretation of Governors' Roles in the 1980s*, Unpublished PhD, University of Leicester.
Thody, A. M. (1992) *Moving to Management*, London: Fulton.
Thody, A. M. (1994) 'Practising democracy; business community governors in the control of schools', *Research Papers in Education*, forthcoming.
Thody, A. M. and Middleton, N. (1989) 'Me and my shadow', in *School Governor*, March, pp.10–11.

Thody, A. M. and Wilson, D. (1988), 'School governing bodies and the pressure group arena', in *Local Government Policy Making*, **15**, 2, September, pp.39–46.
Wagner, R. (1989) *Accountability in Education*, New York: Rochester.
Weston, P. et al. (1992) *The Quest for Coherence*, Slough: NFER.
Whitehead, J. and Aggleton, P. (1986) 'Participation and popular control on school governing bodies: the case of the Taylor Report and its aftermath', *British Journal of Sociology of Education*, **4**, pp.433–499.
Wilson, S. M. (1972) *A participant observation study of the attempt to institute student participation in decision making in an experimental high school*, unpublished PhD thesis, University of Chicago.
Woods, P. (1994) 'The consumer-citizen: A new conceptual framework for understanding key relationships in education'. Paper presented at the American Educational Research Association Conference, New Orleans.
Wragg, E. C. and Partington, J. A. (1989) *A Handbook for School Governors*, 2nd edn. London: Routledge.
Zald, M. N. (1969) 'The power and functions of boards of directors: a theoretical synthesis', *American Journal of Sociology*, **75**, pp.97–111.

# 3 'A rum lot': some aspects of governing a demonised primary school

Charles Batteson and Denise Syndercombe-Court

## The significance of Culloden

In 1991 Culloden Primary School in East London experienced intensive media and political criticism following its prominence as the subject of a six-episode BBC television programme (intended to provide a 'fly on the wall' perspective of inner-city school life). In the immediate aftermath of these broadcasts the school received considerable positive feedback. However, subsequently the *Mail on Sunday* newspaper published an article attacking standards at Culloden, as exemplifying deformations in primary schooling, particularly in the teaching of reading. Martin Turner, a freelance educational psychologist well known as a critic of modern primary teaching methods, was commissioned to run IQ tests on 40 local children, most of whom attended Culloden. Alleged discrepancies between raw intelligence test results and the children's reading performance appeared under the headlines:

> 'Losing the battle at Culloden'; 'A school renowned for its caring fails its children'; 'Modern education "triumph" is turning out a generation fit for nothing', that referred to 'normal boys and girls . . . destroyed by education system', and 'general failure in reading ability' (3 March 1991. Quoted in the Culloden Story Pack).

In the Spring of 1991 Culloden School was incarnated as a 'folk-devil',[1] an object of incrementally more intensive media/political criticism, where different aspects of the school were dissected and discredited. The unsatisfactory schooling provided by Culloden School, discovered or created by the *Mail on Sunday*, had as a particular feature the extension of the guilty or culprit population normally implicated in contemporary educational *scandals* and *scares* (e.g. LEAs, teachers, teacher-educators). The governing body were seen to share responsibility and blame for alleged deficiencies and neglect, illustrated in official responses and informal interactions characterising the subsequent school inspection. Nationally school governors are routinely exercised by concerns with public relations and the reactions of (usually local) press and other media towards aspects of a school's affairs and newsworthiness. Culloden is a potentially informative case study since staff and governors had to engage with, and confront, a relentlessly high profile stemming from intensive press interest that led to direct political intervention. Involvement as voluntary lay governors in such schools as objects of derision poses significant questions about the costs of participatory citizenship. Culloden achieved fleeting prominence, offering pragmatic case law to a coalition of political and media groups reflecting common purposes and preference for outcomes. It fuelled a full HMI inspection where a *Mail on Sunday* article was justificatory, if contrived, evidence of '. . . much publicised concern about reading standards at Culloden School' (HMI letter to Headteacher, March 1991). (The inspection taking place with less than two-weeks notice.)

Against this backcloth we want to explore some of the ways that Culloden illuminated aspects of school government, particularly those of governor involvement in a monitoring process and its press reporting. This review draws on the perceptions and insights from a parent governor at Culloden School, intermittently complemented by views of others working in the area. The intention is to relate some ways that governors were variously involved and apparently became marginalised. Central concerns involve the distribution of power in neighbourhoods; conceptions of 'proper' and 'legitimate' roles and personas for governing bodies; elusiveness in conceptions of parent and governor power: how this is articulated, accepted or rebuffed. In particular we hope to illuminate some aspects of the overt and covert responses of governing bodies to offer some further assessment of Thody's (see Chapter 2) notion of 'illusory democracy' in in school governing processes. The substance of Culloden governors' experiences are neither exotic nor unique. They may illustrate manipulative power relationships often concealed in subterranean underworlds of the politics of education. Exploring these furtive processes may broaden conceptions of school government beyond unproblematical and normative parameters.

In addition to interviews conducted with a parent-governor at Culloden Primary School, in January 1994, we have quoted from the extensive collection of related correspondence (from and to the school) newspaper coverage and supplementary articles fully collected and published as the *Culloden Story Pack* (Culloden Action Group, London, 1991). In the review of events and outcomes of the Culloden affair we provide a brief backcloth to explain something of the nature and content of the school, the prevailing political and educational climate in which the drama unfolded, and some details of how the governors operated and perceived their role prior to the key events of 1991. There is then consideration of how governors operated as a channel for representation and consideration of dilemmas in broadening and fulfilling the imperatives of representativeness. This is followed by illustrations of how Culloden governors came to be excluded from parts of a monitoring process and details on perceptions reflected, for example by HMI, towards governors in a formal inspection process. Finally we relate some aspects of the case study to subsequent experiences of other schools and conclude by suggesting how some of the events at Culloden in 1991 may locate and define aspects of governing schools firmly within parameters of 'illusory democracy'.

## The school in context

Media focus on the credibility of schooling, as total systems failure or as specified sites of mediocrity has been a recurring feature. Dale (1989) described how symbolic imagery of *failed* schools 'proves' anxieties about the corruption of primary schooling. Demonisation of Culloden was perhaps surprising because of the high regard it enjoyed in its locality, and sound academic performances substantiated by LEA records. Additionally it did not reflect the 'teacher politicisation' characteristic of some earlier 'folk-devils' (e.g. William Tyndale in 1976).

The *problem* of Culloden was that it achieved a high profile, by way of television exposure, concurrent with an upsurge in critical political interest in state primary schooling. This was compounded by the relative ease in which both its pedagogy and prevailing ethos lent themselves to easy caricatures of *progressive* and *caring* schooling. In addition school governors did not appear to conform to fresh conceptions of these bodies as fulfilling essentially sceptical and critically vigilant functions.

## Socio-economic and administrative context

Culloden School is located on the southern edge of the Aberfeldy Estate, an area of high density municipal housing adjacent to extensive industrial land use. The immediate local population is predominantly working class including substantial ethnic minority settlement (according to LEA figures, 56 per cent of children have English as a second language). The neighbourhood has been substantially untouched by London Docklands' renewal on its southern fringe. Indications of social and economic deprivation are gauged from LEA estimates showing 80 per cent of Culloden children entitled to free school meals, a local unemployment rate exceeding 50 per cent, and a substantial transient school population (e.g. children living in a Women's Aid Refuge or in temporary 'bed and breakfast' accommodation).

In 1990 Culloden came within the new Tower Hamlets LEA after the disbanding of ILEA. A minority of pupils (approximately 10 per cent) came from professional and middle-class families further afield. Such 'middle-class/professional' children represented parents exercising consumer choices in an educational market place — based on perceived positive qualities that comes through the rationale for selecting the school of one 'in-comer':

> My child used to be looked after by . . . a lunchtime supervisor at Culloden, she couldn't mind him at dinner time. I used to drive from work . . . to look after him whilst she was on duty. I was struck by the quality of the discussions and the communication that was going on between teachers. . . . The educational process that was going on was so impressive that I thought 'this must be a good school to send my child to.' Teachers cared absolutely for the children and went to any length to give them a good education (Culloden parent governor).

Culloden School draws on a powerful residue of local community solidarity and commitment. Traces of support and active participation seem to be at variance with the prevailing experiences in at least some urban, substantially working-class schools. Something of the character of support and participation in Culloden's governing process comes through in this quote:

> There were always people interested, active and wanting to take part (as governors), to talk about the school, to be in and around it . . . there were lots of us with children there. Three of the governors had children at the school and lived on the Aberfeldy Estate. Quite a lot of the rest of us also had children

> there but lived some distance away . . . governors were committed in terms of their communication with the school, all aware of what was going on, knew the teachers well. It was the sort of place that you could come into at any time, you felt you knew what was going on in the local community, what was going on as far as the staff and the children were concerned . . . as if you knew where the school was going. . . . There was a general impression of trust, a partnership between the schools' leadership and the governors . . . a very free flowing system. The headteacher was very open to people coming in to the school and to his room at any time. Governors did and parents did. That was one of his big pluses, he would always talk about anything that people were concerned with. . . . It was a very freely communicating system between teachers, parents, governors, anybody on the staff — very easy to get into. That was very much how the local community worked, it didn't really work to a (formal) middle-class system. If parents wanted to express their feelings they'd come along, go into the Head's room and say 'This isn't right — do something about it'. In a sense the formal representation through governing bodies excludes some groups of people, I don't think it worked for some of that (local) community at all. As governors we did what we thought was best and attempted to represent people who have an interest in the school. . . . But I don't think we found it very easy to communicate freely with other parents. They care about the school as well but perhaps don't have the time or emotional energy because of things going on in their lives (Culloden parent governor).

**Political context**

The precise mechanics explaining Culloden's passage towards a political-educational hall of infamy are elusive. Why, for example, was the school rediscovered and reinvented by the *Mail on Sunday* newspaper after its obvious media value and interest had passed? Why did the Secretary of State come to express hostile interest and personally intervene? However, there seems to be evidence of pragmatic coalescing of interests, where media and politicians reflected a degree of ideological intimacy and common purpose — a common characteristic in educational politics (Wallace, 1993).

London schools may be particularly receptive to periodic attention by national media and politicians as they are in close physical proximity to the centres of both these activities. Historically they also occupy a symbolic importance associated with currently unfashionable notions of experimentation, progressive teaching and repetitive engagement with issues of social class, 'race', and educational achievement. Culloden's exposure cannot be explained by its location in a 'loony-left' LEA, however, as an icon for schooling in general, explanations might be sought in what it could stand for — its symbolism — rather than where or what it was:

> . . . it put its head above the barricades at a time when Kenneth Clarke was looking for somebody as an example to us all — to teach us lessons about the new world . . . it coincided with politicians talking about teaching methods, reading standards and was a convenient stick to beat us all with (London headteacher, interview, February 1994).

This tendency was further illustrated by political and press responses to the OFSTED Report 'Access and Achievement in Urban Education' (OFSTED, 1993). Highlighting 'residents of disadvantaged urban areas . . . poorly served by the education system' and aggregating urban schools' performance and standards as 'inadequate and disturbing' (ibid., pp.6–7) newspaper and ministerial responses to the report sustained a critical chorus about all urban schools, earlier reflected in treatment of single sites like Culloden. Press exposure and the compaction of negative imagery coincided with features of a national educational-political climate stemming from an enduring sceptical approach to state schooling by Conservative governments since 1979. Concurrent with the Culloden TV documentaries was public interest by the Education Secretary, outlining 'further action to improve reading standards among seven-year-olds' (DES Circular No. 4/91 dated January 1991), citing HMI surveys showing 'a deplorable figure of 20 per cent' of schools where reading 'is less than satisfactory' (ibid.).

## Governors

Culloden had few difficulties in attracting and retaining governors. Individual levels of commitment may be indicated by this comment on its chair of governors:

> She had been a governor for 20 to 25 years and Chair for 15 or 20 years . . . had her finger on everything that was going on in the estate . . . worked in the area running the youth club, and set up the community shop . . . knew all about support services within the area and knew all the local people . . . was someone they could all go to (Culloden parent governor).

The Culloden governing body was formed of some twelve representatives, including two parent governors, the headteacher, two elected staff representatives and local authority nominees. Something of the nature and prevailing ethos of the rapport and relationship between the school and governors is inferred below:

> The relationship between governors and the school was always free and easy, a good relationship with the staff. I wouldn't just walk into a class; obviously I would ask someone if I could come in first, but we saw what was going on. We went on school journeys, were involved with the educational process of the school, saw what was happening. When it came to the inspection we all knew things hadn't been done such as some documentation that HMI would expect. We also knew that the presence or absence of these documents was not going to make the difference between a child reading or not because we had faith in the process of education that was going on, knew it was a good one . . . It wasn't something we just thought we knew about, it was good because we had experienced it in classrooms, seen what was going on, not just something we'd been told by the Head (Culloden parent governor).

Culloden governors could be defined as 'supportive' (Thody, Chapter 2) but that did not pre-determine uncritical allegiances. Accessibility and free dialogue might premise collegial and incorporative frameworks indicating degrees of manifest accountability. (In the inclusiveness of the Chair of Governors, freely moving within and across school and neighbourhood.) It is underwritten by a parent governor exercising market choices, then maintaining a vigilance, in overview, confirming appropriateness of initial (consumer) decisions. Within a supportive context, governors simultaneously accommodated and addressed aspects of informal accountability to at least some stakeholders — representative of parents and community.

**Governors as a channel for representation**

In Culloden's unfolding media and political drama, a central criticism was the failure to address parental grievances. It seemed to be implied that governors had been culpable in neglecting a 'silent majority'. Great play was made by the media about concern for the destiny of children poorly served by the school's professional and lay management. Representation, or under representation of working-class, and less prominently, ethnic minority parental views was a central, enduring theme. Difficulties and the attendant frustrations involved in widening participation in procedures of school government has wide, general validity, particularly in dispossessed and alienated communities. The dilemmas of achieving balanced and representative composition had exercised Culloden's governors but they did not feel they had fully resolved them. Informally, a chair of governors originating from the locality, maintaining networks and sharing some cultural affinities, might represent a positive conduit between school and neighbourhood. Additionally there were formal efforts to incorporate parental views into school dialogues:

> We hoped that as a relative outsider, which I was as far as the local community was concerned, different skills could be used to complement those of the chair . . . to offer something good and worthwhile . . . I set up a series of parent–governor surgeries, we held them once a month and advertised them heavily — letters, posters around the school, that sort of thing — and wanted to get parents to feel free to come and tell us their problems. We had meetings in the community shop on the estate so that people wouldn't feel that they had to come into the school in case they had problems with it, like 'My child isn't being taught properly!' We had a whole series of these meetings for about eighteen months but only one person ever turned up before the press and HMI thing blew up . . . When we'd present the Annual Report from the school's governors parents didn't turn up. I'm sure that's not unusual in other places . . . Then we decided to time the annual meeting alongside the school concert so that people who came along for the night might ask questions but nothing happened. It's not that parents didn't care — they do care enormously about their children — but they don't think it's something that they can have influence on: they don't realise that they could have an influence. In the written Governors' Report to parents we'd write a lot about the changes that had been happening in education, the National Curriculum etc., things that were going to happen in the school, we'd try to write about them in a way that would encourage people to come and express views . . . We never got any feedback from anybody — it's very likely that most of the reports were never read at all . . . As a parent governor from 'outside' the immediate local community I tried to set up a system which would look at and respond to needs. To a certain extent the consultative model didn't work — possibly because it's a middle-class system and many local people just don't use 'those types' of system. Instead they'd come in and talk directly to the head. He would talk to us governors . . . we felt we were kept in touch with what was going on. Certainly there wasn't a lot of dissent coming from parents. They'd come in to complain about incidents but they wouldn't come in and complain about the educational process at all (Culloden parent governor).

References to negligible turn-outs for annual reporting meetings, have wider resonance, as do notions of parents preferring face-to-face approaches to headteachers rather than formalities of governor representation. The experience and efforts of these governors to be responsive, and representative of parental opinion were unexceptional and fairly typical, whilst also indicative of consciousness and proactivity in addressing such concerns.

Subsequent charges about deficiencies in Culloden's governing processes need to be correlated with endemic, structural weaknesses in enhancing constitutional roles of governing bodies. In a plethora of rhetoric and documentation there is silence about the residual difficulties of broadening involvement of working-class and ethnic-minority communities. Limited inclusion of Culloden's parents in the formalities of consultative and representative school government reflect how:

> social pressures and legislation have certainly increased the influence that parents may have if they are well informed, articulate, persistent and listened to, but the distribution of these necessary circumstances and characteristics is by no means even (Wragg, 1989, p.132).

A key aspect of the Culloden affair involves the legitimacy of governors authentically representing parental (consumer) interests. Subsequent criticism of governors for their effective unrepresentativeness seems to have ignored the real dilemmas and difficulties in ensuring that deliberations reflect a depth and breadth of perspectives. Citizen involvement and participation in inner urban areas, often with transient populations, is highly problematical. Criticisms of the governors might appear to imply potentially negative and undesirable outcomes for the minority of indviduals able and disposed to assume formally the increasingly time consuming roles and responsibilities of school governing in the 1990s.

## The exclusion of the school's governors

A striking feature of the Culloden case was apparent exclusion of the governors from key parts of the embryonic crisis. Early efforts by a journalist, instrumental in defining Culloden as exemplification of schooling in crisis went on, for example, unknown to either the school management or governors.

> On the Sunday morning at the end of half term, I happened to be listening to a local radio news programme which mentioned the *Mail on Sunday* article. I dashed out and bought a copy. I was horrified to learn that all these children had been gathered together. Nobody in the school — the staff or the governors —

> had any idea of what process had been used. Clearly lots of people went along — forty children, some of them siblings and something in the order of twenty or thirty parents. Soon after some of the parents came into the school and said they hadn't known it was the 'Mail' that had arranged the tests, they thought it had been laid on by the school . . . to find out how well their children were doing, to provide them with extra support! One mother said she'd sent her older child, who had reading problems, but didn't send the younger child because he didn't have problems. One of the children had cerebral palsy, some of the others had special needs. It became clear that the parents weren't aware of what had been arranged or why. It's like somebody had said 'come along for a free test' and they felt curious . . . (Culloden parent governor).

In the aftermath of news coverage of the tests an emergency meeting of the governors was held. Reports had excited considerable interest amongst parents:

> People just arrived in school. There were photographs of some children and parents in the paper. Here was a report saying that 97 per cent of children at Culloden couldn't read. As governors we wondered exactly who'd been involved and what the (media) event was going to mean. Some children in the photos didn't go to Culloden. Not all of the adults shown were currently parents of children at the school . . . There was intense interest among the governing body as to who some of these people were. Immediately we felt how unjust this report had been (Culloden parent governor).

In the aftermath of this exposure 'parent opinion' and 'parent rights' became redefined and represented in different ways. Partiality and selectiveness of emergent 'anti-school' parents, given expression in the press, was keenly felt by the Culloden governors:

> It seemed people had been invited . . . to speak to the paper . . . sending their children to the test . . . we didn't have a sense of exactly who the key people were or how individuals had been approached or chosen. There seemed to be three or four main people who were anti-school. A lot of others, whose children had been sent to be tested, came back to say 'we don't agree with this newspaper — we weren't aware that all this fuss was going to happen, we just went along to see how our children did' (Culloden parent governor).

Such 'anti-school' sentiments assumed considerable political significance. Concerns and dissatisfaction, however partial and unrepresentative, were taken as all-embracing, governors and 'pro-school' parents progressively becoming invisible as the affair unfolded. Momentarily empowered 'anti-school parents' highlighted grievances and popular prejudices which happened to accord with assumptions and perceptions of journalists and politicans. For these, appropriation of the right to define, know and act for 'parent opinion' was an article of faith. This was reflected by the prominent status and the implied universality of critical parents from Culloden. In a key article Martin Turner was quoted on:

> . . . loving, secure homes, mothers and fathers . . . frantic about their children not getting the education they need (*Mail on Sunday*, 3 March 1991).

### Governors and the inspection process

For much of 1991 Culloden governors' were fully occupied in responding to media charges and the somewhat frenetic arrangements for the hastily convened HMI inspection. Pressures were compounded by a pervasive sense of the governors' complicity, inferred in accusations and assumptions of a 'failing' school. Hints were contained in the minister's announcement of an impending inspection simultaneously with condemnation of 'cranky' primary school methods ('Clarke backs phonics against "cranky" teaching methods', *The Guardian*, 7 March 1991, p.2). Culloden's chair of governors responded by expressing:

> surprise and dissatisfaction at (the) Department's approach to recent events . . . It was left to the governors to hear from the press of an inspection . . . (having) overall responsibility for the school, they would have expected to have been informed directly (letter to Secretary of State, 13 March 1991).

Governors were concerned about the impartiality and receptivity to different opinions from the outset of the inspecting process. Indications that there had been resistance by some HMI to a 'political' and hasty inspection were informally passed on. It may have been indicative of some pre-formed attitudes towards all of those associated with Culloden that no letters from governors ever elicited a ministerial reply.

Hints of differences in interpretation and opinion between the DES and HMI, in advance of the formal inspection, appear to be reflected in HMI Rose's letter to the chair of governors (19 March 1991):

> As you know, it is customary though not obligatory for HMI to inform schools in advance about our inspection and visits. . . .

> We certainly had no part in discussing the matter (of announcing the inspection) with the media.

Similar inferences of HMI ambivalence, together with an intimation of how governors were apparently to be procedurally marginalised during the inspection process are contained in another HMI letter. Governors asked for reassurances about the post-inspection arrangements, about consultations with them, and the anticipated time-scale between feedback and public release of the full report. The reply accurately predicted how, in advance of availability to governors, the media would have access:

> The questions you ask should really be addressed to the DES since it is for Ministers and the DES to decide upon the handling of HMI reports . . . convention is that copies . . . are issued by the Secretary of State, in advance of publication to the chief education officer, the clerk to the governors, and the head . . . that is conventional procedure but there are no hard and fast rules . . . when there is particular public interest in an inspection, . . . the report may be issued and published without any intervening delay . . . It is normal practice for HMI to discuss its main findings in confidence with the governing body . . . that arrangement is only blessed by convention and whether or not the meeting between HMI and governors is pre or post publication depends upon . . . the Secretary of State's decision about the handling of publication (20 March 1991, HMI Jim Rose to Culloden chair of governors).

The governors were concerned about the post inspection arrangements. Their concerns appear to have been justified since before the inspection report entered the public domain it was leaked to the *Mail on Sunday* and used to produce a severely critical report ('Failed on all counts — Inspectors critical of showpiece school, 14 April 1991). The governors requested conventional verbal feedback but this was not given. This seems to have stemmed from an aversion to and mistrust of governors that became evident during the inspection. The governors felt they had not merely been neglected or ignored, but came to be seen as part of the schools' malaise, i.e. incapable of acting as partners in a monitoring process since they felt they were visualised as 'part of the problem'.

During their physical presence at Culloden, HMI meetings with governors occurred only when governors specifically asked to meet the inspectors:

> they were all present apart from the local (district) HMI who appeared uncomfortable in the school. They weren't easy meetings, I think that was because of what we saw as their

> hostility and aggression towards the school . . . At the meeting with governors they tried to show a calming influence but they gave the impression of being stressed about it — they weren't comfortable . . . There was something of 'if the governors are supportive of the teachers then they must be bad too, because we know the teachers here are bad' . . . Then there was a comment to the chair about the governors being a 'rum lot' . . . One of the inspectors described the governing body as 'incestuous', as too close to the school and not communicating enough with people outside . . . the chair felt very upset at those sort of suggestions (Culloden parent governor).

The governors' feelings of exclusion were reinforced at the end of the three-day inspection, by a letter from the headteacher to the chair of governors:

> During a brief discussion with . . . the reporting HMI today, she stated that she would prefer if I did not share the content of the report back due to take place tomorrow morning. I did argue that you . . . should be party to such information but she felt that as she had seen you 'around school rather a lot' that this was not appropriate (letter dated 21 March 1991).

Critical conceptions of governors during the inspection process, as variously 'incestuous', a 'rum lot', and being seen 'around the school rather a lot' could be interpreted as attitudes towards how, 'proper' governors are supposed to behave. Throughout the inspection there appear to have been departures from customary practices in how the inspection was convened; the handling of the ensuing report, and to whom, and when, it was made available. Culloden illustrated some of the practicalities and routines of parts of bureaucratic-political cultures that are often concealed.

In analysing parts of the Culloden affair, implied criticism from HMI towards the school's governing body comes through, particularly regarding its composition and the ways it operated. Visibility in and around the school became a negative defining characteristic prefacing excessive intimacy between governors and governed. Some characteristics of governors seemed to conflict with fresh orthodoxies about the ethos and the rationale for freshly empowered citizen involvement in the government of schooling. However, such intimacy between governors and schools may be widely prevalent if we accept Thody's notion (see Chapter 2) of governors operating as 'supporters clubs' for schools. A strand of press criticism in the fallout following HMI's report was criticism of the schools' methodology and philosophy, subsequently parodied by press and politicians as obsessively 'caring'. Comments made by HMI might indicate how governors became tarred with the same brush.

### Other schools

Aspects of experiences and outcomes of the Culloden affair that have wider relevance and utility were reflected in 1993/1994 by close parallels, in press and political treatment, of the first schools labelled 'failing' under fresh 'Office for Standards in Education' (OFSTED) inspection arrangements. Crook Primary School, the recipient of the first 'failing school' report, 'received its copy . . . only the day before publication' (Deputy headteacher, quoted in *TES*, 10 December 1993). Surprise and bitterness was expressed by Crook's governors:

> The governors could not contain themselves when they heard what was in the report. It just doesn't add up . . . it is dispiriting but we've had some tremendous support (Chair of Crook School governors, quoted in *TES*, 10 December 1993).

Further resonations, in the Spring of 1994, came with Kingsmead Primary School in Hackney, coming under intensive press and political scrutiny following a series of events involving the headteachers' professional competence and sexuality (*TES*, 28 January 1994 and 11 February 1994). At Kingsmead, LEA pressures to proceed with disciplinary action against the headteacher were powerfully resisted by the governors. This case highlighted some ambiguity about the legal powers of the DFE, LEA and governing bodies, and the formal distribution of responsibilities for disciplinary procedures. In addition there was considerable tension between an LEA apparently keen to be seen to act decisively in a high-profile and sensitive case set against governors equally determined to maintain the headteacher's tenure. At both Culloden and Crook Primary Schools there were indications of a degree of urgency in publishing highly critical inspection reports, respectively under HMI and OFSTED auspices. Such time scales necessarily restrict opportunities for feedback and dialogue with school authorities, including governing bodies.

## Conclusion

In this chapter we have related some of the experiences and outcomes of a governing body involved in a high profile and sensitive media and political event. We have illustrated some features of the nature and functioning of the governing body. Juxtaposed with this have been apparently conflicting interests in national school inspection arrangements. Schools momentarily caught up as items within broader tensions and debates about the nature and quality of schooling are vulnerable to transient media and political demonisation. This may be particularly so where socio-economic circumstances compound the sensitive and problematical nature of single sites of crisis. At Culloden School governors were criticised for being unrepresentative and held to be out of touch with parents' views. They found themselves progressively excluded as the external monitoring process unwrapped and felt marginalised during the inspection and in the subsequent reporting.

The Culloden case study amplifies some of Thody's suggestions (see Chapter 2) for categorising and analysing aspects of school governing processes. It shows how governors can come to be regarded as unrepresentative to powerful outside groups; as not making, nor adequately policing, school policy nor as sufficiently capable of monitoring the policy makers. In that sense Culloden seems to reveal something of the 'illusion' of the fresh powers formally exercised by governors. Additionally it indicates some limitations in the ways that governors can intervene in normative conceptions of school monitoring. HMI criticisms of the governors' management of the school stemmed from a perception that they were not 'overtly' contributing to managerial efficiency. However, there is strong evidence of Culloden governors' contribution to school management in 'covert' ways, particularly in offering support for headteacher and staff.

Attempts to engage with a hostile and powerful external threat to the school demonstrate governors trying to create some degree of insulation and potential arbitration between inspectors and inspected. At Culloden, and more recently at Crook and Kingsmead, governors have been involved in seeking to ameliorate and offer protection and support for schools and teachers confronted by external pressures. In each case transient high visibility and public notoriety involves governing bodies in fulfilling the imperatives of what Thody (Chapter 2) defined as 'governor protectiveness'. Instances of this role and persona point to highly sensitive and fraught aspects of offering such *protectiveness* when national media and politicians target individual schools as convenient scapegoats, and where lay governor 'judgement is only accepted if other powerful groups agree with it' (Sallis, 1994, p.17).

Understanding the lessons from the Culloden case is helped by a consideration of its broader national context. The scrutiny, and deconstruction of a specific site of schooling helped to consolidate and reaffirm critical ways of 'seeing' and knowing about deformed primary schooling. The periodic identification, and media-political exploitation of convenient 'folk-devil' schools now has well established ancestry and is likely to be a recurring feature. Hall (1993) suggests that such accessible and convenient social sites of crisis will continually be discovered or invented since they offer the prospect of political proactivity, *being seen to do something*, particularly when macro economic performance is sluggish and impervious to regenerative policies.

The reality of involvement in school governing bodies that is sketched in this case study contrast with the bland and somewhat synthetic rhetoric condensed in some official documentation (see for example the *Parents Charter*, DES, 1991 and *School Governors: A Guide to the Law*, DFE, 1993, which both predicate an unproblematical and consensual terrain upon which the act of school governing is played out). The extent to which such perspectives and assumptions might conflict with reality of experiences of governors are recognised in a letter written to the Secretary of State for Education by the Bishop of Stepney (20 March 1991) as part of his efforts to offer some mediation and conciliation in the Culloden affair, and noting a:

> high degree of vulnerability . . . (being) concerned about the governors . . . asked to take on considerable extra responsibilities and . . . only too aware how difficult it is to recruit people who are willing to take on these tasks in our area.

In press and political treatment of Culloden there seems to have been little receptivity to the Bishop's 'hopes and prayers' that ways would be found:

> . . . of dealing with this precious human community, which is creative and sustaining of their best efforts (ibid.).

Instead a prevailing maxim seems to be that where governors offer support and protection to their schools and are seen to have 'gone native' they become incorporated with, and treated in similar ways to other strands of a discredited educational system — as integral parts of an 'enemy within'.

## Note

1. In referring to the demonisation of Culloden and other schools we have drawn on Cohen's (1972) work exploring how in 'moral panics' particular 'folk-devils' are picked out for critical attention and censure, as exemplars typifying a wider malaise or crisis.

## Bibliography

Cohen, S. (1972) *Folk Devils and Moral Panics*, London: Paladin.
Culloden Action Group (1991) *Culloden Story Pack*, London: Culloden Action Group.
Dale, R. (1989) 'The case of William Tyndale' in *The State and Education Policy*, Milton Keynes: Open University Press.
DES (1991) Circular 4/91 (Dated 9 January 1991) *Kenneth Clarke announces further action to improve reading standards*, London: HMSO.
Hall, S. (1993) *Moving On*. Full edited transcription of a lecture given at Conway Hall, London, 19 November 1993, London Democratic Left.
Sallis, J. (1994) 'No exceptions to responsibility' in the *Times Educational Supplement*, 11 February 1994.
Wallace, M. (1993) 'Discourse of derision: the role of the mass media within the education policy process'. *Journal of Education Policy*, **8**, 4, pp.321–337.
Wragg, T. (1989) 'Parent power' in Macleod, F. (Ed) *Parents and Schools: The Contemporary Challenge*, Lewes: The Falmer Press.

# 4 Interests, accountability and representation: a political analysis of governing bodies

Kevin Brehony

The theme of this chapter is the democratic control of schooling and the question that I shall attempt to answer during the course of my discussion is how might governing bodies be restructured in order to enhance the democratic control of schooling by the population it serves. The assumption is that changes are needed which confirms the suggestions of Thody in Chapter 2 that governing bodies are not democratic in the mainstream understandings of the term and that what they typically exhibit is an appearance of, or an illusive, democracy.

In the course of discussion, I shall draw upon data collected while working on a UK Economic Social Research Council funded research project entitled 'The Reform of School Governing Bodies — a sociological investigation'. This project was co-directed by Professor Rosemary Deem of Lancaster University and the research assistants were Ms Sue Hemmings and Ms Suzanne Heath (formerly New). As a former chair of governors myself and as a researcher interested in the issues of citizenship and participatory democracy (Brehony, 1992), I have definite views about the governance of schools and the way the education system is governed. These views have been derived from other experiences and sources as well as from data collected during the ESRC project, so that the scope of my discussion will range beyond a discussion of the research evidence itself. Nevertheless, as the project lasted from 1988 to 1993, it could not fail to be enormously influential in shaping my thinking about school governors, the role of lay actors in the administration of public goods, and participatory democracy.

I shall begin therefore by briefly describing the research project and following that I shall identify and describe three perspectives on governing bodies. These perspectives are not hermetically sealed; in real, concrete governing bodies, aspects of all three may be detected but in varying degrees. I shall then go on to discuss notions of the representation of political and social interests and relate that discussion to the current social composition of governing bodies. In the final part of the chapter I turn to the consideration of possible ways in which, from the point of view of participatory democracy and democratic accountability, school governing bodies may be reformed.

## The reform of school governing bodies: a sociological investigation

As I have already mentioned the reseach project began in 1988. At this stage it was a pilot study of fifteen school governing bodies. The date was significant as in this year governing bodies were re-established according to the requirements of the 1986 Education (No 2) Act. 1988 also saw a massive Education Reform Bill become an Act of Parliament. We were curious to see how governors would cope with their newly acquired powers and duties, and wanted to discover how they would accomplish the working of the new arrangements and relationships with schools. Our research design was constructed to ensure that the governing bodies investigated contained differences as well as having features in common. The fifteen schools were selected from two contrasting local education authorities (LEAs) and the sample making up the case study contained roughly equal numbers of primary and secondary schools so that there were contrasts relating to both size and sector in the governing bodies chosen. A further contrast was provided by the areas from which the schools were chosen. One set of areas were leafy, suburban and middle class, whereas the other areas were urban, predominantly working class and displayed characteristics conventionally associated with the inner cities.

From the autumn of 1988 we attended all the formal meetings and some sub-committee or working group meetings of the selected governing bodies in the two LEAs, to which we have given the pseudonyms of Northshire and Southshire. After April 1990 the number of governing bodies being studied was reduced to ten; this was in order to allow us to focus in more depth on how the governing bodies were enacting their roles and to reflect the proliferation of sub-committees and working groups which most of our research sites adopted to facilitate their work. The two LEAs related to governing bodies in very different ways. Whereas Northshire took a fairly paternalistic attitude to its governing bodies but also offered them a lot of support, Southshire was a more post-modern local education authority as it had a 'hands off' approach and provided correspondingly less support and guidance to governors than did the more modernist Northshire.

The methods we used included observation of meetings, sub-committees and working groups, attendance at governor training sessions, and the use of two questionnaires, sent in summer 1989 to all members of the fifteen pilot case-study bodies and in 1992 to all members of the ten governing bodies that constituted the main project. We carried out semi-structured interviews with 43 of the governors out of around 170 governors in the main study. Those interviewed included headteachers, chairs of governing bodies, chairs of finance and other sub-committees, parent-, LEA-, co-opted- and teacher-governors. In addition to the interviewing and observation we collected a large range of documentation, including agendas, meeting and briefing papers.

## Perspectives on governing bodies

School governing bodies in their present form may be seen to be both the product of, and legitimised by, three differing perspectives. This allows them to be supported by groups who in other respects are politically opposed. This eclecticism extends to the purposes of governing bodies and to governors, many of whom were, and remained, unclear as to what they were supposed to be doing and what governing bodies were for. If Maclure was right (Maclure, 1989), and there are good reasons to believe he was, then the restructuring of school governance that occurred in the 1980s should be seen as both emanating from, and being legitimised by, ideologies of the market that celebrate and privilege the figure of the consumer and denigrate its binary opposite, the producer. Through the provision of more competition between schools and choice for the consumers, embodied in the form of parents, these ideologies suggested that thereby standards would be raised and education improved. However, in this new right scenario, governing bodies have little or no role other than to be a part of a general and desired tendency towards decentralisation and the devolution of decision-making, since their composition would include not only parents (who are centrally involved in the new quasi markets for education (Le Grand, 1991)) but also business people, politicians and other LEA representatives and teachers. Right wing views about school governance had not in the past always been so limited. Thus in 1984 Sir Keith Joseph's Green Paper, 'Parental Influence at School' proposed that parents be given an absolute majority on governing bodies. Leaving aside the problem that, as Le Grand argues with respect to voucher schemes, parents are the 'agents' of their children's choice of school and are therefore not direct consumers (Le Grand, 1991), the 1984 Green Paper was consistent with the view of education as a market place in that the consumers were to predominate over the producers (teachers) on governing bodies. The answer as to why governors are of relatively little interest to the new right since 1984 seems to be that markets do not require consumer and producer interests to be politically represented on organisations like school governing bodies.

## A political science perspective on school governance

If school governing bodies are not essential to the requirements of state funded schools which are to operate in a quasi market but at the same time have been reconstituted so that consumer interests in the form of parent and co-opted governors are predominant, then the question arises of how precisely they are to be seen. Rather than provide a single answer to that question, it is perhaps more useful to see views of governing bodies as being intersected by at least three perspectives. The first I shall call the political science perspective. In this view, governing bodies are sites for the making of decisions about the allocation of scarce resources to various aspects of schooling. They are also places that permit conflict over the allocation of those resources to be regulated and absorbed. Moreover, as the size of the majority of the resources to be allocated is determined by the central state through its control over and regulation of the local state, governing bodies are places where conflicts over resources are radically displaced. That is to say, conflicts over the size of the resources, instead of being fought out between parents and teachers on the one hand, and the central state apparatus for the regulation of schooling on the other, tend instead to become channelled into conflicts between governing bodies and increasingly weakened local authorities. That is when governing bodies are not absorbed and defused through a recognition of powerlessness by governors themselves. Many of the governors we interviewed would probably reject the label 'political' being attached in any way either to their governing body or to their activity within it. This is because 'political' is a term that most governors we interviewed associated with party politicians and the following reaction to politicians was widespread in our research:

> I would be very unhappy if there were overtly political people serving on our governing body with no interest in this area and no interest in this school. And I see there have been a couple and they're the sort whatever the problem you just get the current government's party slogans coming out, and there's no real communication with them. So they're the ones I mind.

Nevertheless, political interests of a non-party kind were at the forefront of the Taylor Committee's deliberations as evidenced in its report published in 1977 (Report, 1977). At the centre of its recommendations was the view that five interests should be equally represented on school governing bodies; the LEA, teachers, parents, older pupils, and the local community. For this reason, the Taylor Report is a good example of the political science perspective.

## A participatory democracy perspective

This is also a political perspective but instead of looking first at the functions performed by governing bodies the primary focus is on the activities of agents, the governors themselves. In this perspective, school governing bodies open up opportunities for the participation of many citizens in decision-making about the allocation and form of a major 'public good' namely, state schooling. This perspective is akin to that identified by Thody in Chapter 2 as 'overt democracy'. There are a number of sub variants of this perspective, which may be identified although they exist more at a discursive than a material level.

Few signs of this perspective were to be seen among the governors researched in our case study. The variants of the participatory democracy perspective are associated with a continuum that runs from somewhere a little to the left of the centre of UK party politics, to positions occupied by libertarian Marxists and anarchists. Common to most, if not all, of these variants is the notion that democratic participation in all organisations, whether they be in the structure of organised consumption or that of production, gives power to the participants and is, at the same time, also educative and an essential part of citizens' self-development (Pateman, 1970; Ransom, 1992). This position first emerged in ancient Athens and is to be found in the work of such diverse figures as Rousseau, John Stuart Mill and Marx and Engels (Brehony, 1992).

Recently in the United States a similar position has been advocated by Stivers. She mobilises some of Giddens' work on structuration and his stress on the knowledgeability of human agents in order to argue that the construction of a *polis*, 'a public space where administrators and lay people share in the good life' is not only realisable but it is also highly desirable (Stivers, 1990, p.97). The *polis* in her account bears a very close resemblance to the 'ideal speech situation' advocated by Habermas (Habermas, 1976, pp. xiii–xviii), with the main exception that Habermas actually specified the conditions which needed to be present before an 'ideal speech situation' could materialise.

What citizens actually do in a participatory democracy is a significant axis of differentiation among those who could be assimilated under the participatory democracy perspective. Many see a major obstacle to participation as inhering in the power that professionals possess by virtue of their knowledge and occupation of permanent positions within educational institutions. Thus, like Sallis, they stress the need to make professionals more accountable to the communities they serve (Sallis, 1988). Others like Stivers, who follow the classic model of participatory democracy, want to see administration become the work of citizens or lay people acting jointly with professionals.

## The new managerialist perspective

In the 'new managerialist' perspective, school governing bodies are intended mainly to act in the name of consumers in order to regulate, discipline and conduct surveillance upon teachers, who are regarded as the producers of a public good. During the research project we encountered numerous governors who thought that this was the *raison d'être* of governing bodies. Some but not all of the people with such views were co-opted governors. This category consists of governors who are selected by the other members of their governing body. Governing bodies when making co-options must, according to the 1986 Education (No 2) Act, have regard to the extent to which those they are considering for co-option are members of the local business community. This is an important departure from the Taylor Committee's recommendations as Taylor did not specify who should be co-opted other than that they be from the school's immediate community.

The requirement that business governors should be co-opted can be understood in two differing ways. First there is the view expressed by a business governor of a primary school who said that:

> The teaching profession consists of people who have gone to schools and have gone to university without actually having gone out into the business world to see what it was like. It would worry me whether — and obviously the general point about managing — whether they are sufficiently aware of what the business community, the general employment community actually requires from the people as they leave school to move into employment themselves.

It follows from this that business governors in LEA maintained schools, as *de facto* employers of teachers and heads, can represent the views of a set of 'customers' and make known to schools the kinds of labour they require. Yet, since the specification of what the schools' output should be is tightly controlled by the Central State through the National Curriculum, there are obvious limits on business governors' capacities to act in this way.

A second way of understanding the intentions which lay behind the requirement is to begin with the point made in the interview just quoted that teachers are generally unaware of life in business organisations. The position of teachers has been graphically presented by Strain (1993) who says of them, with a welcome attention to the *longue durée*, that:

> They belong to, and have themselves, within universities, schools and colleges, contributed to the formation of a pastorate of knowledge and human development, the post-Enlightenment legatee of the mediaeval church's universal mission to teach.

The values of this 'pastorate' are deeply at odds with the 'enterprise culture' an 'ongoing programme of reform' which aims at changing the way all of us, and particularly teachers in this context, understand ourselves (Heelas and Morris, 1992). Thus the co-option of business governors may be seen as having primarily to do with helping to change the cultures of schools and teachers in directions consonant with the 'enterprise culture'. That this was how the following governor from business saw his role is made clear in the following extract when the respondent was asked to reflect upon what schools might learn from industry:

> You can't sack teachers readily, they know that, and they feel that they are in a cloistered community anyway. They live by a set of rules. Well this, at the end of the day, is a business. It's been a business protected by — it's not nationalised, municipalised. Just in the same way as the gas industry, the electricity industry and other industries were owned by the municipality, and run by the municipality, and then they were nationalised and then privatised and the culture shock for

> anybody who'd been around over that period of time is quite frightful. And I think that's the problem for the teachers, this culture shock, this threat as they see it of being managed in a sense, and their competence called into question. But mine is anyway. It's no wish to boast, but nobody's better qualified as I say. I admit I'm up as high as educational facility will take me, but I'm only as good as the last decision, and the next one, if it doesn't suit the manager, you can wave goodbye as I disappear into the dust. I'm not suggesting it's a good system, a good scheme, but it's something that needs to be brought in I think, to education.

This 'new managerialist' perspective has little in common with the participatory democracy one and in some senses it departs radically from the political science perspective in its specification of the need to ensure that business interests are represented.

## Interest representation

Typically, in liberal democratic societies, social and political interests are held to gain representation through the election of representatives. Those who share an interest or a spectrum of interests with others, seek to promote and advance them by getting their representatives elected to deliberative bodies. It is nevertheless commonplace for representation not to be secured through the process of election. Interests in corporatist arrangements such as quangos are represented by people selected by power holders who, by doing so, exercise a degree of control not only over the range of interests represented but also the representatives (Brehony, 1995). This is partly the case with co-opted governors. Whom they should be in terms of interests to be represented is dictated by power holders through the 1986 Education (No 2) Act and whom they should be as individuals is decided by those with power among the already existing governors. LEA governors also conform in part to corporatist arrangements for representation except that they are usually selected by the political party in power at the local level. These semi-corporatist and anti-democratic, arrangements sit rather uncomfortably alongside those for the selection of teacher and parent governors who are elected.

In the case study what was noticeable was that only on very few occasions did the arrangements for representation consequent upon the post 1986 Education (No 2) Act restructure attract any criticism within the meetings of the governors. That parents, teachers and LEA appointees should be present appeared to be 'taken for granted' and 'natural'. When there was any questioning of the arrangements for representation it usually concerned the co-opted governors. Nearly all the governing bodies in our study experienced difficulties in making co-options. At an early stage, it was perceived that people from certain categories of occupation would be useful to the governing body. These included, as might be expected from the new arrangement for site-based management intended to come on stream in the 1988 Education Reform Act, accountants, solicitors and bankers. This was not so much a case of enthusiasm for the 'new managerialism', as a desire to get free services in areas where it was thought such services would be needed in the context of the impending transition to Local Management of Schools (LMS) and a decline in the powers and services of the LEAs. However, schools in working-class areas found particular difficulties in attracting governors in any category other than teacher governors but their problems were greatest in attracting business people. What happened was that the required business people were found but in most cases they were parents or had been parents of pupils at the school. In no sense could they be seen to be representative of the local business community.

At a primary school we call Birchdene, a teacher governor tried to encourage the acceptance of a teacher from a secondary school as a co-opted governor. This practice had advantages for both the primary and the secondary schools and the head of one of the secondary schools in the case study was himself a co-opted governor of one of the schools in the pilot study. The other governors, among whom the ideology of the 'new managerialism' had strong roots, vigorously opposed this suggestion on the grounds that the 'producers' already had too much power. Unlike the teacher governor, the majority of the other governors held the view that business people were the only fit people to be co-opted to the governing body of a primary achool.

## Who are the governors?

Interest representation is not confined to the categories defined in law. Many governors we interviewed, for example, wanted to see more governors from ethnic minorities, especially in those areas where the concentration of ethnic minority groups was relatively high and the school population contained many ethnic minority pupils (Brehony, 1995). This desire, in the main, indicated a recognition that ethnic minority communities may have particular interests that needed representation on governing bodies. In some cases, as has always been the case with democratic arrangements, the desire was motivated less by democratic sentiment and more by a need to try to incorporate and control ethnic minority interests. Whatever the intention, there was a general feeling from our research that ethnic minorities, particularly those that are black and Asian, are under represented on school governing bodies. We found also that once on the governing bodies we studied, black and Asian governors, unless they constituted a majority, were less likely than white middle-class governors to be on the important subcommittees such as finance or staffing, where many of the key decisions are taken prior to being presented to the main meeting. This was also true of women, who were less likely to be on the major subcommittees than men and also less frequently chaired governing bodies (Deem, 1994). Survey research studies since the 1980s reforms have shown that lay governors in England are predominantly recruited from the white, middle-class, highly educated and qualified sectors of the population, although within this, both women and men are reasonably well represented (Keys and Fernandes, 1990).

Governors turn out to be recruited disproportionately from a rather narrow sector of society, namely those that have the resources of time, money, cultural and political capital to enable them to assist others in a voluntary capacity. Does it matter that what I have called, following Stedman Jones, the 'urban gentry' have tended to dominate governing bodies? Stewart for one, thinks it does and he sees what he prefers to call the 'new magistracy' as a growing non-elected elite that is taking over large parts of local government which is not locally accountable (Stewart, 1992). Elected governors find it difficult enough to find ways in which they might be accountable to their constituencies and this is especially so of parent governors but there is no possible means for the appointed LEA and business governors to be accountable either to the LEA or local business.

## Making spaces for voice: some suggestions for reform

Viewed from both the political science and the participatory democracy perspectives the current situation regarding school governing bodies is untenable. The contradictions between the forms of representation and the purposes of governing bodies are such that, disregarding the tensions between lay governors and the professionals, governing bodies are failing to provide either local accountability or local control. Does this imply that governing bodies should be abolished, with the control of schools reverting to teachers who would once more be subject only to professional accountability? I think not, as what I think is needed is something like the 'critical professionalism' argued for in 'Education Limited' (Education Group II 1991) that requires a restructuring of professionalism so that it becomes open to alliances with parents and community groups. As Hodge has argued in relation to other public services, we need in education to move from a culture which traditionally has put bureaucratic and professional interests first, to one that prioritises customers and citizens (Hodge, 1991, p.11). Among heads of schools we interviewed, now that the school system is fragmenting and access to local networks of power becomes more important than ever, there was considerable support for the principle of governing bodies as a way of involving local lay people in schools. As one head put it:

> It is quite right that society should be represented by people in the running of a public service of this sort which is so vital to the future formation and the local community and that professionals, especially headteachers should be accountable to such bodies. On the whole, therefore, I approve of the legislation of eighty six eighty eight and it is the matter for on-site agreements and working relationships locally. I suppose, to make the optimum benefit out of the legislation and situation which we find ourselves. It is useful to have Governors who can, act not only as a sounding board to my ideas for the future and my interpretations of events as they unfold in the school, but to give me more authority.

The solution proposed by the right to the problem of the accountability of public services is that of 'exit', which is one of Hirschman's three options; the other two being 'loyalty' and 'voice'. (Hirschman, 1970)

Loyalty, occurs when those in receipt of public services are either satisfied or their dissatisfaction is not sufficient to motivate them to act in a critical way. Voice is the expression of dissatisfaction. Thus the parents of pupils in a school may make representations to the school's management about issues that they feel critical of. If parents or pupils do not like their school then, runs the logic of 'exit', they can leave and choose another (Flew, 1991). Apart from the fact that for every choice secured another is potentially denied, the logistics of 'exit' are such that it makes a rationally organised system of schooling virtually impossible. Free parental choice of schools is a fantasy and a cruel deception practised on those gullible enough to believe in it by cynical Tories looking for political advantage. What then of the alternatives? Skidelsky, who rejects 'exit' and solutions based on an unregulated market in general, nevertheless charges the Left with having failed to develop 'a plausible story' of how accountability may be secured through the exercise of 'voice' (Skidelski, 1989). This is the challenge I turn to in the rest of this chapter.

## Accountability and education: whose voice?

Public services are provided and run for reasons other than just meeting the needs of those who work in them. Therefore other constituencies have a right to be consulted as to the direction that service should take. Nevertheless, if change of any significance is to occur it is clearly important that those who work in schools whether they be teaching or non-teaching staff are represented on any body that has power over the direction that the school may take. While in our study non-teaching staff were sometimes regarded as in some way subordinate to teachers, a teacher governor we interviewed put the case for their representation by arguing:

> I would like to see I think — I'm thinking aloud here — some form of representation for the non-teaching staff, who know the mechanics of the school. We've got very good ancillary staff here. I mean it seems to me you've got ancillary in-class staff, and you've an ancillary staff to do with the services, and they don't have a voice, and they certainly don't use me as a voice. And yet a lot of what's decided has ramifications on their day-to-day working lives.

It is also the case that schools and parents need to co-operate, if pupils are to derive the maximum benefit from schooling. The ways in which co-operation may take place are numerous and diverse but the representation of parents on governing bodies is one way that co-operation might be developed. The Taylor Committee also recommended that older pupils in secondary schools should be represented on governing bodies. From several points of view but particularly that regarding education in citizenship, this is a laudable notion and one that needs to be reasserted. One of the governing bodies in our case study continued a long standing tradition of inviting older pupils as observers to its meetings without any opposition from anyone.

Public services must be accountable to those who they are meant to serve and parents and pupils should be at the forefront of that category. The circle of accountability, should then widen so that schools should give an account of their actions to the community or communities that they serve. This does not mean as at present that business or commerce should be in any way privileged. In order to ensure that this does not happen all categories, teachers, non-teaching staff, parents (and pupils where appropriate) and community figures should all be elected.

In many areas there will be problems in finding sufficient people to contest an election as the practice of citizenship is not one that the population of England has been taught much about or is very familiar with, aside from the occasional ritual of voting at election time. This, and the low poll, were used to criticise the school boards that were established through popular election in the late nineteenth century (Brehony, 1985). However, in Chicago elected schools' councils currently appear to function well. In circumstances where there were insufficient numbers standing for election those who had been elected could co-opt others to represent the unfilled categories. The point to be made here is that co-option should be a second line strategy and not as now one that acts as a conduit to ensure that business ideals and business ethics enter the school.

Community is, as many have pointed out, a very slippery notion. Within a geographical area such as that from which a school draws its pupils there may be not one but many communities and even aggregations of the population in which the social ties we recognise as accompanying the term community have ceased to exist. How then can we begin to ensure that communities are represented fairly? Our suggestion is that quotas be established in order to encourage those members of our communities like women and blacks who, as our research shows, are frequently under represented on governing bodies. The argument for quotas has already been advanced in the Labour Party (Brooks, Eagle and Short, 1990) and there is, in my view, no good reason why the principle should not be applied to other arenas in which citizenship is practised in order to spread the load of representation. Such a change would incorporate similar arrangements to those in New Zealand, which Cusack describes in Chapter 7.

## The purpose of school governance

Having outlined who ought to be on the new school governing bodies I shall now turn to address the question of their purpose. Our research has convinced us that the volunteers, who have taken on the task of governing schools and who have, under LMS shouldered much of the burden formerly carried by the local authorities, have a task that in most respects is impossible to perform. It is impossible in terms of the extent and scope of the work required of them and also due to the absence of material and human resources. Personnel issues, for example, place governors in the position of employers who have to carry out policies originating elsewhere and this may in due course lead to industrial conflict. As Monck et al. have argued (Monck et al., 1992), the right to determine teachers' pay, for example, is not something that should be left to governors. Much of the work of management and administration associated with devolved budgets is best left to teachers and others hired for their expertise in coping with it.

Governors on the other hand should, as they are supposed to in Spain, set the broad policy direction that the school is to take. In addition they should be partners with schools in chains of accountability. Given that resource scarcity is likely to be a permanent condition facing schools in the future governors also have a vital role to play in representing the school in political processes associated with the allocation of resources. They should occupy a place at the interface between the boundary of the school as an organisation and its immediate environment and play a major part in the representation of one to the other.

## Conclusion

I have attempted in this chapter to consider three perspectives on governing bodies that have emerged from the research I have been involved in on school governing bodies. I argued that the perspectives, elements of which are to be found in combination on most governing bodies, are contradictory. The reason for this lies in the ideological provenance of the 1980s legislation. The political science perspective of the Taylor Report was yoked to the new managerialism and market philosophies of the new right to create an unstable mixture which has left governors uncertain as to the intended purposes of the restructured governing bodies. For this reason, as well as a commitment to more democratic forms of controlling schools, I proposed changes in the way in which interests are represented on governing bodies. I also suggested that their purposes should also change. None of these changes could occur in a vacuum. For them to be successful, changes are also required at the local level. Instead of LEAs being abolished they should be restructured and their membership opened up to popular election. At the same time, in order for communities to make substantive decisions about core activities of schools such as the curriculum, the centralising tendency in education must be reversed. Of all the contradictions surrounding the conduct and place of school governing bodies in the school system none is greater than that between the rhetoric of local decision making and the reality of expanded state power.

## Acknowledgements

The research project described here was funded by an Economic and Social Research Council Grant (R000 23 1799). I am indebted to my co-director of the project, Professor Rosemary Deem of Lancaster

University, for her help and critical comments on an earlier draft of this chapter. A version of the chapter was presented at a meeting on the Education Group of the Fabian Society in July 1993 and I would like to thank the members of the Group for their willingness to think boldly about how the education system may be revitalised.

## Bibliography

Brehoney, K. J. (1985) 'Popular control or control by experts? Schooling between 1880 and 1902' in Langan, M. and Schwarz (Ed) *Crisis in the British State 1880–1930*, London: Hutchison, pp.256–273.

Brehony, K. J. (1992) '"Active Citizens": the case of school governors'. *International Studies in Sociology of Education*, 2, 2, pp.199–217.

Brehony, K. J. (1995) '"Race", ethnicity, racism and the governing of schools' in Tomlinson, S. and Craft, M. *Ethnic Relations in Schools in the 1990s*, London: Athlone (forthcoming).

Brooks, R., Eagle, A. and Short, C. (1990) *Quotas now: women in the Labour Party*, Fabian Tract 541.

Deem, R. (1994) The organisational practices of school governance: modernist or post modernist'. Paper given at the CEDAR International Conference, April, University of Warwick.

Education Group II (1991) *Education Limited*, London: Unwin Hyman.

Flew, A. (1991) 'Educational services: independent competition or maintained monopoly' in Green, D. G. (Ed) *Empowering the Parents: How to Break the Schools Monopoly*, London: IEA, pp.15–53.

Habermas, J. (1976) *Legitimation Crisis*, London: Heinemann.

Heelas, P. and Morris, P. (1992) 'Enterprise culture: its values and value' in Heelas, P. and Morris, P. (Ed) *The Values of the Enterprise Culture*, London: Routledge, pp.1–25.

Hirschman, A. O. (1970) *Exit, Voice and Loyalty*, Cambridge Mass: Harvard University Press.

Hodge, M. (1991) *Quality, Equality, Democracy: Improving Services*, Fabian Pamphlet 549, London: Fabian Society.

Keys, W. and Fernandes, C. (1990) *A Survey of School Governing Bodies*, Slough: England, National Foundation for Educational Research.

Le Grand, J. (1991) 'Liberty, equality and vouchers' in Green, D. G. (Ed) *Empowering the Parents: How to Break the Schools Monopoly*, London: IEA, pp.77–90.

Maclure, S. (1989) *Education Re-formed*, 2nd ed, London: Hodder and Stoughton.

Monck, E. and Kelly, A. (1992) *Managing Effective Schools*, London: IPPR.

Pateman, C. (1970) *Participation and Democratic Theory*, Cambridge University Press.

Ransom, S. (1992) 'Towards the learning society'. *Educational Management and Administration*, **20**, 2, pp.68–79.

Report, T. T. (1977) *A New Partnership for Our Schools*, London: HMSO.

Sallis, J. (1988) *Schools, Parents and Governors*, London: Routledge.

Skidelsky, R. (1989) *The Social Market Economy*, London: Social Market Foundation.

Stewart, J. (1992) 'The rebuilding of public accountability'. Paper given to European Policy Forum Conference, Westminster.

Stivers, C. (1990) 'The public agency as *polis*: active citizenship in the administrative state'. *Administration and Society*, **22**, 1, pp.86–105.

Strain, M. (1993) 'Education reform and defamiliarisation: the struggle for power and values in the control of schooling: towards a postmodernist critique'. *Educational Management and Administration*, **21**, 3, pp.188–206.

# 5 'Voice' trumps 'choice': parents confront governors on opting out

Stephen Brigley

## Introduction

Educational reforms of recent years have disturbed established relationships of power and responsibility amongst central government, local education authorities and teaching professionals. The legislation of 1986–93 has transferred much of the control of the curriculum, governance and management of schools, previously divided between teachers and LEAs, to governing bodies and the Secretary of State. Under local management (LMS), many of the financial and managerial responsibilities previously fulfilled by local education authorities have been delegated to school governing bodies. But statutory measures do not necessarily give an accurate guide to practice. In the transition from a mainly honorific or symbolic role to a closer collaboration in school management, various styles of governorship have emerged: community participation, managerialism, consumerism, bureaucratic control and para-professional involvement (Brigley, 1991). These strongly suggest that the formal changes are being assimilated within local traditions of governorship at different rates and with varying results.

Under the onerous responsibilities of LMS, many post-1988 governing bodies have retreated to a supportive model of governorship (Kogan, 1984), characterised in Thody's Chapter 2 above as the covert roles of giving consent, offering protection and providing legitimation to schools' full-time leaders. For the most part, governors defer to the headteacher in the complex business of running secondary schools, but some preserve a trusteeship role in the primary sector (Golby, 1990). One new development seems to be the re-casting of governing bodies on business lines (Baginsky, et al., 1991).

> Here the government of schools is equated with enterprise, the governors act as a board of directors and the Chair as managing director (Appleby and Golby, 1992).

Enterprise requires flexible and responsive strategies to satisfy the market and adapt to the changing environment of education. Governors as directors will be concerned with quality assurance and efficient management in their schools. Thus, the impact of LMS has probably been to divert governors' attention away from child-centred concerns and towards the detailed management of finance and personnel, and (increasingly) marketing the school.

The participation of parents has also become an increasingly important feature in the landscape of local education systems, but the nature of their role and influence *vis-à-vis* their children's education is still unclear (Munn, 1993; Woods, 1993). Governors are expected to be democratically representative and accountable to parents and the community. Thody has described this expectation as having been transmuted to illusory democracy (Chapter 2 above), although another contributor to this book (Macbeth, Chapter 11) considers that it should not be too difficult in England to use channels of communication with parents and ensure accurate and linked representation. Batteson and Court's study in this volume (Chapter 3) demonstrates, however, that differences between parents and governors can emerge which complicate the meaning of 'representation' and 'accountability'. Parental opinion barely registers as significant in many schools, but stronger assertion by some parents has revealed contrasting educational values and views of accountability (Golby and Brigley, 1989) and potentially makes for an unstable environment in school governorship.

The reforms contain much ambiguity regarding the relative distribution of power between central and local institutions, and about whether schools are to satisfy private interests or the public good. At times, conflict has replaced consensus as local groups of governors and parents have begun to contest the control of education. As the difficulties of new working relationships, responsibilities and accountabilities become apparent, professionals and administrators in education have called for the re-establishment of partnership in the service. However, a new consensus in support of 'what is best for the children' may not be simple to achieve with parental groups who do not show unanimity of values and interests among themselves.

## Parents: consumers or citizens?

The prospects for schools are linked more closely to parents' wishes than ever before. Some of the choices given to parents under the reforms are politically controversial. The 1988 Act requires a majority of parents at a school to vote in favour of its governors' resolution to opt out, if the proposal is to go forward for consideration by the Secretary of State. The attainment of GM status in turn can help governors to change a school's character (this has been facilitated by the 1993 Education Act). Thus, the decision to opt out may carry considerable importance for the continued existence of a school and its standing in the local community. The long-term effects of the opting out policy are not certain, but could include: the reinforcement of the managerial control of headteachers (Fitz, et al., 1993); the obstruction of local authorities' attempts to maintain balance and equity of educational provision (Pryke, 1993), and the ultimate break-up of the system of comprehensive, publicly-maintained schooling (Maclure, 1988).

The intent behind much of the legislation appears to be the empowerment of parents as consumers through the provision of a wider choice of schools and more detailed information on them. With school funding linked mainly to pupil numbers and ages, the cumulative impact of parents' choices will be to compel schools to improve their performance. The new market discipline injected into the running of schools will in effect influence policy as an invisible hand, causing the elimination of 'inferior' institutions and the elevation of those of 'quality'. The apparatus for the exercise of consumer choice is outlined in the Parents' Charter, with its statutory rights of parents to information, choice of school and access to complaints procedures. Parental choice on opting out and other matters is presented as an analogy with a competitive market model. The parental view is assumed to be individualistic: fundamentally orientated around the interests of the individual child, and widened to that of the individual class or school as and when appropriate.

This combination of consumerist empowerment, school self-management and centralist restructuring of what remains principally a national system, locally administered may not be satisfactory to all parents. Consumer choice does not permit the level of participation in policy-making which some would like (O'Connor, 1994), nor does the Parents' Charter cover all matters on which they may seek redress in education (Cordingley and Kogan, 1993). Parents are citizens with civil, social and political rights. As such, they may wish to hold the education service publicly accountable, using their rights to freedom of speech and association, to vote in national and local elections and politically to influence public institutions. Within the broader accountability framework, parents are influential users of public services and, therefore, an important source of legitimation for them. Public education authorities have long been accountable to parents *via* the ballot box, and open to pressure-group influence, but governing bodies too may find that parents as 'active citizens' press them to become more open and accountable to the community.

The following case study will help to illustrate uncertainties surrounding the extent to which governors can be described as representing parents, and the effectiveness of mechanisms to enable this accountability to operate. Underlying this study are expectations about governors as mandated representatives or governors as trustees, raised by Macbeth in this book. The case concerns a school where a policy for 'opting out' into grant-maintained status had to be decided. In describing governors' policy-making powers, Thody (above) concentrated on internal divisions between headteachers and chairpersons, delineating governing bodies as deferring to heads in policy making. In the case discussed here, the governors did make common cause with the headteacher, as Thody inferred was likely, but its special interest lies in the wider political divisions between those who might be described as constituents (the parents) and those who might be termed their representatives (the governors). The case is also of interest in the light it may shed on governing bodies' capacity to learn how to function politically (Thody suggested that governing bodies were politically immature).

## The opt-out case

(Note: the author was a participant observer in the events described below.)

In September, 1992, at their Annual Meeting with parents, the governors of a voluntary-aided primary school in the West of England announced that they were going to commence a fact-finding investigation on opting out of LEA control. The school concerned, referred to as 'VA School' in this account, is situated in a residential part of a town in which grant-maintained (GM) secondary schools have a presence. It is recognised locally to have a good reputation, to be happy, well-run, and popular with middle-class parents. It has over 200 pupils and is placed in a local authority which is more generous in its education spending than the government would wish.

For nearly a year the matter remained dormant. Then, on 6 September 1993, the governing body at VA School passed its first resolution to ballot the parents on opting out. This announcement came as a surprise to some parents, who sought immediate clarification and information. The governing body replied that it would present its findings on opting out and discuss the matter with parents after its second resolution had been passed at least one month later. Thus began a period of discord between governors and parents over consultation and the provision of information on the opt-out decision.

At an early stage, some parents felt uneasy at the prospect of an opt-out vote. One of them recalled:

> I felt sick when I first heard that the governors were going to look into opting out. I know what awful upheavel and divisions it can cause in a school.

Another questioned the 'morality' and 'commonsense' of opting out, but also the wisdom of the governors in putting the school through the 'trauma' of the process. After the resolution of 6 September, a parent expressed objections to GMS in a letter to the governors, followed by a more detailed statement to parents. Soon a small group of parents had formed in opposition to the proposal to make VA School grant-maintained.

To make up for what they saw as the governors' failure to consult and make information available, the anti-GMS parents gathered their own information from various sources, and published their views regularly in a user-friendly bulletin to parents, which was distributed up to the date of the opt-out ballot. They held meetings for parents at a local pub, at which officials of teachers unions and a representative (the present author) of the Campaign for State Education were invited to speak. They campaigned at the school gate in discussions with parents and occasionally with teachers. They lobbied key personnel, not only the governors themselves but also the diocesan director of education, the director of education of the county concil, the local MP, and the bishop of the diocese. These strategies were clearly aimed at making the governing body pull back from making a second resolution. However, on 26 October, the governors' decision to put the matter to a parental vote was unanimously reaffirmed. Attention now switched to winning the hearts and minds of parents.

The opposition group of parents sensed that the headteacher at VA School, though maintaining a publicly neutral 'face' on GMS, was very keen to see the school leave LEA control. They complained that the head refused to allow them to distribute their communications through the school, whereas this facility had been offered to a former governor who wrote a letter in defence of the governing body (the offer was declined). The teachers' views on opting out were more difficult to fathom, though they were reported to have discussed the matter among themselves and concluded in favour.

Unusually the teachers' associations had not been allowed to discuss opting out with them at VA School, and no ballot of teachers at VA School was held. Apparently, the views of ancillary staff at the school were never canvassed.

After the second governors' resolution, the 'gloves came off' in the political contest for the future of VA School. The anti-opt out parents became more outspoken and strident in their pamphlets and stepped up their campaigning in the school playground. Some governors were clearly irritated by the note of alarm sounded by the parents. They retaliated with regular canvassing of parents on the school premises. They branded the opposition parents as 'troublemakers' and 'politically motivated'. There were some angry exchanges between parents and governors, including one in which a parent was singled out accusingly by a teacher at the school gate and told 'My job is on the line'. The governors' own publicity included an annotated version of one of their opponents' bulletins, making amendments, corrections, criticisms and derisory allegations of 'distortion' and 'incomprehension'.

It was in this atmosphere of confrontation that the governors held a meeting on 23 November to discuss opting out with the parent body. The governing body's findings and recommendations on GMS were distributed to all parents prior to the meeting, but only fuelled the controversy. The anti-GMS group felt that the governors' statement was biased and issued too late to assist informed, democratic debate. The governors cited financial and managerial advantages, suggesting that under GMS VA School would gain £70,000. This figure was vigorously disputed, but the opposition could not obtain detailed figures from the school with which to refute the claim. By this time, opposition parents were of the opinion that the governors wanted to stifle open discussion of the opt-out decision. They noted with irritation that the Annual Meeting of parents and governors had been postponed twice (in September and November). Moreover, their participation was confined at the governors' meeting with parents on 23 November. The meeting was advertised as consisting of presentations of the governors' view, the LEA's view, and that of the diocesan education authority, followed by a question-time for parents.

The meeting on the 23rd produced a big turn-out of around 150 parents. They queued to enter the school hall, while the school secretary and a governor checked off names from the electoral roll. Inside the hall some parents were surprised to see a uniformed police officer. At the front of the hall was a raised dais occupied by the chair of governors, the speakers, and, as if to emphasise their unity, slightly to the side of them sat the teaching staff. The governors were ranged around the sides of the hall (though it was only at the end of the meeting that their identity was made known). The parents occupied the floor of the hall. Seemingly to give the proceedings an air of impartiality, the meeting was chaired by an outsider. Parents were lectured on how to conduct themselves during the meeting, especially in asking questions, when they would be required to speak into a microphone and to preface their question with their own names, their children's names and class group. The evening commenced and ended with prayers led by the parish priest. At the start of proceedings a governor was seen to switch on sound recording equipment. Only when someone from the floor queried the recording was an explanation given by the chair of governors.

To some parents the meeting appeared deliberately stage-managed to intimidate the audience. The governor presenting the governors' case for going grant-maintained used OHP slides, but the lighting was dimmed very low for an unnecessarily long period. This increased the sinister atmosphere in the hall and made it impossible to take note of the OHP data. The annotated anti-GMS bulletin was displayed, and opposition parents berated for their 'scaremongering' and false claims. There was even a disparaging remark about their meeting in a local pub (which happened to be run by VA School parents). The vehemence of the governor's attack became so extreme at one point that the chair had to intervene.

Feelings in the floor were already running high when the governor suggested that the school would have to lose three full-time teachers if it stayed LEA-maintained, and then proceeded to name the candidates for redundancy. This, along with the final message of the presentation ('Don't let politics dictate the future of this school'), created uproar in the audience. If there was a feeling before the meeting that the governors were remote and unresponsive to parents, they were seen to have alienated themselves still further from the audience by this high-handed approach. In later contributions, an LEA spokesperson emphasised the harmful effect of opting out of schools under the LEA and urged parents to place fairness before finance. The diocesan director of education tried to be even-handed, suggesting that for parents the choice was between opting out, which on balance would probably be better for VA School, and not opting out which would probably be better for other schools in the area.

It became apparent during question-time that the parents had not been cowed: critical questioners from the floor were moved by concerns about the governors' handling of the opt-out process, the apparent plight of the named teachers and financial issues. The meeting concluded amid a rising tide of parental indignation. The question 'Who are these governors?' went around the hall, whereupon the governors were all asked to stand up. At this point, it seemed that parental opinion clearly turned against them, causing a rapid realignment in the stances of key individuals within the school and church foundation.

Subsequent fall-out from the meeting was swift. The school's opt-out issue had been covered in the local press for some time, but now it was front-page news. Under the threat of legal action by the teachers' unions over the naming of teachers for redundancy, the governors publicly admitted their mistakes and apologised to the three teachers. The governors also abandoned a legally dubious plan to play the recording to parents who could not attend the meeting of the 23rd. To disgruntled parents, the speed of their response to union pressure contrasted sharply with their obdurate response to parents' requests for access to important information, such as the OHP transparencies and the tape recording of the meeting.

Diocesan guidelines recommended that governors give balanced and objective information on opting out to parents, but by now both sides were engaged in an open, political contest. New voices entered the debate: one parent sent a letter to parents (via the school) in support of the governors, having witnessed parents 'berating a governor in a very aggressive manner'. According to one parent, a belligerent governor made comments which displayed 'outright contempt' for individuals in the anti-GMS group. The anti-GMS group was still incensed by the governors' patronising and objectionable treatment of parents at the meeting, but could not see any way to obtain redress. They felt that an apology was called for, and possibly some governors' resignations.

The result of the parents' ballot on 14 December 1993 was not a foregone conclusion, but a comfortable 60/40 majority against the opt-out proposal was returned. The aftermath contained the usual calls for the re-establishment of unity among those in the school and all concerned with it. There was general physical and emotional fatigue among those closely involved with the campaigning. Parents had never had any reason to withdraw their trust in the teachers and confidence in the quality of education at the school. But they had put a big personal stake on the outcome of the opt-out ballot, as well as a considerable investment of time, energy and money in the campaign.

In February, 1994, the chair of governors was quoted as saying of the opt-out episode that everyone had forgotten about it and the subject was closed. This did not prove to be the case. In a letter from the chair to parents, a short paragraph on the issue mentioned the governors' 'regret' about the mistaken budget figures and their apology 'to all concerned'. In March, the long-postponed Annual Meeting was held. It seemed that the absence of any mention of the GMS proposal in the governors' Annual Report and the meeting's agenda would pre-empt any further discussion. But there was an outstanding question from the postponed November AGM about the governors' funding of their opting-out publicity. Further parental criticism of the governors' conduct during the episode and their managerial competence followed. This caused the head to rally to the governing body's defence. Parents were told by governors that if they had wanted more representation in the running of the school they should have voted to opt out, and if they did not like the way the school was run they should take their children elsewhere.

## Theoretical issues

The VA School opt-out case may be seen as something of an aberration on the governorship scene. It was located in a church school with an 'unreconstructed' governing body, comfortable with a 'hands-off', supportive role and insulated from the new climate of accountability (it is worth noting that many rural primary schools fit this description). However, the case study raises issues about relationships between governors and parents which have wider importance in the current policy context. These relate to long-standing difficulties in theorising the powers and responsibilities of governing bodies in relation to the school, its management and professional teachers, in relation to parents and the community and to local and national political authorities.

The ambiguities and complexities of these multi-faceted relationships have been worked through in the case study mainly from a parental perspective of a critical incident in the life of a school. They may not have quite such a fine point in schools of a different character or in other localities. VA School as a church school had a foundation majority in the composition of its governing body. Moreover, there were only two parent governors, one elected and one nominated by the foundation. However, it will be argued that this episode highlighted incompatibilities of values and interests which, given the ambiguities of the policy framework noted earlier, have the potential to cause conflict in situations other than opting out and in schools which are not voluntary-aided.

## Effectiveness and authority

The unfolding of events at VA School clearly raised important questions in parents minds about the governing body, particularly its competence, ethics and accountability. The comment 'Who are these governors?' from parents at the meeting and their reactions to the governors' presentation were tantamount to questioning their authority as a management group. The effectiveness of interested 'amateurs' in governorship not only raises practical problems, but is also linked with the theory of governance. In practice, the problem of managing complex and unpredictable relationships in the changing, very public and unfamiliar environment of education may prove taxing even for governors who have considerable managerial experience. At VA School the governors tended to allow legal regulations to dictate their strategy. This approach was fraught with dangers, as soon became evident when some of the players introduced moral values and emotional attitudes into the opt-out drama.

Governors, especially chairs of governing bodies, are normally in close working relationship with the headteacher on managerial decisions. However, the head at VA School seemed intent on remaining above the politics of the opting out process, and perhaps left governors too much to their own devices. It is a matter of conjecture whether or not the head was consulted on some of the more aggressive tactics used by governors against the parental anti-GMS lobby. The fact that parents felt patronised and manipulated by the governors bears testimony to their clumsy handling of the situation. It could take some time before relationships between the governors and parents are repaired.

The theory of governorship effectiveness goes to the heart of the nature and purpose of school governorship. The 'effective school governor' may still be a vague and ill-defined notion: fulfilling their legal obligations and doing their best for the school may sum up the view of many governors. But that conception of governorship may not translate easily into effective strategies in unusual and testing political decisions. The recent promotion of governors as partners in the management of the school did not resonate with the parents' lack of confidence in the governors' handling of the opt-out inquiry, communication and consultation. Parents, many of whom had never seen the governors before, were dismayed at the opt-out meeting that the governing body appeared to have such an important say in the future of the school and their children's education, and questioned its right to do so. From the parents' point of view, the governors may have had formal legal authority to advance the opt-out proposal and possibly gleaned further legitimacy by association with the headteacher and teaching staff, but they had lost moral authority by failing to consult and inform the parents in such a way as to enable their full participation in the decision.

## Accountability

The governing body's detailed document on opting out was prefaced with an explanation of its role, including its responsibility to parents and the LEA for the running of the school. But responsibility is a weaker notion, unlike the term preferred by the anti-GMS parents, which was accountability. The first steps towards accountability require the acceptance of the obligation to inform the party to whom the account is rendered and then to be open to question on it. The governing body recognised the first element by informing parents on opting out, though the quality and balance of the information was seen as questionable and only sufficient to fulfill its legal duties on the opt-out arrangements. The governors' willingness to answer parents' questions was doubtful in view of their limitation to a single meeting, followed quickly by the issue of ballot papers as if to discourage further discussion. Stricter levels of accountability which would have obliged governors to consult, listen to advice and even to act upon it were clearly not entertained. The most vociferous opponents of opting out would probably have been satisfied if all sides of the issue had been fully aired. Instead, they felt frustrated at every turn by governors who seemed worried about losing control of the opt-out initiative and unsettled by the cleverly orchestrated campaign of a few middle-class parents.

Accountability relationships and assumptions of authority were closely connected for the anti-GMS parents. At VA School the governors by their own actions succeeded only in undermining their moral and managerial authority in the eyes of parents. The exercise of accountability presupposes that an accounting body has the authority to do so in a social activity. But this means that the body has more than just formal authority: it must have real or substantive authority and be seen by others to do so (Brigley, 1991). It was probably not far from parents' minds that some of the present governors would be members of the GM governing body, if the school opted out. The prospect that governors, whom they now saw as lacking substantive authority, could have the most important accountability role in relation to the school under GMS, did not fill them with enthusiasm.

Most parents are not school managers, governors or teachers, but they all draw upon sources of authority as parents ('parents' rights') and citizens. The anti-GMS group were predominantly from professional backgrounds, and could be loosely described as 'active citizens' in that they shared a sense of civic responsibility. This lent authority to their moral and political arguments and helped to explain why they sustained their critical voice long after the opt-out ballot was completed. For them, the opt-out vote was not merely a case of 'winners and losers': wider values and interests which underlie the governance of schools had to be considered. Their perspective on the issue diverged from a narrow consumer focus of parents on their own children's interests. It was with the voice of concerned citizens as much as parents that they made their contribution to the opting-out debate.

## Representation

Representation of parental opinion is obviously a problem in a governing body with only a 'lone' elected parent governor (Golby and Brigley, 1989). The parent governor at VA School was criticised by parents for failing to recognise any need to consult with or represent them during the opt-out affair. The difficulty for a single individual in vigorously communicating with parents and canvassing their views on school policy and practice is considerable when this tradition has not been strong in a school governing body. Indeed, over-protective governors may wish to insulate the school from external stakeholders, and invoke collective responsibility, rules of confidentiality and corporate loyalty to dissuade governors from actively representing outside views.

The law does not encourage the active canvassing and representation by governors of parents' views. The 1986 Act omitted to make any regulations on such matters as reporting back to parents or the right to set up a parents' association. Many governing bodies have introduced routine channels of consultation with parents usually through the PTAs, including some with advanced participation structures at year group and class group levels. What the 1986 Act did seem clear on was that all governors have the same rights and responsibilities by virtue of membership of the board, and that members of the governing body always speak and act as one. This appears to militate against independent attempts to represent parents' wishes.

For some parents, the dispute was aggravated by the failure of the whole governing body to take heed of their wish for an informed and free debate on opting out. The resulting absence of a broad cross-section of opinion on the issue raised an old problem for democrats: the distortion of the process by elite groups. Only a small group of parents had the facility to present their views and wield strategies of influence to make a major impact on the debate. Active campaigners in the pro-GMS lobby who could match them were similarly few in number. The most commanding personality in the affair was probably the headteacher, who understandably did not want to be seen confronting parents. The role of the school foundation was ambiguous: at the meeting the diocesan director presented a fairly impartial view, while encouraging parents to take account of the consequences for the wider community in their decision. Views given in conversation, however, showed that members and clergy of the local church did not see anything immoral about opting out. Some parents found it curious, others were disappointed that no-one from the Church seemed to give any credence to the ethical case against opting out.

## Values contrasts

The body of law and related orders and regulations, the Instrument and Articles of Government, all provide a framework within which schools are governed. If traditions of governance can be sustained within that framework which reflect a local consensus on educational values, the system may run smoothly. Radical changes in the framework, however, tend to upset traditional ways of governing and magnify divisions within that consensus. The opting out policy has already caused major restructuring of local education systems and brought contrasting sets of moral and social values into opposition. Thus, it was hardly to be expected that all parents and governors at VA School would see things the same way.

The contemporary polarity of values in education and society which was exemplified in the VA School opt-out debate invests the case with wider relevance. The individualist values of the Right were clearly visible in the way the governors saw the decision before them. They promoted their case by citing the advantages which would narrowly accrue to VA School. These were mainly market-driven and managerialist in inspiration: enhancement of the prestige and popularity of the school locally (presumably, they believed all GM schools to have higher social status), financial gains to the school, greater managerial autonomy for the head and increased responsiveness to parents (the 'consumers'). Thus, when pressed, they slipped from the supportive model into the business model of governorship.

The parents against opting out espoused collectivist values of the liberal Left. Education for them was seen as a public good, to be provided in comprehensive schools which are part of a wider system, publicly funded and controlled. Fundamental values which were implicitly threatened by the opting out policy were equity, social unity and altruism. Mass opt-outs would defeat LEAs' attempts to create balanced and fair educational provision across a range of institutions with different circumstances and needs, if only because the governing mechanism and management system by which to do so would no longer exist. If local, publicly maintained school systems were destroyed in their area, the parents thought it likely that the values of partnership, community and participation would disappear with them. Their preferred model of the governing body was a democratic forum through which parents might participate in decisions on school policy.

The leading players acted out these conflicting values in their respective opt-out campaigns. The governors saw GMS as a cost-benefit decision for the parents to consider in relation to their own children in the school. The provision of correct information was all that was necessary for parents individually to make a quasi-market choice. As long as it stays within the perimeter of the law, consumerism does not require democratic debate, any more than buying a jar of coffee in the supermarket. By contrast, the collectivist arguments of the anti-GMS parents dictated rational discussion of the wider impact of the exercise of individual choice by their school. They acknowledged that schools are not all equal in the educational market place, and the long-term effect on other schools of opting out could be so harmful as to be morally unacceptable. For these parents, participative procedures were vital to enable open exchange of information, the free expression of opinion and proper consultation. They saw citizenship values embedded in the opt-out process: expressing a democratic voice was as important as exercising a consumer choice.

## Conclusion: the politics of choice

The commonplace criticism that those who contest the decisions of public authorities are 'politically motivated' was much in evidence in the VA School opt-out affair. It is clear that the values of those who favoured opting out were as political as any held by their opponents. It would require a deeper investigation than this to determine which people, on each side of the controversy, were driving those values and with what motives. Indeed, they may have been only a handful of powerful individuals with very divergent moral and political aspirations for the school.

The case study raises in an extreme form many of the long-standing theoretical issues of legitimacy, accountability, representation and effectiveness which affect governing bodies and have probably been made more confusing by the current policy rhetoric of choice and diversity in education. The confusion is at bottom connected with different values and goals, such as were previously uncovered among parent governors and gave rise to correspondingly varied and opposing views of the nature and purpose of governorship (Golby and Brigley, 1989). As in VA School, these divisions were sometimes demonstrated in political engagements between well-informed, organised and capable individuals, which constituted critical incidents in school governorship. However, there was a crucial difference: formerly, conflicts were more likely to arise between governors and officers of the LEA, or between parent governors and LEA nominees.

This case study has highlighted differences of values and interests between parents and governing bodies, which some might see as illustrating the illusory democracy (Thody, Chapter 2 above) that governing bodies make possible. On the other hand, the active involvement of parents may indicate that the long-term effect of devolution under LMS is to lower the point of political engagement. Governors may find increasingly that they are in the front line, fielding the kind of complaints which the LEAs used to receive from them, and feeling singularly ill-equipped to do so.

## Bibliography

Appleby, R. and Golby, M. (1992) *School Governors: End of Term Report*, Devon: Fair Way Publications.

Baginsky, M., Baker, L. and Cleave, S. (1991) *Towards Effective Partnerships in School Governance*, Slough: NFER.

Brigley, S. (1991) *Education Accountability and School Governors*, unpublished PhD thesis, University of Exeter.

Cordingley, P. and Kogan, M. (1993) *In Support of Education*, London: Jessica Kingsley.

Fitz, J., Power, M. and Halpin, D. (1993) 'Opting for grant maintained status: a study of policy-making in education'. *Policy Studies*, **14**, 1.

Golby, M. and Brigley, S. (1989) *Parents as School Governors*, Devon: Fair Way Publications.

Golby, M. (Ed) (1990) *The New Governors Speak*, Devon: Fair Way Publications.

Kogan, M. (Ed) (1984) *School Governing Bodies*, London: Heinemann.

Maclure, S. (1988) *Education Re-formed*, London: Hodder and Stoughton.

Munn, P. (Ed) (1993) *Parents and Schools: Customers, Managers or Partners?*, London: Routledge.

O'Connor, M. (1994) *Giving Parents a Voice: Parental Involvement in Educational Policy-Making*, Report of Research and Information on State Education.

Pryke, R. (1993) 'Opting into irrelevance', *Times Educational Supplement*, 1 October, pp.12–13.

Woods, P. (1993) 'Parents as consumer-citizens', in Merttens, R., Mayers, D., Brown, A. and Vass, J. (Eds) *Ruling the Margins: Problematising Parental Involvement*, University of North London Press, IMPACT Project.

# 6 Effectiveness and efficiency: views from South Oxfordshire

Anne Curtis

> There is too much for a part-time, unpaid amateur to do if the job is to be done properly.

This was one of the comments made by several respondents in a 1993 survey of governors from nine schools in southern Oxfordshire. The survey aimed to discover how governors interpreted their roles, in particular in relation to the management of their schools and the potential division of responsibilities with school principals. Reports made by governors generally supported Thody's thesis in Chapter 2 that governors are adopting the covert managerial roles of support through consent, protection and legitimation. Further, covert democracy provides the illusion of control over professionals with governors still politically immature. There were, however, some interesting signs of possible developments away from these roles in that the structures for a more overtly effective position were at least in the process of being put into place, if not yet operative. The research demonstrated that the organisation of governing bodies is a complex system going through a period of disturbance, as it attempts to adjust to the changing culture that is being demanded of it by the increased powers and duties.

Seeking a way to assist governors' passage through the changing culture was the original focus for this research since it was seeking to ascertain what training initiatives might be developed by the South Division, which forms part of Oxfordshire's Governor Training organisation. The needs analysis for this resulted in a wide ranging commentary on governors' roles seeking to provide a benchmark against which future developments, in making governing bodies 'fit for purpose' (to use the 1990s popular jargon of quality management), could be measured.

The research took place in nine schools which together provided coverage of all different types of schools, bar voluntary aided, within the area of Oxfordshire local education authority (LEA) which is an LEA in the south of England. The research used questionnaires and semi-structured interviews[1] with 46 governors responding, representing the full range of different types of governorships.[2] The schools involved were a special school (3 governors completed questionnaires), a secondary school (5 governors), two voluntary-controlled primary schools (9 governors) and five county primary schools (29 governors).

The results obtained from this survey are first outlined below and then their implications for managerial efficiency and democratic effectiveness are discussed.

## Research outcomes

**1.** Three-quarters of governors expressed varying degrees of uncertainty and frustration about the changing emphasis of their role. This was further exacerbated by the demands made on them, particularly in terms of time, in relation to their functioning as a board and the necessary commitment involved. Certain governors recognised that a new culture in governorship was evolving, based on management principles, but that the transition period, to incorporate such a change in philosophy, needed to be better managed.

**2.** A majority of parent, staff and all foundation governors felt their role was special, and should be that of representative of their constituents of interest, whilst still retaining their individual viewpoints. Parent governors stressed the importance of a more productive relationship with their external group, with several disillusioned about this lack of opportunity. A structured communication network to allow parents to voice their concerns was considered important.

Co-opted and LEA governors stood for a 'voice' which represented 'objectivity' and 'expertise', indicating a trend in recruiting 'useful' individuals, rather than constituent representatives. In addition, there was a feeling amongst a cross-section of governors that a 'business' voice needed to be represented as a uniting force; which could help to manage the change of culture. This would enable 'best practice' management principles to be openly discussed within governing bodies and provide a catalyst to become 'fit for purpose'.

3. Governing bodies saw their role primarily as being supportive, advisory and a critical friend. Only a minority of governors regarded the role as one of a board of directors or watchdog. Governors' overall management styles operated effectively within both supportive and advisory modes. However, the increased demands being placed upon boards were causing them to shift towards an accountable management style, which incorporated the concept of a critical friend.

Although a working partnership was being sought through shared management, this was mostly one-sided, with governors yet to define a significant place for themselves alongside staff, an area recognised as one area for improvement. Working in partnership with the head was considered effective. No governing body had formally discussed their governing body's purpose and management style, suggesting possible fragmentation within boards.

4. Over half of governors felt their structure was effective, and just under half used committees with delegated powers to make informed decisions. *Ad hoc* working groups were widely used often to help draw members into the decision-making process. Certain boards, however, were considering restructuring as they acknowledge the necessity of terms of reference to support the structure. All governing bodies, bar one, had established subgroups but their efficiency and value varied considerably depending on the qualities of the chair.

Although three-quarters of governors felt morally and professionally accountable, organisational structures to foster the development of a sense of accountability for tasks were difficult to identify. Certain governors also felt that insufficient emphasis was currently being placed with regard to the importance of the curriculum and personnel committees. Few governing bodies, as yet, used the school development plan (SDP) as a basis for structure or as a mechanism for joint governor/staff involvement. None had considered an integrated approach to school management where decision-making was based around a single policy formation body supported by temporary team and task groups.

5. The majority of governors felt that their meetings were effective, reaching decisions by consensus, where they delegated and actioned decisions appropriately. However, three-quarters wanted to see a change in the way they conducted their work. There was little evidence of any formal code of conduct or meetings' charter to act as a

guide to efficiency, or acknowledgement of an established communications network to support the reporting procedures, other than for formal meetings.

**6.** Whilst many governors used their expertise, of mainly managerial and professional qualities, to make informed decisions, others, however, were finding it difficult to realise their potential and contribute effectively. Boards lacked a systematic approach to identify strengths and weaknesses to establish governors' skills.

**7.** Governors expressed concern at their lack of detailed knowledge and the difficulties of 'lay' governors becoming informed participants, although the flow of communication was felt to be effective. The fundamental issue that should be addressed, is that of governors having to accept responsibility for becoming fully involved within the school.

**8.** Although governors felt that they were effective in working in groups and as a team, new governors found entry difficult. Governors were concerned about the new balance expected in relationships, with traditional attitudes and behaviour creating tension, especially between the professionals and the consumers.

**9.** The majority of governors considered that they were making a worthwhile contribution, but few thought that they were effectively monitoring their effectiveness, and sought development in this area. Regular monitoring of effectiveness could become part of a continuous improvement programme.

**10.** Two-thirds of governors saw their main training need centred around issues in education, whilst a third requested duties and local management of schools (LMS). These topics indicated that, at all levels of experience, governors were seeking knowledge based skills to cope with the change in culture and to improve the quality of their decision-making. Less than a quarter of governors, looked to the functioning of the governing body as a training requirement, despite the research data.

## Managerial efficiency

### 'Rank amateurism'

This could be deemed the summation of the concerns of governors in this survey. Most concern was related to the functioning of the governing bodies, but group behaviour, time constraints and poor decision-making were contributing towards the struggle and anxiety governors were experiencing in fulfilling their responsibilities. Other frustrations were:

> financial and numerical changes imposed by central government (parent governor).

and:

> the difficulty of getting decisions from the LEA — in one instance it took two years (parent governor).

Both were felt to impose externally driven restrictions, inhibiting governors from implementing change.

Maintaining the necessary commitment proved to be difficult for some. Several governors believed that it was:

> too much for a 'part-time unpaid amateur' to do if the job is to be done properly (LEA governor).

One parent governor summed up the situation regarding his own board, which he felt was not atypical, and that was that 'rank amateurism' existed compared with management in other sectors of the economy:

> Where it doesn't happen, and this is the biggest frustration, is in organisations that really work in business, in commerce, in industry. Targets are set, targets are met, things are done.

In recognising their rank amateurism, governors appeared ready to adopt the covert managerialism described by Thody in Chapter 2 above but they overtly stated this as their role, rather than it emerging as Thody described. The research clearly indicated that governors saw the board's role as a supporter, adviser and critical friend, in that order of priority, both currently and in the future. Although the governing bodies researched appeared to operate in different modes at different times, it was evident that all boards saw themselves operating primarily in the advisory or supportive modes. This confirmed the Kogan view (1984), that one of the most important functions of the governing body — to support and advise — was still widely held. A mediating mode appeared 'not to be relevant' (parent governor), although governors could be said to be moving in that direction, since there were requests to have a voice in how education was provided.

What complicated the picture however, making the situation more complex and difficult to resolve, was that the perceptions of role varied considerably within the same board. Interviews confirmed that governing bodies' various purposes, and subsequent management styles, had not been formally discussed. This raises a fundamental problem if a clear understanding of the direction and necessary goals are not openly established.

Amidst this uncertainty, governors identified their boards as being effective in undertaking the advisory, and particularly the supportive modes of operation. In these circumstances governors viewed the professionals as running the school effectively:

> the head and teachers have the expertise — we're here to support (LEA governor).

and:

> individual governors have been very good as consultants in particular areas — e.g. finance, liaison with the LEA but not as a board (staff governor).

Governor expertise, especially managerial strengths, was felt to be helpful in advising on planning but this advisory role appeared not to continue into the organisation and implementation stages of development. Does that mean that governors are recognising that the supportive and advisory management styles should be confined to particular parts of management? If so, then does this undermine the views of governors in this study who stated, quite clearly, that they saw their role as maintaining the status quo? Staff governors were felt particularly to demonstrate this view:

> If people don't agree (in meetings) there is deadly silence and then we move on . . . e.g. staff governors only seem interested in maintaining 'the status quo' — no change in anything, anywhere (no governor training, no effective governing body session etc. . . . silence (parent governor).

Amongst parent and co-opted governors interviewed there was an emerging awareness that the status quo was insufficient and a different perception was required from governors:

> I thought I'd be a supportive, almost nodding helper. A person to back up the head and staff, but its got much more complicated . . . I just feel that there are things we ought to be doing which we aren't doing, I'm not quite sure what they are (co-opted governor).

This confusion was felt to have stifled creativity and opportunities for innovation. Where there was no mechanism to challenge the status quo and improve managerial efficiency, 'breaking the china' (Johansson, et al., 1993, p.xi) i.e. stepping back and challenging the very organisation and questioning what should be the real basis for managerial strategy appeared a somewhat daunting hurdle.

Governors in this survey clearly felt inadequate.

> . . . I certainly have come far short of my own standards. I have 'coped' but there is far more that could be done. I have insufficient educational knowledge and insufficient time to acquire it since like many/most people who serve as governors, I am already heavily involved in the community in other ways (chair and LEA governor).

and:

> lack of expertise means several governors, myself included, cannot participate fully in the decision-making . . . (parent governor).

Their views coincided with those of Taylor (1991) and Hinds (1992) who both reflected on the difficulties facing governors in the 1990s being unpaid, unrewarded volunteers, yet who were emerging as 'part-time' managers with performance related workloads (Curtis, 1993).

The governors' reflections concerning the supportive element of their roles also reflected those of Baginsky, et al. (1991) and Kogan (1984). Such views appear to indicate, as Thody implied above, that the roles of governors have not yet changed significantly. Perhaps as Douglas (1989) suggested, the key to change may lie in the extent to which governors see themselves as executive or non-executive directors of schools. There is a need for governors to consider the possibility of playing what the Oxford Centre for Education Management (OxCEM) (1991, p.6) described as the 'pivotal role'. In examining that, governors might look to the general literature on management (Peters, 1988; Drucker, 1990) which postulates the importance of commitment to a vision for organisational effectiveness. What, however, is the vision for governing bodies?

## Business analogies

The evidence from this survey presented a contrast between the views of government and of governors. Whilst most governing bodies were adopting the traditional, educational protective view, recent legislation has injected a competitive dimension into school management forcing governors to adopt a new management culture based on business concepts. Governors could, therefore, assume the role of a board of non-executive directors with the head as the chief executive.

The board of directors' role, however, emerged as one of the least favourable options for the governors in this survey. They suggested that:

> the role of the governing body is to support the head and the staff . . . *If* governors have any expertise in finances, building, etc. they can advise and support the school (staff governor).

These feelings were particularly felt by the staff governors and governors with educational expertise, one of whom felt that:

> By 'supporters' I accept governor responsibilities but we are not a 'crisp' factory nor a private school so cannot act in the general sense of 'directors' (parent governor).

implying perhaps that state schools were unique from any other organisation, and therefore isolated from normal management practice.

What was of interest, was the contrast with the opinions of the consumers who felt that although the term:

> board of directors is a little too strong — more of a steering group with executive powers (parent governor).

there was the realisation that business directors, like governors, were given legal powers to control the management of the organisation.

> I hesitated about (using the terminology), 'board of governors' because it exaggerates our directing role *viz-à-viz* the headmaster. But in the end we must take decisions and take responsibility for what goes on in the school (LEA governor).

There was clearly tension and potential conflict between the professionals and the consumers over the issue of the governing body's role, with one head identifying tension regarding:

> the cloudy issue of 'who's in charge/who's school is it?'

Governors' views could exacerbate this tension, in that the popular role they identified was that of 'critical friend'.

Resolving the cloudy issue of who is in charge was just beginning in the governing bodies, in this survey. Three different management styles adopted by the governing bodies — supportive, advisory and a weak model of accountability appeared to be currently in operation. A fourth style, that of partnership, was at the embryonic stage. Evidence of shared management indicated that there was a genuine effort to develop such a relationship. This was acknowledged by 'staff representation on board and in sub-committees' (co-opted governor) but some governors also recognised that:

> governors and staff both share but not often together. Some sub-committees co-opt extra staff members (co-opted governor).

It appeared that staff were prepared to either serve on committees or present 'papers' at governors' meetings but staff governors were more pessimistic about the realities of shared management:

> staff, I think believe — shared management — more meetings and more work at a time of great burden.

and:

> there is a limit to how much management can be shared in the busy day to day life of the school.

and believed that until there was a well defined management structure, with terms of reference, in which staff could become constructively involved and have some influence they would be reluctant to be drawn further into the process.

Some governors reported that:

> As governors, we are now responsible for many areas, but we have little control if the head and staff argue that they are the 'professionals'. Two meetings a term means many weeks can go by before a matter is discussed (LEA governor).

Yet the certainty that change will take place and will require a new perspective was anticipated by Coopers and Lybrand (1988) and reiterated by a staff governor in this survey who believed that:

> our body of governors have not yet defined clearly our roles and tasks. Therefore lack of clarity of purpose means energy is sometimes expended unnecessarily.

implying that changes would have to take place, leading to a clearer definition of purpose and management style. This has become more important as the boards are being asked to become more accountable for their decisions and are being forced, if reluctantly, towards the accountable style of management, particularly with inspection, where a board of directors analogy sits more appropriately.

This aspect of the research highlighted a developing area for the new roles of governing bodies — that of their relations with the staff as a whole and not just the headteacher. Adams (1989) noted that governors would have to join internal school committees and working parties in ways that previously had been unheard of and which would be viewed with suspicion by staff. Evidence from the survey supported this viewpoint with governors stating that:

> formal discussions occur between governors, head and teacher governor. Only informal contacts between governors and other members of staff (LEA governor).

Some schools were encouraging governing bodies to partake in in-service training days (INSET) acknowledging that a greater involvement by governors was required, although this had not extended into any internal group structures.

In alleviating this suspicion, Morley-Jones' (1989) thoughts might give a lead to ways for development since he suggested using sub-groups or boards prior to decision-making. Such a proposal mirrors ideas of delegation and team working common in business management but presupposes some rethinking of the structuring of governing bodies.

**Structures for effective management**

Governors' enormous workloads and the large amount of business to transact at meetings, raised the issue of delegation and management of devolved functions. Considerable variations in working practices amongst governing bodies have been reported (Cleese, 1993; Baginsky et al., 1991; Kogan, 1984), as has the expectation that arrangements made should enable governors to function efficiently as administrators (Lea, 1991). It is worthy of note, therefore, to report that governors in this survey, felt their governing body structures worked well. The benefits of:

> wide participation — to harness individual expertise — joint decision approval (parent governor)

and:

> subcommittees reflect areas of concern for the school. Governors straddle committees — therefore good cross-fertilisation (staff governor)

built a picture of strengths.

Governing bodies represented in the survey were undergoing various degrees of structural change. These changes varied from those forming informal committees, to others who were critically examining their structure, based on business practice, to find the most appropriate framework.

> Subcommittees are time-consuming. It has been proposed that the present five should be reduced to two to reduce the number of meetings. However, if each subcommittee covers all that is suggested, its meetings risk being extraordinarily long (foundation governor).

Giving governing bodies the power to appoint committees with delegated authority was seen as an answer to the additional workload. Data showed that all boards had taken the opportunity to establish a basic framework comprised of mainly finance, premises, and curriculum committees. *Ad hoc* working groups were also used as part of the delegation mechanism as:

> . . . with more and more responsibilities — more meetings (working parties for specific tasks: special needs, bullying, health and safety and devolution) were needed (staff governor)

with several governors suggesting, like Davies and West-Burnham (1990) the elimination of sub-committees and replacing them with 'small temporary groups having clearly identified issues on a minimum of occasions' (LEA governor).

There was some uncertainty about the necessity to establish personnel committees; one co-opted governor reported not having heard of the idea nor of understanding its remit. Where such committees did not exist, or met infrequently, it was reported that:

> Having no committee meetings, as yet, it is difficult to know what's going on, what should be on the agenda and where we should be going i.e. the problems — there seems to be no preparation. Also having been nominated onto a committee, it would be useful to get to know each other (parent governor).

Some governors believed that, in the absence of committee activity:

> all the decisions (are) made in advance by the head (LEA governor).

and:

> decisions are often made by the head and chairman of governors without reference to other governors (parent governor).

Certainly there was confusion about who made the decisions and whether or not the governors were a rubber stamping agency. This issue was a sensitive one which is why terms of reference were felt to be vital if managerial efficiency in Thody's overt interpretation (Chapter 2 above) was to be realised.

## Working procedures for management structures

Evidence revealed that decision-making was being devolved to committee level, but without the committees having terms of reference, suggesting that few had got to grips with this important task. Boards of governors had made *ad hoc* decisions about delegation but without defining exactly what was to be delegated. However, the majority recognised the limitations in their efficiency with the need to generate:

> More delegated powers to sub-committees, but with written

> reporting procedures to aid in (the) decision-making process by (the) main board (parent governor).

Some appeared to have been deterred from devising terms of reference by their lack of administrative knowledge. One wonders whether some governors were aware of the need for terms of reference.

The disadvantages of this lack of knowledge were openly acknowledged, during the survey interviews, by governors whose full-time occupations were in business. They stated that the current system was flawed, since setting up committees without stipulating the terms of reference first, tended to generate more aimless work. Guidelines, they felt, would have been a significant asset in coping with the onerous tasks arising from the major changes in recent years. One wonders why there was failure to adopt terms of reference for committees. Was it due to lack of knowledge, or to lack of creativity? Why did not headteachers advise governing bodies of the value of the terms of reference?

Ineffectiveness caused by lack of terms of reference of committees appears to have been compounded by inefficient meeting procedures. Although over half of the governors considered the existing committee structure generated a capacity to share ideas, workload and decision-making, three-quarters wanted to see a change in the conduct of business. One parent governor felt that his governing body was:

> Unwieldy — decisions are too often deferred to future meetings and sometimes abrogated totally — rule by committee is slow and largely ineffective — agreed action is not expediated with enough urgency — 30 to 40 per cent of the governors are passengers.

Not having terms of reference on which to build an appropriate way of operating appears to have led to an informal approach being adopted by some boards, often breaking the law in the process through lack of knowledge (Sallis, 1990; Doe, 1991). One governing body, in particular, seemed reluctant to change:

> I was staggered. I'm on the finance committee and it still doesn't have minutes. Its not only illegal its ridiculous (parent governor).

There was little evidence of boards having introduced a code of conduct or meetings' charter to ensure an efficient way of working. Several co-opted governors felt that:

> . . . some decisions should be based on calm assessment of

arguments i.e. written report plus recommendations (not very often done).

Reliance on well run meetings centred around the qualities of the chair. One governor commented on the:

> excellent chair, who runs the meetings efficiently and who has done his 'homework' before the meeting (LEA governor).

If such expertise were not present, the boards' performance suffered:

> poor chairmanship — too long an agenda — unhelpful time spent on minor issues.

reported a different LEA governor in the survey. The quality of chairmanship appears to be a critical factor in attaining a well organised governing body.

Boards are responsible for the effectiveness of their decision-making structures and the efficient conduct of their own business. Establishing ground rules for their process of working would help offset any decisions reached being put at risk of being challenged. Governing bodies could be encouraged to discuss openly how to conduct their business professionally.

## The team solution?

One county primary governing body seemed to be achieving involvement through the SDP with:

> the different expertise of governors is used in relevant delegated tasks and committees (LEA governor).

and:

> staff and governors work by setting objectives through the SDP (co-opted governor).

Involvement centred on the SDP is a constructive way of generating discussion and improving the decision-making process for governors. By participating at the initial and final stages, i.e. with the audit of the school's strengths and weaknesses and the evaluation of the plan, boards would generate a structured involvement. This would legitimise the request for progress reports, clarify roles and responsibilities and enhance a constructive working relationship towards partnership (Browning, 1990). This does not appear to be common practice amongst this group of schools.

Despite the lack of evidence of this type of corporate activity, the governors in this survey considered that they were effective in working together as teams even though they also recognised their differences. This evidence created a dilemma. Why did boards state that they were more effective in working together as a team than they really were? Was it that boards had not fully explored the benefits of developing the team approach? Relationships within the governing body were of concern particularly from new parent governors, who expressed difficulties in becoming part of 'the team' with:

> I hated being a parent governor in the first year ...

and:

> I have found it harder than I anticipated to feel part of the 'team'.

This raised the question concerning the composition of governing bodies. Field (1989) found that they varied considerably with widely differing views and experience. The different values held by individual governors caused a lack of a clear organisational identity and presented a fragmented group image (James, 1990).

Whilst the majority of governors felt that they made a worthwhile contribution, evidence suggested that both the effectiveness and the efficiency of governing bodies were being undermined by the failure of these governors to work at optimum levels — a theme identified by Baginsky, et al. (1991). Also, although governors felt that they were making a worthwhile contribution, the quality of that contribution becomes questionable when half of the boards felt that they did not monitor their own effectiveness and sought help in this aspect of their work, an area previously noted as requiring development (Curtis, 1992) and one which is considered of the utmost importance for achieving effectiveness (Handy, 1985; Drucker, 1990). The commitment of governors to managerial efficiency may be noted, however, from the statement of one co-opted governor responding to suggestions that governing bodies might monitor their own effectiveness 'as long as it doesn't take too long'. This statement may be less a resistance to achieving efficiency but may add even more to the governors' workload — which is where the search for efficiency began.

## Democratic effectiveness

Although legislation has provided equality of representation on governing bodies, albeit in numbers, it is questionable to what extent such constituencies actually exert influence on the governance of schools. How do parent governors, for example, see their role, as delegates, representatives or trustees of the parent constituency?

How do other interest groups, particularly co-opted governors who have no constituency, interpret their part in democratic effectiveness? If school governance is to offer more than the illusory democracy described by Thody in Chapter 2, then governors need to examine the networking established between themselves and their constituencies.

In this survey, issues of democracy were examined from both questionnaire and interview data which raised aspects such as the governor's role and whether they considered it special compared with the other categories of governors. The extent of their contribution to the work of the governing body and whether they felt accountable to both internal (pupils, fellow governors and themselves) and external (parents, community, LEA and the Secretary of State) interest groups were sought.

It was clear from the research that the different categories of governors felt that their role was to represent a particular viewpoint, although most co-opted and LEA governors considered that this meant 'bringing specific skills or experience' (co-opted governor) and 'being objective' (LEA governor) rather than being linked to any specific community of interest. However, for staff, and especially parent governors, the issues of whom they represented and how they fed back to the groups were important concerns as other research has highlighted (Golby and Brigley, 1989; Sallis, 1993). The majority of parent governors specifically stated that they were elected to represent parents' views and felt responsible for reporting back to parents.

In interviews they considered that there were inadequate facilities to generate a constituent voice. One parent governor reported that:

> there is no formal access of parents to governors, no structure exists — there should be mechanisms in place.

There were no commonly agreed strategies amongst members of the same governing body concerning the ways in which parents might be contacted and parental liaison was *ad hoc*, showing no change, therefore, from patterns reported by Kogan in 1984. The question of how parents are in future to communicate with governors, to get their voice heard, is as Sallis (1991) believes, a matter that can be channelled in a positive direction allowing the overt democratic function, described by Thody in Chapter 2, to develop through suitable mechanisms, that not only legitimises the process, but strengthens parental influence.

Co-opted governors, selected by the other governors, are intended to represent 'consumer' interests, either that of local business or local community. In this survey, it was found that only two out of seven co-opted governors represented local industry as 'official' community representatives. There were, however, governors with business occupations in all the other categories as has been found in other surveys (Thody, 1994, forthcoming). Business did appear, therefore, to have significant representation on these governing bodies although it was less clear what, if any, elements of the local 'community' were represented. Since most of the governing body members would live locally, this was perhaps deemed to infer local community representation but whether or not there should be representatives from local groups such as Women's Institutes or sports groups for example, is a question that needs some research.

Two issues concerning representation have caused controversy since the changes in governing body composition produced by the legislation of 1986. First, there was debate over the extent to which political parties were dominating governing body deliberations because it became accepted that whichever political party held power in the local authority could appoint all the LEA governor representatives. In Oxfordshire, the LEA at the time of the research was a hung council but whatever its political character, only three of the LEA governors surveyed expressed personal involvement with the political system having 'personal involvement in Education committees of the County Council', 'the role of the LEA of which I am a member (has enabled me to specialise in) the budget and conditions of service' and 'it helps the community role of the school with the town since I am a Town Councillor'. It appears unlikely, therefore, that political parties found these governing bodies to be significant channels for their influence.

Secondly, a number of governors from all categories had occupations related to education. Some parent governors, for example, were teachers at other schools or colleges. This *de facto* extension of the category of teacher governors increased the political dominance of education professionals as discussed by Thody in Chapter 2. In the late 1980s the government attempted to prevent educationalists standing for governorship except as teacher governors at the schools where they were employed, in order to avoid this dominance (in part of Australia, such a ban is in force) but this attempt was thwarted and education professionals remain potentially a very powerful and large group. Their power may be enhanced by the idiosyncratic nature of the behaviour of other groups amongst the governors. No groups appeared to offer the possibilities of concerted action.

One co-opted governor, for example, in interview, recognised the importance of 'like-minded' governors uniting to produce a strategic plan based on business concepts to improve the quality of governance. The governor, however, emphasised the sensitivity required in sharing school management with the professional staff, thus demonstrating Thody's educational protectiveness. The governor was also unclear how it would be possible to organise action amongst the fragmented groups on governing bodies. This could be seen as a recognition of the political immaturity described by Thody in Chapter 2 above.

The question is, how long will these governors take to negotiate entry — this term, next term or will they simply abdicate responsibility or resign in frustration? Although Thody (1994) found governors operating at higher levels of management in schools, the real issue is surely one of 'gatekeeping' by the professionals reluctant to build an appropriate framework for shared management.

A perceptive parent governor recognised that the relationships between the governors, who represent the wider audience, and the external groups they represent, was of considerable importance in facilitating an effective customer care service and considered that:

> I should be as informed as possible about parental views and worries, but allowed to express my own; and make sure that the governing body is aware of them, as far as possible.

These external groups cover all those who 'buy' a school's product (the product being the child) such as staff, parents, employers, government and fellow citizens. Companies who listen to their customers and provide excellent customer care have proved the most successful (Peters and Waterman, 1982) — and there is an assumption now that schools who listen to their consumers will be similarly successful.

This listening may be impeded if governing bodies continue, like those in this survey, to be dominated by professional educators. There was evidence of decision-making being controlled by the '"experts" sometimes leaving the "lay" members behind' (foundation governor). The necessity to involve lay governors in the work of the school in order to provide a solid base of knowledge for effective decision-making was reflected in the attitude of governors concerned with their:

> lack of knowledge about the key issues/awareness of pressures teachers face/government moving goalposts (co-opted governor).

and the need for training in this area.

Some structures had already been established to create governor involvement in the work of the school but again this was on an *ad hoc* basis, with no clear structure or built in accountability to the system. The development of a code of practice, to avoid possible conflict, has been voiced (Sallis, 1991) but is there the necessary entry point for possible discussion? A structured involvement in all aspects of school life would then enable governors to:

> discharge their responsibilities as an integral part of the management team of the school rather than being imposed upon it (Watkins, 1989, p.233).

Although it will only succeed if heads, their staff and governors view it positively and initiate new working relationships creating a sense of 'usness', rather than 'them' and 'us' in the management of schools.

This 'usness' is of importance not just within the school but also in relation to the wider community which is supposed to be represented through the democratic mechanism of governance. Although three-quarters of the governors in this survey felt very much accountable locally, both morally i.e. to the parents and community and professionally — not just to other governors but equally to themselves, organisational structures to foster the development of a sense of accountability for tasks were difficult to identify. Such structures need developing if governors are to extend the illusory level of democracy.

## Conclusions

To achieve overt managerial efficiency, it can be suggested that guidelines should be developed to clarify how governing bodies should function and how democratic effectiveness could be helped by delineating how representative mechanisms might better indicate customer views. Divisions of functions between staff and governors could be made more obvious and the practice of setting terms of reference for committees could be established. Governors might audit their own skills, practise team building, devise action plans and follow school-based governor training.

Achieving such laudable aims will take time due to the fundamental change in emphasis needed to implement any recommendations associated with 'best practice' management principles, considerable thought as to how they can be successfully adopted for implementation will need to take place. One of the problems is the traditional view held by non-profit organisations that 'management' meant 'business' management and as schools have no 'bottom line' they were not businesses and therefore did not need management (Drucker, 1990). Schools, like any other organisation, need management as a tool to survive the recent innovations and concentrate on their mission. Governing bodies, as organisations within the school system, have realised that there is a need to become effective. Within this new management culture, 'best practice' in management techniques also calls for efficiency in governance, an area in which most of the governing bodies in this survey felt they needed help. Within this new management culture, governing bodies also have to accommodate the democratic imperatives of their roles.

There is no single correct model of 'the governing body' and how it should operate just as there is no 'best way' to manage and organise (Trompenaars, 1993). Governing bodies will have to examine the models of 'best practice' that hopefully will become available to them and adapt them to the members and the process within that particular environment, thereby unlocking the potential in their situation, their technology and, especially, their people to become a well governed school.

## Notes

1. Governing bodies were invited to take part in the research in November 1992. The questionnaires were sent by post on 1 February 1993 to those governing bodies that had agreed to participate. Individual governors were asked to return them, in a self addressed, stamped envelope by 22 February.

   The questionnaire format gave governors the opportunity to respond primarily in a quantitative (controlled choice) mode but qualitative (open ended) questions were asked. Additional comments were sought throughout to enrich the data.

   The 14 semi-structured interviews were conducted between March and June 1993. They were taped by the researcher although where time and distance was a constraint, a framework was prepared to conduct the interviews by telephone.
2. Six categories of governor can make up the composition of a governing body dependent upon the type of school. They are parent, LEA, minor authority, found in all primary and voluntary-aided secondary schools, (in the survey these have been incorporated with LEA governors being a political nomination), teacher, head (in the survey these were combined to represent staff governors) and co-opted or foundation dependent upon whether the school is respectively county or voluntary.

## Bibliography


Adams, N, (1989) 'Climate of trust', *Times Educational Supplement*, 17 February 1989.

Baginsky, M., Baker, L. and Cleave, S. (1991) *Towards Effective Partnerships in School Governance*, Slough: NFER.

Browning, E. (1990) 'Keeping an eye on progress', *Times Educational Supplement*, 23 November 1990.

Cleese, M. (1993) 'Equal partners? A study of relationships between governors and teachers', in: Wallis, G. (Ed) *Local Management Central Control: Schools in the Market Place*, Bournemouth: Hyde Publications.

Coopers and Lybrand Associates (1988) *Local Management of Schools: a Report to the Department of Education and Science*, London: HMSO.

Curtis, A. E. (1992) *Improving Governor Effectiveness through Training*, unpublished BA dissertation, Wheatley: Oxford Brookes University.

Curtis, A. E. (1993) *Efficiency and Effectiveness in School Governing Bodies*, unpublished MA dissertation, Wheatley: Oxford Brookes University.

Davies, B. and West-Burnham, J. (1990) 'School governors — an effective management force or another bureaucratic layer of school management?', *School Organisation*, **10**, 2 & 3, 1990, p.253.

Doe, B. (1991) 'Panels with a sound constitution', *Times Educational Supplement*, 9 December 1991.

Douglas, B. (1989) *Local Management of Schools*, Sheffield: Sheffield City Polytechnic.

Drucker, P. (1990) *Managing the Nonprofit Organisation*, New York: Harper Collins.

Field, L. (1989) 'School governing bodies', *Curriculum*, **10**, 2, Autumn 1989.

Golby, M. and Brigley, S. (1989) *Parents as School Governors*, Tiverton: Fair Way Publications.

Handy, C. (1985) *Understanding Organisations*, 3rd Edn. Oxford: Facts on File.

Hinds, T. (1992) 'How to boost the numbers of would-be recruits', *Times Educational Supplement*, 28 February 1992.

James, K. (1990) 'Approaching the unfamiliar', *Times Educational Supplement*, 15 June 1990.

Johansson, H., McHugh, P., Pendlebury, A. and Wheeler, W. (1993) *Business Process Reeingeering*, Chichester: John Whiley and Sons.

Kogan, M. (Ed) (1984) *School Governing Bodies*, London: Heinemann Educational Books.

Lea, J. (1991) 'Caught in a tangle of words', *Times Educational Supplement*, 3 May 1991.

Morley-Jones, R. (1989) 'Increased responsibilities of governors. Aspects of school governance', in Fidler, B. et al., *Effective Local Management of Schools*, Harlow: Longman.

OxCEM (1991) *Governors and LMS*, Wheatley: Oxford Polytechnic.

Peters, T. J. (1988) *Thriving on Chaos*, London: Macmillan.

Peters, T. J. and Waterman, R. H. (1982) *In Search of Excellence: Lessons from America's Best-Run Companies*, New York: Harper and Row.

Sallis, J. (1990) 'Agenda, poor service', *Times Educational Supplement*, 5 January 1990.

Sallis, J. (1991) *School Governors — Your Questions Answered*, London: Hodder and Stoughton.

Sallis, J. (1993) 'Governors' agenda for the new year', *Times Educational Supplement*, 1 August 1993.

Taylor, Lord (1991) 'Not yet a perfect partnership', *Independent Newspapers*, 18 April 1991.

Thody, A. M. (1992) *Moving to Management, School Governors in the 1990s*. London: David Fulton.

Thody, A. M. (1994) Business Community Governors in the Control of Schools, *Research Papers in Education*, forthcoming.

Trompenaars, F. (1993) *Riding the Waves of Culture*, London: The Economist Books.

Watkins, M. (1989) 'Getting governors involved in the work of a primary school', in Fidler, B. et al., *Effective Local Management of Schools*, Harlow: Longman.

# 7 Future shock: prospects from New Zealand

Brian Cusack

*New Zealand's school governance reforms came into effect shortly before those in England and Wales and included the abolition of the LEA equivalents, Education Boards, thus leaving school governing bodies as the sole school administrators. The reforms have also attempted to delineate more clearly than in England and Wales, the division of roles between school principals and school Trustees. There is major parental representation on New Zealand's governing bodies, and there is provision for racial and gender representation. The outcomes indicate that New Zealand's governing bodies make much more contribution to democracy 'overtly' than 'covertly' in the terms identified by Thody in Chapter 2. There are signs of real accountability and of Trustees beginning to emerge into political maturity. In the division of responsibilities with school principals, there have been numerous disputes but these in themselves indicate that there appears to be less of the 'consent, protection, legitimation and support' functions performed by New Zealand's governing bodies than Thody suggested was the case in England and Wales. (Editor.)*

New Zealand school governors have substantial legal powers for decision making in their schools. They are entitled 'school trustees' and hold global responsibility for school governance. Trustee numbers vary according to school size and type but are predominantly parents of students currently attending the school (Lange, 1988). Trustees are the employers of all professional and auxiliary staff, and in approximately 3 per cent of cases control 100 per cent of the school finances, including professional staff salaries. Trustees who do not control professional staff salaries have discretion in the choice of staff for appointment to the fixed salary scale. Principals' contracts often allow additional flexibility for performance based salary payments. As a consequence, schools are 'self-governing' with fully devolved responsibilities for the expenditure of public funds.

The structures and powers for school governance underwent radical change on 1 October 1989 (Macpherson, 1990). School governance arrangements had reflected 120 years of spasmodic evolutionary growth and were diverse even within different school sectors (Picot, 1988a). The central issue of the reform was power and the reconstruction of participatory democracy. Power was to be redistributed to plural groups of stakeholders and to be exercised in contractual arrangements. It was proposed to unify the governance structures for all schools, to devolve resources and decision-making responsibilities, and to balance powers with a plurality of lightweight central agencies. The method for reform was direct political intervention which was colloquially termed the 'earthquake model' (Taylor, 1991). New governance powers and structures were hence imposed across the schools sector (Cusack, 1992a).

Such radical change was not without controversy. Numerous lines of resistance developed. Some were adopted into the process of change and others polarised into new lobby groups (Jesson, 1989; Lauder, 1987). Schools became sites for the exercise of parent power over professional conduct and for new accountabilities. School Trustees were hence positioned at the cutting edge of change in New Zealand schools. In this chapter, evidence from research reports, legal cases and academic publications is drawn together to articulate a vision of school governance in the 1990s. The text is structured to first, briefly review the rationality for structural change, second to elaborate controversial issues, and third, to extrapolate from contemporary controversies into a pragmatic future for school governance.

## Radical change

A political watershed of radical social and economic change swept New Zealand during the mid-1980s (Palmer, 1979; Jesson, 1987, 1989). The Picot Report on educational administration was one of many far-reaching reviews designed to restructure the state, to reposition the government and to enhance economic performance. Education was perceived to be 'creaky' and 'cumbersome' and educational administration ripe for reform. Urgent attention was required to redress the alleged poverty in decision-making, confusing school governance structures, lack of systems control information, the quality of management practices and client dissatisfaction (Picot, 1988a). The Government chose to act on most of

Picot's recommendations which were later consolidated in the 'Tomorrow's Schools' White Paper (Lange, 1988). On 1 October 1989 the radical legislation for the restructuring of New Zealand school governance came into force. School Trustees were to have new powers and influence in school decision-making processes. They were to have new authority for the employment of professional staff, for school strategic planning and for the expenditure of public funds. The Department of Education and the former middle management agencies (equivalent to LEAs) were to close (Picot, 1988a; Education Act of 1989). The new Boards of Trustees were to be weighted in favour of a parent majority and to have a balanced representation of the diversity of roles, culture and expertise in schools.

The devolution was achieved by giving school Trustees full powers to manage all resources at a local level (with the exception of teacher salaries in most cases). School Trustees were to be the school policy-makers and the employees the implementors of policy. In practice policy making became a consultative process guided by consultants and the school Trustees. School Trustees consequently, took over work which had formerly been done by Education Department and Education Board employees, and school principals. In exchange for a bulk grant of government monies the trustees undertook to achieve various educational outcomes contained in a document entitled, the 'school charter' (Codd, 1991). The school charter specified a range of responsibilities including community consultation, financial management, property management, employment responsibilities and oversight of the efficient delivery of the National Curriculum. Alteration to the employment law had put school principals onto employment contracts with annual review clauses. Hence, the school principal had responsibilities as the school's professional leader to implement a raft of national and local school policies to a standard acceptable to the Trustees (Breakwell, 1993).

In the new devolution of decision making powers the government retained control through a proliferation of central agencies. It was the purpose of government to withdraw from the role of 'provider' in the education market place and to achieve a different stature in government by making policy and by judging the quality of policy implementation (Codd, 1991). The former Department of Education and the Educational Boards were to close and two very different principal central agencies were opened. These agencies were to report directly to the Minister of Education. The Ministry of Education was to advise the Minister on education policy and to oversee its implementation, and the Educational Review Office was to report the performance of education organisations (a role similar to OFSTED in England). Further central agencies and associations also formed (initially six and then nine), for example, to oversee all non-university qualifications, to certify teacher registration and to provide an association for school trustees (Ministry of Education, 1990; Ramsay, 1992; Monitoring Today's Schools Reports).

The net effect of the Government repositioning was a stratification of education providers and interest groups into distinct lobbies from which the government might purchase competitively priced services. The separation of powers also served to enhance accountability (Macpherson, 1989b). For example, the parent–professional separation in schools provided close scrutiny of professional performance, and in reciprocation, the Education Review Office provided regular scrutiny of trustee compliance and school performance. Consequently, the school charter and the employment contract became the basis for legitimation in school affairs and the touchstones for accountability. The new arrangements for the management and administration of education cut across previous divisions and powers to 'flatten', diversify and to down-size the central agencies, with the express purpose of providing a choice of resources in schools. The new diversification of central agency structures and the unification of school governance structures turned the former government department pattern upside down. As a consequence, many of the matters of concern which had formally been passed up the hierarchical line of accountability were to be processed at a local level — by school trustees. Accountability for the provision of schooling was hence fully devolved (Caldwell and Spinks, 1988; Rae, 1989; Cusack, 1992c).

The new and radical changes were a successful implementation of many of the aspects of restructuring in education attempted elsewhere in the world (Beare, 1989). The New Zealand reform was marked out by the speed with which it was implemented and the extent of the devolution of decision-making powers (Mitchell, 1991). The closure of former central and middle management agencies was a radical shift in government policy with lasting implications for the way in which education ought to be managed. Changes to employment legalisation and the shift of the employer into the immediate proximity of the employee also radically altered the industrial condition. Researchers have conceptualised the reform to be an experiment, a lived experience by participants and as pragmatic action by government. The model of an 'earthquake' has also been postulated to simulate the destruction of the former management structures and the rebuilding of the new. School trustees and their school principals were identified as being central for the successful implementation of the new structures and crucial for the ongoing operation of the new system. The compulsion for trustees to consult fully with their communities in the making of policy and to provide open reporting has also changed the nature of schooling in New Zealand (Monitoring Today's Schools Reports).

## New and critical edges

School trustees were to be the employers of all the waged and salaried people in their school, including the professional staff. This was a new and radical shift in government policy (Rae, 1991). Formally the responsibility for the employment of professional staff had been shared by regional Education Boards, High School boards and the Department of Education. School trustees became accountable in a new legal framework shaped by three principal acts of parliament; the Education Act 1989, the State Sector Act 1988 and the Employment Contracts Act 1991. The implications for the day to day running of education were far reaching (Towner, 1993).

The Education Act 1989 specified trustees' responsibilities through the aims, objectives and purposes contained in their school charter. Each charter contained compulsory National Guidelines for the employment of staff and these were signed for as an undertaking by the trustees. Consequently, the undertaking by the trustees to the Minister of Education was enforceable by the Ministry of Education through the courts. The key compulsory employer undertakings for trustees were (Education Act 1989):

- To enhance learning by staffing the school with teachers and ancillary support staff to meet the curriculum objectives
- To be a good employer, abide by the industrial awards, and endeavour to maintain harmonious industrial relations
- To develop sound personnel policies, which treat staff fairly, protect students and promote staff performance and the effective use of resources
- To provide equal access, consideration and equal encouragement in the areas of recruitment, selection, promotion, conditions of employment and career development.

The Education Act 1989 further granted to trustees the powers to appoint, suspend and dismiss staff, subject to the restraints of a limited total number of staff and the right of employees to bring personal grievance action against the trustees.

The State Sector Act 1988 applied to all state sector employees and in particular to education employees. It specified the actions of employers in regard to (State Sector Act 1988):

- The duty to be a good employer
- Codes of conduct
- Performance criteria
- Equal opportunity
- Reinforced the general powers and duties contained in the Education Act 1989.

The Employment Contracts Act 1991 altered the basis of employment of all employees by placing them into a contractual environment. The choice of contract varied from employee to employee. The employee could appoint a bargaining agent on their behalf (for example, a union) or attempt to negotiate a personal contract with their trustees. In practice most employees opted for one of the six relevant education collective contracts and accepted the group's bargaining agent. The Employment Contracts Act 1991 further detailed the specifications for personal grievance claims by employees and the lawfulness or otherwise of strikes and lockouts (Towner, 1993, pp.4–7).

The framing legislation for school governance has been well tested in the courts since 1989 (Rishworth, 1993; Cusack, 1994). The challenges have come both from parents testing the scope of trustees' powers in providing discipline and control of their children, and in far greater numbers, employees challenging the new employers justification for dismissal. Rule making and the enforcement of school rules has always been contested by parents in the courts (Breakwell, 1993). The new trustees were given powers under section 75 of the Education Act of 1989 for complete discretion to control the management of the school subject to any enactment or general law. Section 76 of the Education Act of 1989 further specified the school principal to be the governors' chief executive with complete discretion to manage the day-to-day administration of the school. Parental challenges have been comparatively few in number and have focused attention on the trustees power through the school principal to enforce rules and codes of conduct. The cases have played an important part in interpreting the new legislation and the extent of the new administrative arrangements in schools.

By far the greatest challenge to the trustees' new powers has come from employees, particularly school principals. An 18 month survey completed late 1993 showed that a little over 10 per cent of all New Zealand schools had significant conflict between the trustees and their principal (NZ Herald, 17 February 1994). The magnitude of the industrial dispute has received significant television and press coverage. Personal grievance claims by employees against trustees increased 4,000 per cent, prompting industrial insurers to lift premiums by 1,000 per cent and in other instances to withdraw services from school employees entirely. The central issue of contention has been the distinction between professional matters and that of governing matters (Codd, 1991: Cusack, 1992d, 1993). The new legislation eroded principal's previous powers to have complete discretion in certain areas of the day-to-day running of a school and reduced control in governance matters. The immediate scrutiny of principals by an employer with varying expertise in matters of education has highlighted differing value positions represented in a school community. A president of a school principals' association argued that the level of conflict was to high and that students were being overlooked while principals and their trustees attempted to resolvc their differences (Cusack, 1994). The need for people to work harmoniously together has come against a sharp edge of value difference. Professionals are long-term stake holders in education whereas trustees have a high personal stake holding in a single school for only as long as their son or daughter is in attendance. Consequently, the trustees are concerned with obtaining measurable results from school processes and evidence that teachers are enhancing their sons' and daughters' future life chances. Teaching staff on the other hand, have been experts in a National Curriculum and assessment which has been nationally the same for all schools and students. The professional–lay difference is deliberate on the part of the reformers and serves as the cutting edge of change in New Zealand schools (Cusack, 1992d).

The new and critical edges have developed on a multiplicity of fronts. Trustees have experienced the intervention of the Minister of Education exercising his statutory powers to dissolve trustees under certain conditions of disharmony, mismanagement and incompetence. The cases have been well publicised and have elaborated the conditions under which trustees may be disbanded and a statutory manager appointed. Other cases have arisen where trustees have legitimately removed members from their number, including one non-compliant chairperson who was physically removed by police after receiving a vote of no confidence. Democracy is being well served by the new governance boards and schools have gained a renewed vigour and vitality (Cusack, 1988–1991). The active short-term parent stake holding has destabilised the historical professional control of school matters and accelerated diverse change. The value of these changes are yet to be measured in terms of student learning gains but in the short term, communities are gaining the benefit of parents becoming experienced in large scale business management practice, the dynamics of conflict management and the ways of democratic leadership (Mitchell, 1991; Cusack, 1994).

## The redistribution of power

The central concern of the restructuring of educational administration in New Zealand was that of power. The reformers expressed dissatisfaction with the political processes in education and the dominating participation of provider groups in the administration of education. Democracy was to be improved by the inclusion of a wider range of participants in the decision-making processes in educational administration. It was argued that interest group capture had undermined effective administration.

> Consultation with interest groups has come to be confused with the seeking of consensus. This process has led to a paralysis of action and in effect become an abdication of responsibility (Picot, 1988b).

The reformers were concerned that power had to be redistributed so that the control of education would be put firmly in the hands of different groups of people who would be mutually accountable for their administrative actions. The reform proposals, consequently, implicated providers who were perceived to have captured administrative resources with the perceived deficits experienced by other education groups. In particular the articulated sense of 'powerlessness' experienced by some groups was to be balanced and redressed by changing the structures of educational administration (Picot, 1988a). In practice parents, students and school communities were to be empowered, and Education Boards, teachers, and other education employees were to be de-powered. Considerations of gender and ethnicity were of importance. The re-balancing of powers occurred by legitimating parent control of schools, distancing employees from the terms of their employ and by implementing open reporting and consultation with school communities (Cusack, 1990). The long-term effect of the changes was for the local control of schools (Ramsay, 1992).

The power for decision-making shifted from the top of an hierarchical non-political department of education and beyond government agency control, to school trustees. The government was to retain the power to evaluate school performance, to ensure compliance with national guidelines, and to intervene in the case of non-achievement. The radical devolution effected the primary schooling sector most dramatically. The former primary school administrative structures depended upon a regional Education Board to maintain the appointment of staff, the maintenance of properties and distribution of teaching resources. In the new order these functions were to be the responsibility of trustees. In all school sectors collegial professional support networks were ruptured. The previous role of school inspectors with its dual components of professional guidance and assessment, ceased, as did all middle management agencies (Cusack, 1992b). As a result stratification occurred along position lines and across previous demarcations. School principals networked with other principals, and deputy principal associations flourished. The New Zealand School Trustees Association was initially formed to assist with governor training and employer matters, and later developed a more independent stance as an effective political lobby group. Trustees, hence, became major stakeholders in education at both local and national levels.

## Network structures and conversations

The stratification of New Zealand education into new interest groups and lobby groups completed the restructuring of educational administration. The perceived problems in the former structures had been redressed and the government had repositioned from the role of education provider to a purchaser of services. The former central Department of Education had been divided into numerous mutually exclusive agencies, down-sized in personnel numbers and 'flattened' in management structure. At the periphery of state management, school trustees operated independently, and autonomously implemented national and local policy in education. The metaphor for the administration of New Zealand education had changed from 'family' to 'network' (Rae, 1994). A secondary reform agenda was then engaged. The National Curriculum content, assessment and qualifications structures were radically altered to fit the pattern for education which was to take New Zealand into the twenty first century. The administration of education could hence proceed as a large number of peripheral networks with loose knit central co-ordination (Cusack, 1992d).

Education conversations also changed. The players were no longer family but often protagonists, antagonists and strangers. People came in to play the game of education who had not bothered on the previous field and in some cases had been barred from participation under the former rules. The new codes for conduct allowed exponents of law, economics, plant management, financial expertise and marketing to talk in schools. The mother tongues of sociology, psychology, curriculum theory, paedology and politics were heard less and often only in a hush of lowered voices behind closed doors. One of the loudest calls in school hallways and principals' offices became, 'But they are *my* kids!!!' Policy was made by parents in the board room, implemented by principals, done by teachers and assessed by parents. Jargon became the speak of the day. Teachers structured 'delivery vehicles' to 'deliver modules' of work which came from the 'National Framework' for 'NZQA' (New Zealand Qualifications Authority) qualifications recognition. Schools were to be 'reviewed' on their 'charter' undertakings and 'strategic plan' achievements by 'reviewers'. The school 'executive officer' (principal) was to be reviewed annually by the 'board of trustees' (trustees) against the 'contract' provisions and 'performance agreement'. Employers and employees conversed in court rooms and in formal hearings, and employment contracts were arranged by 'bargaining agents'. Education became a multi-lingual jargon spoken by a diverse range of adherents.

Conversations in schools reflected new role expectations and the stress individuals felt during rapid change. Sentences beginning with 'Some of this is madness . . .', and concluding in generalities such as, 'Many babies have gone out with the bath water', and 'Things have to improve', were common. In interviews school principals acknowledged role shifts and a new emphasis on 'community sponsorship, market planning, public, relations, strategic plans, policy development and implementation'. Principals were conscious of their new accountabilities and spoke about the 'limited resources', the 'written list of criteria' for professional performance, and the 'job description'. Others commented that 'a lot more people wanted to influence events' and that it was 'hot in the office'. The 'paper war' enveloped school administration and managers 'taking time', and adding to the 'telling' 'tensions and stresses'. The 'work load' went up and more time was to be used 'negotiating'. Principal's had to 'sell' their schools to the communities to 'get students' and 'manage public relations'. In the new order 'decisions' took 'longer because of the process'. Compulsion for consultation, public reporting and non-curriculum activities left some principals pining for 'hands-on' activity, and the desire to 'get back to the classroom'. Many saw the changes to be 'an improvement' which brought a 'far greater focus' to planning. A 'better fit' between 'programmes and resources' was possible with control over the school budget (Cusack, 1988–1991).

Trustees' talk was official speak. To be a school trustee was to control large budgets, many employees and the future prospects of many students. Trustees spoke with authority through publications, reports and school newsletters. They addressed employees, gave speeches and performed ceremonial roles. Annual Reports carried financial statements, performance outputs and strategic plan updates. Trustees convened the committees for 'important decision-making'. Trustees also spoke out on matters which affected them. Concern was expressed at the 'excessive' work load and the 'level of expertise' required for the successful functioning of a board. Some mentioned the amount of time required to 'read and digest' the 'mountain' of paper and the 'hours' spent in meetings. Others noted that most trustees were parents who 'feel inadequate' in schools and 'really do another job' as their first priority. They expressed concern for adequate support and training, and for 'enough' funding to do 'the job' well. Some mentioned their 'frustration' at not being able to achieve the changes and control in the school they had anticipated prior to election. The 'hype' of public advertising gave rise to 'unreasonable expectations' and overlooked the 'high degree of commitment and responsibility' required by a governor. Suspicions were voiced that 'the whole exercise' was a 'cost cutting' move by government, whereby trustees would do and take the government's responsibility for education. Most trustees considered the changes for greater 'parent involvement' in education to be 'a good thing' and 'much better' than the former arrangements for school governance (Cusack, 1988–1991).

## Future prospects

The future of New Zealand schooling is in no doubt. The current structures are here to stay and the ongoing debate of professional and local matters is destined to develop the shape of schooling in the next few years. Protracted industrial disputes will no longer disrupt the effective running of schools but rather the resolution of values will go to arbitration in the district courts. School trustees are to play an increasingly important role in the education of the children of their communities. They will continue to shoulder full responsibility for the expenditure of public education funds and the governance of their schools. The work load is unlikely to diminish and the school reviewers are to be concerned with compliance and with student examination results. The effective de-skilling of professionals is to be balanced by standardised assessment, a re-constructed National Curriculum and a unified qualifications framework. Skilled and disenchanted professionals will continue to leave schools for more demanding employment and the positions will be filled by newly trained staff who are prepared to work on specific contracts and in lesser and more transient roles.

The annual school budget will still be crucial. Trustees are to play an increasingly more important part in the future of the students and the economic well-being of their school. The on-going growth of school-business partnerships will spell success for a school in terms of the quality of material provision available to students. Trustees will need to ensure expertise in financial matters, planning, and marketing are available on their boards. The seven factors displayed by successful school trustees are unlikely to change (Cusack, 1992c):

> The trustees and the principal develop a relationship of trust and respect so that they, and the school staff work together as a team
>
> Key functions and services are delegated within the board and school
>
> An executive officer or equivalent is employed to separate teaching and professional roles from administrative tasks in the school
>
> The principal separates professional leadership tasks from school management tasks by delegating responsibilities to appropriate divisional leaders
>
> Trustees have confidence in their principal to manage the school. They also monitor the danger of the principal doing too much in the new and expanded role
>
> Financial management and administrative tasks are delegated to experts
>
> Trustees make provision for the purchase of support services.

Successful trustees will need to clearly define the fine line between policy-making and policy implementation so that employees can be certain as to the expectations in their school. Schools in general will continue to polarise along a variety of social, economic and curriculum lines, but it is the trustees who will have the overall direction of the school in their control. Schools will become more local and community orientated, but again it will be the trustees who can ensure that the standards of the school are in keeping with national norms. Trustees will need to cultivate effective working relationships within their schools and with their communities in order to retain support for the school programmes. The relative strengths and weaknesses of any school will continue to be publicly available in the annual report and the review documents. Open reporting and public scrutiny will pervade all practices. Consequently, the direction for the future of New Zealand schooling has already been set in the radical reforms of the last five years. To a large extent that future is in the control of school trustees.

## Bibliography

Beare, H. (1989) 'Structures for managing schools and school systems in the next decade: some lessons from the education reform movement', *New Zealand Principal*, **4**, 1, pp.3–13.

Breakwell, J. (1993) 'Control and management of schools: disciplinary powers of school boards of trustees', *Legal Research Foundation Seminar*, 20 April 1993, Auckland.

Caldwell, B. J. and Spinks, J. M. (1988) *The Self-Managing School*, London: Falmer Press.

Codd, J. (1991) 'Managerialism: the problem with today's schools', *Delta*, **44**, pp.17–25.

Codd, J. et al. (1991) 'School charters: the contractualist state and education policy', *New Zealand Journal of Education Studies*, **26**, 1, pp.21–34.

Cusack, B. O. (1988–1991) Unpublished field notes.

Cusack, B. O. (1990) 'Philosophical research into agency and structure in New Zealand education: using Foucault to understand post-Picot power' in Macpherson, R. J. S. and Weeks, J. (eds), *Pathways to Knowledge in Educational Administration*, Armidale: ACEA.

Cusack, B. O. (1991) 'Rethinking school development along personnel lines' *Educational Management: Theory and Practice*. Auckland: Kohia Teachers Centre.

Cusack, B. O. (1992a) 'Collecting trustworthy data in turbulent times: field recollections', Pathways Series, **3**, Brisbane: ACEA.

Cusack, B. O. (1992b) 'An end to school inspection: the New Zealand experience' *Management in Education*, **6**, 2, pp.6–8.

Cusack, B. O. (1992c) 'Radical changes in New Zealand', *Governors' Action*, **19**, p.15.

Cusack, B. O. (1992d) 'Structural change, professional change: the New Zealand school principal', ERIC Data base, ED 354579 Portland, USA.

Cusack, B. O. (1993) 'Political engagement in the restructured school: the New Zealand experience'. *Educational Management and Administration*, **21**, 2, pp.107–114.

Cusack, B. O. (1994) 'School trustees: too powerful by half?', *Management in Education*, **8**, 1, p.29.

Easton, B. (1988) 'From Reagonomics to Rogernomics'. Fulbright Seminar, National Library of New Zealand, 15 September, 1988.

Education Act 1989 (& Amendments) The Government of New Zealand, Wellington: Government Printer.

James, J. and McRobie, A. (1990) *Changes? The 1990 Election*, Wellington: Allen and Unwin

Jesson, B. (1987) *Behind the Mirror Glass — The Growth of Wealth and Power in New Zealand in the 1980s*, Auckland: Penguin.

Jesson, B. (1989) *Fragments of Labour — The Story Behind the Labour Government*, Auckland: Penguin.

Lange, D. (1988) The New Zealand Government, 'Tomorrow's schools: the reform of education administration in New Zealand'. White Paper, Wellington: Government Printer.

Lauder, H. (1987) The new Right and educational policy in New Zealand', *New Zealand Journal of Educational Studies*, **22**, 1, pp.3–23.

Macpherson, R. J. S. (1989a) 'Why the politicians intervened into the administration of New Zealand education', *Unicorn*, **15**, 1, pp.38–43.

Macpherson, R. J. S. (1989b) 'Radical administrative reforms in New Zealand education: the implications of the Picot report for institutional managers', *Journal of Educational Administration*, **27**, 1, pp.29–44.

Macpherson, R. J. S. (1990) 'The reconstruction of New Zealand education: a case of high politics reform' in Beare, H. and Boyd, W. (Eds.) *Restructuring Schools: An International Perspective on the movement to transform the control and Performance of Schools*.

McKenzie, D. (1988) 'Responses to Picot: education after the Picot report', *New Zealand Educational Administration Society Journal*, **3**, pp.1–9.

McLeod, M. (1989) 'The cutting edge', *New Zealand Listener*, 4 March 1989.

Milne, D. and D. (1987) *Your Government — A Guide to the Way New Zealand is Run*, Auckland: Wilson and Horton.
Mitchell, D. (1991) 'Monitoring today's schools: a score card after 18 months', *New Zealand Journal of Educational Administration*, **6**, pp.48–61.
Ministry of Education (1990) *Introducing the Education Family*, Wellington: Government Printer.
Monitoring Today's Schools Reports, 1990, University of Waikato.

New Zealand Government Publications:
*A Review of the Bulk Funding of Schools*, MoE, April 1991.
*A Review of the Early Childhood Development Unit*, MoE, April 1991.
*NZ Qualifications Authority*, MoE, 18 March 1991.
*A Review of the Parent Advocacy Council*, MoE, April 1991.
*A Review of the Teacher Registration Board*, MoE, April 1991.
*Administering for Excellence*, A summary of the Report to Review Education Administration. DoE, 1988.
*Charter Framework*, and subsequent Amendments 1989–1993.
*Contracts for Secondary Principals*, Secondary Principals' Association of NZ, 21 April 1989.
*The Role of the Principal*, BoT Training Notes, 1989.
*Todays Schools*, A Review of the Education Reform Implementation Process, Government Printer, April 1990.
*Tomorrow's Standards — The Report of the Ministerial Working Party on Assessment for Better Learning*, MoE, Wellington 1990.
*Towards Self Management*, Ministry of Education, September 1991.
*Twenty Thousand*, Summary of Responses to the Review of Education Administration, September 1988.

O'Brien, T. (1990) 'A critical analysis of industrial relations for primary teachers in New Zealand', Unpublished Masters Thesis, Victoria University, Wellington.
Palmer, G. (1979) *Unbridled Power*?, Wellington: OUP.
Picot, B. 'The Picot Report' (1988a) The New Zealand Government, 'Administering for Excellence: Effective Administration in Education', Report of the Task Force to Review Education Administration, Green Paper, Wellington: Government Printer.
Picot, B. (1988b), 'Life after Picot', *New Zealand Listener*, 21 May 1988. Interviewed by McLeod, M.
Rae, K. (1989) 'New principles and models for reviewing New Zealand education: a critique', *New Zealand Educational Administration Society Journal*, **4**, pp.1–10.
Rae, K. (1991) 'Industrial relations for New Zealand teachers', *Educational Management: Theory and Practice*, Auckland: Kohia Teachers Centre.
Rae, K. (1994) 'New Zealand's self-managing schools and five impacts in 1993 from the ongoing restructuring of educational administration', New Zealand Educational Administration Society Conference, Auckland, 16–19 January 1994.
Ramsay, P. (1991) 'Creating conditions for shared decision-making: the role of the school principal', The First New Zealand Conference on Research in Educational Administration, Auckland, 4–6 July 1991.
Ramsay, P. (1992) 'Local school management: a New Zealand view', New Zealand Educational Administration Society Conference, Massey University, 12–15 January 1992.
Renwick, W. L. (1986) *Moving Targets — Six Essays on Educational Policy*, Wellington: NZCER.
Rishworth, P. (1993) *Education and the Law in New Zealand*, Auckland: Legal Research Foundation.
Schools Trustees Act 1989, *Government of New Zealand*, Wellington: Government Printer.

State Sector Act (1988) Government of New Zealand, Wellington: Government Printer.
Taylor, W. (1991), 'Global and national trends in educational administration', ACEA National Conference, Gold Coast, 15–19 September 1991.
Towner, R. (1993) *School Boards as Employers: Employment Law in Education*, Auckland: Legal Research Foundation.
Wood, G. A. (1988) *Governing New Zealand*, Auckland: Longman Paul.
Wylie, C. (1992) 'Making it work or making work? — some possible lessons from the first 20 months of tomorrow's schools', New Zealand Educational Administration Society Conference, Massey University, 12–15 January 1992.

# 8 School governance: Australian perspectives

David Gamage

*School governance systems are emerging variously in the Australian states, ranging from Victoria with a long established tradition to Tasmania which has only recently adopted the idea. None have quite such extensive powers of those in England and Wales and some states have made the formation of School Councils optional, a freedom not permitted in England and Wales. Devolution of power to schools has occurred concurrently with the establishment of School Councils and the thrust of the Australian reforms appears to be concerned with the achievement of overt democracy and with the role of councillors in securing the efficiency and effectiveness of the management of the newly empowered schools. The evidence from this chapter indicates satisfaction with the models emerging and apparently less indication of the covert functioning described in Chapter Two. (Editor.)*

In the contemporary world decentralisation and devolution has become a common phenomenon. It is a concept first implemented in the political sphere and then by the corporate giants in the business world. Now, in the 1990s it is fast spreading to the education sphere and is known as school-based governance (SBG) or school-site management. However, if SBG is to be effective, the devolution of adequate decision-making authority to school level should be considered as a pre-requisite. The term devolution could be defined as the transfer of authority from a central authority to a lower or local level unit/s to manage their own affairs with a common set of guidelines. This could be effected with or without a legislative base. Yet, it becomes most effective if devolution is effected through legislation.

Devolution could be categorised into two types: administrative or bureaucratic and political or democratic devolution. When it is applied to schools, the administrative devolution could be referred to as the delegation of authority to the principal or headteacher whereas democratic devolution could be referred to as the transfer of authority to an elected group of stakeholders of the relevant school community. It is believed that democratic devolution leads to more effective decision-making resulting in increased local autonomy, flexibility, economy, productivity, and accountability. In this chapter, the author proposes to examine: the development of the concept of SBG: implementation of SBG in different Australian school systems; research undertaken in Victoria until 1992; outcomes of two research projects by the author in New South Wales (NSW) and Victoria, and a discussion on the extent of success achieved.

## Development of the concept of SBG

The origin of decentralisation of educational administration to the local and district levels could be traced to the establishment of local education authorities in England and School Districts in the United States. The first public legislation towards democratic devolution was enacted in Massachusetts where the General Courts Act of 1647 required each town to establish a school and a school district board to manage the education system. Thus, a district board of education became a quasi-corporation authorised or established by a state vested with responsibility and considerable autonomy for the organisation and administration of all public schools in the district. Yet, over the years rather than devolving authority to smaller units, the smaller school districts were amalgamated to create bigger and more centralised units of control. This process of consolidation resulted in the reduction of the number of school districts from 127,244 in 1932 to 16,000 by 1977 (Morphet et al., 1982, pp.238–241).

Opposed to the concept of decentralisation, the Australian system from its inception in 1789 showed a tendency for centralisation and bureaucratic forms of management. However, in the 1970s the Australian systems took the initiative in moving towards SBG with both the democratic and administrative types of devolution of authority to the school levels.

In an historical analysis of the community participation in SBG, it is evident that the Australian Capital Territory (ACT) played a significant role in the development of this concept. The report on *An Independent Education Authority for ACT*, released in 1967, by a voluntary committee headed by Sir George Currie could be considered as an important milestone on the path to community participation in SBG. The report recommended not only the establishment of a representative schools' authority for ACT but also the formation of school boards consisting of the principal and representatives of the parents, teachers, and community, and in the case of secondary schools, the students (Currie, 1967). Prolonged discussions on the report both at public and government levels mainly resulting from the opposition of the NSW Teachers Federation (NSWTF) delayed the establishment of school boards.

In 1972, the establishment of an interim committee on Australian Schools Commission headed by Peter Karmel and the release of its report in 1973 provided a further boost to the public debate and government initiatives. The Karmel Report supported the community involvement as a means of extending its educational influence and reinforcing student motivations and also in bringing reachers and parents closer to each other (Karmel, 1973). In 1973, the federal government commissioned an official panel headed by Philip Hughes to report on the recommendations made by the Currie Report. The Hughes Report which supported the main thrust of the Currie Report was adopted by the government resulting in the establishment of an Interim Schools Authority for ACT in 1974 along with school boards at school level (ACTSA, 1986, pp.1–7). The implementation of school governance with community participation was expected to improve the administrative efficiency and teaching/learning environment resulting from the flexibility and autonomy in decision-making and also increased commitment to the implementation process because of the resulting ownership and accountability for the decisions made.

## Implementation of SBG in the 1970s

In the meantime, the winds of change on SBG had a more cordial reception in South Australia (SA). In 1971, the Director General of Education (DGE) in a memorandum to the Committee of Inquiry recommended the establishment, in state schools, of school councils with extensive powers. On the basis of the recommendations made by the committee, the South Australian Education Act was amended in 1972, leading to the establishment of school councils in the form of mandatory, corporate bodies (Education Act, 1972).

This move in the direction of school-based governance was followed by Victoria with the enactment of the Education (School Councils) Act of 1975 and the establishment of school councils as mandatory, corporate bodies in 1976. The Victorian legislation enabled the devolution of a greater degree of authority to thc councils including maintaining accounts, entering into contracts, employment of non-teaching staff, teacher-aids, and even part-time teachers (Education Act, 1975). In 1976, the ACT became the third Australian schools system to institute SBG with school boards in the form of mandatory, corporate bodies (ACT Schools Authority Ord., 1976). In Tasmania, the Department of Education adopted a policy of permitting those schools which desired to have community involvement in school level decision-making to experiment with school councils (Clinch, 1976, p.19). Thus, by 1976, SA, Victoria, and ACT implemented democratic models of SBG while Tasmania permitted its schools to take similar steps.

## Further developments in the 1980s and 1990s

Between the mid 1970s and the early 1980s, the major Western economies experienced a severe economic recession which pushed the then prevailing fairly liberal policies to much more conservative socio-political and economic values. Hence the education policies of Malcolm Fraser, Margaret Thatcher, and Ronald Reagan reflected this swing. Thus, the policies that were implemented in Australia, UK, and USA came to be known as the New Right Agenda. This agenda contained such elements as: promotion of policies supporting educational excellence; emphasis on the right of parental choice and involvement in education; promotion of private schools; return to basics and discipline in schools; and emphasis on narrow vocational roles through schools and their links with the economy as against broader social and integrative roles in society (Boyd and Smart, 1987, p.21).

In 1981, the Victorian Government undertook a major restructuring process of its education system. In the midst of the reform process, at the general elections held in 1982, a new government was elected to office. Because of the differences in political philosophies, it halted the reform process and instituted a review of the public education system with the involvement of all relevant stakeholders. The result was the publication of six ministerial papers with the major objective of devolving authority to the school councils. In this process particular emphasis was placed on (1) genuine devolution of authority and responsibility to school communities; (2) collaborative decision-making; (3) a responsive bureaucracy; (4) effective educational outcomes; and (5) the active redress of disadvantage and discrimination (Fordham, 1983, pp.104).

In 1983, the Victorian Education Act was once again amended to enable the school councils to determine the general education policy of the school within the general guidelines issued by the minister.

The amendments to the Act emphasised the importance of local responsibility and shared decision-making on educational policy. The council's authority was reinforced by providing for a school council to act on behalf of the Crown in the performance of its legal functions thus according legal protection to councillors (Gamage, 1992a).

In South Australia, the Keeves Committee of Inquiry of 1981, recommended the gradual and planned extension of the policy of decentralisation and devolution with a view to providing the schools greater freedom and autonomy. Accordingly, some of the DGE's authority was delegated to the principals and councils. To make this authority fully effective, the schools were given block grants to cover expenditure on equipment, grounds and teaching materials. However, further progress had to be halted when the department was unable to index the expenditure in keeping with inflation. Yet, the reviews instituted by the department revealed that even though the devolved system was a little more costly, the quality of decision-making in relation to schools were both quicker and markedly superior to a centralised system (Steinle, 1983).

In 1983, the Northern Territory (NT) legislative council amended the Education Act to enable NT schools to incorporate school councils on an optional basis. The functions devolved included the determination of schools' educational policies and educational needs of the community and advisory functions on buildings and facilities, budget, external use of school facilities, and fund raising. In terms of the proposed devolution package for the 1990s, NT wants its councils to accept greater responsibility, flexibility, and accountability by accepting block grants, participating in the selection of staff, controlling the school's operational budget, and involvement in several other areas of school management (NTDE, 1983, pp.18–22).

In Western Australia (WA), school decision-making groups (SDMGs) were established by amending the Education Act in 1990. These SDMGs were expected to participate in the formulation of the school's educational objectives and priorities but were not authorised to hold accounts and employ staff to provide amenities. (WAME, 1990, pp.2–8). In 1990, NSW also enacted legislation enabling the establishment of school councils. The final report of the review instituted by Queensland's new Minister of Education entitled *Focus on Schools* was released in 1990. It recommended that schools should move towards self-management and that education should be a partnership between the school and the community. Initially, it recommended advisory councils on a trial basis (Dempster, 1991, pp.124–125).

In Tasmania, on the basis of a paper entitled *School and College*

*Councils* state schools were encouraged to form councils to make them self-managing entities with the involvement of local communities. Councils were expected to take a decision-making role in areas such as buildings and grounds, staffing, finances, and monitoring school performances (TDEA, 1990, pp.1–5). Accordingly, by 1990, six Australian systems had legislated for the establishment of different models of SBG while the other two systems were taking similar steps.

## Research on SBG in Victoria until 1992

The main objective of the first research project conducted by Chapman in 1984 was to develop a research instrument for investigating the relationships between principals and members of school councils. The instrument consisting of 24 items was administered to 372 council members including principals in 21 schools. According to the 297 responses received, there were statistically significant differences between the attitudes of principals and council members in one third of the councils sampled while principals' scores were significantly higher than those of other members (Chapman, 1984, pp.47–56).

In 1985, Chapman investigated the factors associated with teacher involvement in decision-making. The first phase of the survey included 26 schools and the second phase 44 interviews with teachers in 6 schools. The outcome supported the proposition that the involvement-influence distinction was the key to restructuring worthwhile opportunities for teacher participation in decision-making. Further, it revealed that because of the inadequacy of resources for the implementation of proposals there was a deep seated malaise at school levels associated with the ultimate powerlessness (Chapman, 1988, pp.39–71).

The main aim of a project commissioned by the Victorian Board of Education in 1987, was to identify the ways and means of supporting the educational role of school councils/boards in State and Catholic schools. The sample included seven state and two Catholic schools. The findings revealed that all schools had made significant progress towards the implementation of their educational role while the committee structure had reflected the needs of the schools for enhancing wider community participation (Hunt and Stewart, 1990, pp.35–40).

The main objective of the project undertaken by this author in 1989, was to ascertain the effectiveness of school-based management through the process of collaborative decision-making. The sample was limited to a secondary college and a primary school. The findings revealed that both principals were dedicated to the concept of collaborative decision-making and were in daily contact with council presidents and had excellent relations with the councils. Each council had constituted sub-committees in dealing with specialist and/or time consuming subjects enabling the council to function as an effective and efficient instrument of governance (Gamage, 1990, pp.95–108).

The project by Watkins was a case study of a secondary school. He investigated the role of the local administrative committee (LAC). The findings revealed that the LAC established on the basis of an industrial agreement had brought a sense of involvement in decision-making to a wider range of staff and gave them a feeling of empowerment and a sense of ownership over policy decisions. LAC had played a significant and responsible role in the administration of the school (Watkins, 1992, pp.35–40). Thus, it is clear that until 1992, except for several small-scale projects, no significant research had been undertaken to ascertain the effectiveness of the Victorian schools councils.

## Research on SBG in New South Wales (NSW)

Once in 1973 and again in 1983, the NSW state schools system made two unsuccessful attempts to establish school councils. Yet, the new Government elected to office in 1988 on a manifesto based on the New Right Agenda decided to restructure the education system. The main objective of the reform was the establishment of a school-centred education system with the involvement of the school communities via the concept of school councils. Accordingly Brian Scott, a business consultant, was commissioned by the Government to review the whole system. The Scott Report released in June 1989 recommended that the principals should be encouraged to establish school councils.

In September 1989, the government started the process of dismantling the centralised bureaucracy and the inspectorial system. By April 1990, most central staff were transferred to ten regional offices and 150 clusters were created. Each cluster consisted of 14–17 schools and was headed by a cluster director (CD) who was expected to play a collegial role with the principals as a resource person. In keeping with the recommendation in the Scott Report, CDs were required to encourage the principals to establish school councils in consultation with their school communities (Gamage, 1992b).

However, in spite of the two unsuccessful attempts, the proposed councils were made neither obligatory nor corporate bodies. Besides, the councils were to be constituted with representatives of the parents, parents and citizens groups, local business and industry, and where considered appropriate students (Scott, 1989, p.29).

NSWTF which opposed the concept since 1972 was further prejudiced by this requirement to exclude teacher representation. The final Report on 'School-centred education', published in 1990, made provision for the inclusion of only one teacher representative in a council of 7–11 members. Yet, on the basis of the public debate that was initiated by the media, the Minister for Education increased the number of teacher representatives to three. Thus a council of 11 consisted of the principal, 5 parents, 3 teachers, and 2 community members. In spite of the compromises, NSWTF adopted an attitude of non-cooperation towards the process.

Even though the Department of School Education set an annual target of establishing one fifth of the total or 440 councils from 1990, by December 1990, there were only 117 councils (Chadwick, 1991, p.1). In 1991, perhaps in recognition of the slow progress made, DSE revised its annual targets for the establishment of councils to: 150, 250, 650, and 500 from 1991 to 1994 (DSE, 1991).

It was in this context that the author established a research project in 1991, supported by the Department of Education to determine: (1) the process through which councils were formed; (2) reasons for the delays in the formation of councils; and (3) operational effectiveness of the councils. The research sample included all councillors of 21 councils (50 per cent of those already established) in state schools in the Hunter Region. The research instrument included 24 Likert-type multiple-choice questions along with open ended ones and produced a 75 per cent return.

According to the analysis of the data, 78 per cent of the respondents reported that it was the principal who took the initiative while 11 per cent stated that several parties contributed to the formation of councils. Fifty-four per cent reported that the formal decision to establish a council was taken at a special meeting of the school community while 25 per cent indicated that the decision was taken at a meeting of the Parents and Citizens (P&C) group. They perceived that the departmental guidelines, personnel from other councils, cluster director, and departmental officials facilitated the formation of councils. School newsletters, special meetings, principal's letters addressed to the community, and public addresses by departmental officials were employed to enlist the support of school communities (Gamage, 1993, pp.52–53).

In a study of the causes for the delay and slow progress, it was clear that the complexity of the sample constitution issued by the department, the opposition of the P&C groups, and lack of interest on the part of the principal were the prominent ones. One principal stated that even after three meetings running into several hours each, it was not possible to finalise a draft because of the complexity of the Sample Constitution. Most P&C groups felt that they would lose their power once a school council was established through the electoral process.

The study revealed that 96 per cent of the councillors were satisfied with the current composition of the councils while 94 per cent felt that no particular individual or interest group dominated the decision making process at council meetings. They perceived the council proceedings as a fair go for everyone. Seventy-five per cent of the councillors were satisfied with the power and authority they enjoyed while 94 per cent indicated that no meetings were cancelled due to lack of a quorum. Most importantly 53 per cent reported that the establishment of the council had improved the teaching learning situation. Finally, 88 per cent were happy to devote their time for council business while 91 per cent of the respondents were satisfied with the overall functioning of their councils.

Data also revealed that in spite of the fact that the Sample Constitution made no provision for a committee structure that 65 per cent of the councils had instituted a committee structure. In discussions relating to the problems faced by the councils some members who were interviewed by the author pointed out the reluctance of some principals to provide adequate information. They stated that the principal had the monopoly of relevant information and it was very frustrating when information was not forthcoming in spite of repeated requests. This sort of situation made the member realise that the principal was still in charge and the council was only a back-up. At times the concentration of elite groups of parents was the result of lack of interest of apathy of particular groups of parents rather than a deliberate act.

Those who were prepared to come up with suggestions to improve the current system wanted to diversify the membership with the inclusion of students and general staff and also allowing the school communities to determine the size of a council. That the duties, responsibilities and the role of the councils be more clearly defined enabling the members to be a more involved team. To avoid the possible conflicts between the councils and P&C groups it was suggested that more authority be given to the councils and make the P&C the fund-raising committee of the council (Gamage, 1992c). It is clear that still there are some teething problems in the NSW system which could be attributed to the optional and non-corporate nature of the schools councils.

## Latest research on Victorian system of SBG

Except for the small scale research projects on some aspects of the operation of Victoria's system referred to above, there has been no significant research undertaken to evaluate the overall effectiveness of the system. It was in this context, that the author assisted by two school executives undertook a study of the operational effectiveness of Victorian school councils in 1992. It was a two-year project funded by the Research Management Committee of the University of Newcastle. The overall aim was to prepare an exemplary model of SBG based on one of the longest surviving, democratically devolved systems of school administration. The more specific objectives were to examine: (1) the characteristics of more effective councils; (2) the devolution package and the extent of bureaucratic influence; (3) the different models of councils, operational structures, and procedures; (4) the process of decision-making and opportunities for participation; (5) the extent of parental and community participation; and (6) the overall effect of the system on the operational efficiency and effectiveness of the schools (Gamage, 1991).

During the first phase of the project, a research instrument consisting of 27 questions was dispatched to 965 councillors belonging to 66 (42 primary and 24 secondary) schools located in four educational regions, of whom 53 per cent responded to the call. In the second phase, 75 interviews were conducted with the principals, council presidents, and one from each category of representatives of teachers, parents, community, and students of 17 schools. In addition, sample copies of archival material such as council constitutions, minutes, agenda and connected papers, newsletters, and annual reports were also collected to obtain a more accurate picture. However, the author would like to emphasise that these findings are limited to the state schools system that was in operation until February 1993, as a new set of reforms were to be implemented in 1993.

An analysis of the respondents of the sample revealed that 55 per cent were parents and community members; 26 per cent teachers; 10 per cent principals; 3 per cent general staff; and 6 per cent were students (of whom 58 and 41 per cent were males and females respectively). The composition of each council was prescribed by law while the size of a council could be determined by the school community. In primary schools not less than one half the members were parents, not more than one half were staff members while not more than one fifth were community members. In secondary schools: not less than one third were parents, not more than one third staff, not more than one fifth students while another one fifth were community members. In both categories, the principal was an ex-officio member and executive officer. The parents, staff, and students were elected by their respective electorates while the community members were co-opted by the principal and other elected members. The vast majority of primary schools had 12, 14, or 16 member councils while secondary schools had 21 or 24 member councils whereas one particular council had 32 members.

The data relating to the eight items included in the criteria for the identification of more effective schools revealed that 91 per cent of the respondents perceived the current composition of councils as either good, very good or excellent. Ninety-four per cent of the councillors were prepared to grade the committee structure as either good, very good or excellent while 75 per cent considered the power and authority vested in the councils as adequate. Ninety-one per cent considered that the information received for decision-making as either good, very good or excellent. Fifty-nine per cent perceived the time available for council business as adequate while 15 per cent considered it to be more than adequate. Sixty-six per cent perceived that there was some improvements in the teaching/learning environment, of whom 35 per cent were bold enough to state that there were significant improvements as a result of the implementation of the school council concept. Ninety-three per cent were prepared to grade the council decision-making process as either good, very good or excellent. Finally, 93 per cent perceived the overall functioning of the councils as either good, very good or excellent.

## Discussion and conclusions

In an examination of the data relating to the model of democratic devolution in Victoria, it is clear that in the case of five of the features out of the eight included in the criteria (current composition of the councils, the committee structure, adequacy of information for decision-making, the decision-making process itself, and the overall functioning of the councils) there was overwhelming satisfaction as was evident from the expression of opinions of well over 90 per cent of the respondents. Even with regard to the authority vested in councils and time available for council business, three fourths indicated their satisfaction. Most importantly 66 per cent of the councillors were convinced that SBG resulted in some or even significant improvements in the teaching/learning environments of the schools. It is also important to remember that these opinions have been expressed by a group which consisted of all relevant stakeholders who were directly affected and interested in the business of schooling.

Similarly, in an examination of the data relating to the model of administrative devolution in the NSW state system, the effectiveness (realisation of the set goals) of the system was evident as confirmed by the respondents who consisted of the principals and representatives of the teachers, parents, community, and students. Ninety-six per cent were satisfied with the current composition of the councils, 94 per cent indicated that no meetings were cancelled due to lack of a quorum and no particular individual or group dominated the decision-making process. Most importantly, in spite of the short period that the system was in operation, 53 per cent of the councillors perceived that there was some improvement in the teaching/learning situation as a result of the implementation of the concept of school councils. On the other hand, even though the councils were optional and advisory, 75 per cent were satisfied with the power and authority they enjoyed especially in the context of the moral obligation binding the principals to implement the council recommendations in view of the strong system-wide support for the concept of community participation. Finally, 88 per cent were happy to devote their time for council business while 91 per cent were satisfied with the overall functioning of the councils.

In a careful examination of the operation of the concept of SBG since 1976 in Victoria, and from 1990 in NSW, it is clear that school communities have gained a considerable degree of autonomy and flexibility in making policy decisions on the basis of their needs, interests, and resources at the school level. In the past, when the Department was paying the water, electricity, and gas bills, the schools were not interested in minimising the wastage but when block grants were given to the schools, the school authorities took action to prevent wastage and utilise such savings to improve the school facilities and programs thus improving the efficient utilisation of the limited resources.

The opportunity for participation in decision-making by all stakeholders gave them a feeling of empowerment and enabled them to claim ownership of the policies which increased their motivation and commitment to implement the policies more effectively. As the representatives of all relevant stakeholders were included in the composition of the councils they had to be accountable to their electorates as well as to the department for the funds placed at their disposal. School newsletters, annual reports, and special meetings of the school communities were utilised to render this accountability. Thus, it could be seen that according to the perceptions of the councillors who were the elected representatives of the stakeholders, the set goals of the concept of SBG have been realised to a considerable degree. It was also clear that structures, procedures and processes are well established in Victoria while there are some teething problems in the NSW system.

However, it must be emphasised that these results may not be equally applicable to all schools in these two systems or other systems as the contexts could be different. In order to obtain a more comprehensive general picture, it is desirable to undertake more extensive and significant research which should include the school community members other than the councillors. Yet, the popularity of the concept is evident from the fact that apart from the reforms of school governance that are being implemented in countries such as New Zealand, England and Wales, USA, and Hong Kong, even some Canadian Provinces such as Quebec and British Columbia have already taken steps to establish Orientation Committees and Advisory Parents Councils in 1988 and 1989 respectively (Levin and Young, 1993) while Manitoba and Alberta have announced the establishment of School Committees in 1993.

## Bibliography


ACT *Schools Authority Ordinance*, 1976.

ACT Schools Authority, (1986) *School Boards: Partnership and Participation*, Canberra.

Boyd, W. L. and Smart, D. (1987) *Educational Policy in Australia and America: Comparative Perspectives*, New York: Falmer Press.

Chadwick, V. (1991) *A Letter to the Parents* on Community Participation in Education By the Minister of Education, Sydney.

Chapman, J. (1984) 'Relationships between principals and members of school councils: an attitude scale'. *The Journal of Educational Administration*, **2**, 1, pp.47–56.

Chapman, J. (1988) 'Decentralisation, devolution, and the participation by teachers in the decision-making of schools'. *The Journal of Educational Administration*, **26**, 1, pp.39–72.

Clinch, R. M. (1976) 'School Boards for Queensland Schools', *Unicorn*, **2**, 2, pp.11–19.

Currie, G. (1967) *An Independent Education Authority for the Australian Capital Territory (Currie Report)*, Canberra: Department of Adult Education, ANU.

Dempster, N. (1991) 'Restructuring education in Queensland'. *Unicorn*, **17**, 2, pp.124–126.

Fordham, R. (1983) *Ministerial Papers 1–6*, Melbourne, Ministry of Education.

Gamage, D. T. (1990) 'The changing role of leadership of the Australian high school principals in a changing environment'. *Perspectives in Education*, **6**, 2, pp.95–108.

Gamage, D. T. (1991) 'School-based management and operational effectiveness of school councils; a comparative study'. A research proposal submitted to the University of Newcastle, Australia.

Gamage, D. T. (1992a) 'A comparative study of the school-based management pursued by Victoria and New South Wales'. *Melbourne Studies in Education*, pp.82–95.

Gamage, D. T. (1992b) 'School-centred educational reforms of the 1990s: an Australian case study'. *Education Management and Administration*, **20**, 1, pp.5–14.

Gamage, D. T. (1992c) 'Challenges facing school councils'. *Education Monitor*, **iii**, 3, pp.23–28.

Gamage, D. T. (1993) 'Establishing school councils in New South Wales: some teething problems', *Studies in Educational Administration*, **58**, Winter, pp.49–55.

Hunt, R. and Stewart, R. (1990) 'Supporting the educational role of school councils and boards', in the Board of Education, Victoria (Ed), *Working Papers on Public Education*, **2**, Melbourne, pp.33–38.

Karmel, P. (1973) *Schools in Australia: Interim Report of the Australian Schools Commission*, Canberra.

Levin, B. and Young, J. (1993) *The Organisation of Public Schooling in Canada* (final manuscript delivered to HBJ Holt Publishers), Faculty of Education, the University of Manitoba.

Morphet, E. L., Johns, R. L. and Reller, T. L. (1982) *Educational Organisation and Administration*, Englewood Cliffs: Prentice Hall.
NSW Department of School Education (1991) *School Education News*, 17 April.
NT Department of Education (1987) *Towards the 90s: Excellence, Accountability, and Devolution in Education*, Darwin.
Scott, B. (1989) *Schools Renewals Report: The Management Review NSW Education Portfolio*, Milsons Point.
Steinle, J. R. (1983) 'Structural change in South Australia' in Harman, G. (Ed) *Managing Structural Change in Asia and the Pacific: A Blue-Print for Action*, Canberra.
South Australia, *Education (Amendment) Act*, 1972.
Tasmanian Department of Education and Arts, (1990) *School and College Councils: Admission Paper*, Hobart.
Watkins, P. E. (1992) 'Representative committees in Australia's secondary schools: a case study of local administrative committees in Victoria'. *Studies in Educational Administration*, 57, pp.35–40.
Victoria, *Education (School Councils) Act*, 1975.
Western Australian Ministry of Education, (1990) *School Decision-Making Groups: Policy Guidelines*, Perth.

# 9 Culture, consent and contestation

Richard Hatcher

*This study of governing bodies indicates how issues of 'race' appeared to be blocked, deflected or rendered invisible in governing bodies' agendas. The findings demonstrate an additional dimension to the illusive democracy identified in Chapter 2. The representative process, combined with the way governing bodies operate as protective of educational professionals, appeared to collude, and thereby to exclude, the particular concerns that were the subject of this research. The evidence presented supports Chapter 2's expectations that governors will legitimate, through consent and protection, the professional staffs of their schools. On the other hand, this chapter offers evidence that contradicts Chapter 2's assumptions of governing bodies' lack of political maturity and contrasts also with the idiosyncratic and individualistic nature of the behaviours of governors reported in Curtis's Chapter 6 in this book. The parallels drawn by Hatcher with developments in New Zealand can be further studied in Cusack's Chapter 7 in this book. (Editor.)*

## Introduction

This chapter arises out of a research project on 'LMS and Racial Equality' which Barry Troyna, Deborah Gewirtz and I carried out in 1992 and 1993 (Troyna, Hatcher and Gewirtz, 1993).[1] As is often the case, the issue of 'race' serves to exemplify and illuminate wider school processes: in this instance, the processes by which patterns of power and inequality are reproduced by school governing bodies, and it is on these that I want to focus here. I'll begin by briefly outlining our findings about issues of 'race' at local education authority, school and governing body levels, in order to open up a wider discussion about school governance.

In the four comprehensive secondary schools in our study we identified a number of issues of racial inequality. These included: an under-representation of teachers from minority ethnic groups; a tendency for pupils who had initially had English as a Second Language to remain trapped in the bottom band; racist behaviour and ethnic hierarchy among pupils; cuts in ESL and pastoral provision as a result of budget reductions; unmet demands from Asian parents for more community language teaching; and the low involvement of these parents with the school. These aspects of racial inequality were of great importance to ethnic minority pupils and parents, and to a number of teachers. What was striking, when we observed governing body meetings, was the virtual absence of these concerns from their discussions.

The reasons for this marginalisation of 'race' were multiple and complex. Some of the factors were 'race'-specific. Others were general in scope, but with significant consequences for issues of 'race'. They worked at LEA, school, and governor levels, but their efficacy lay in their combined and cumulative effect.

## Filtering out racial equality

I will use the concept of *filters* to describe the various factors which served to block, deflect or render invisible issues of 'race' in the agendas and discussions of governing bodies. These factors ranged from the impact of budget cuts to the ideological and cultural formations of individual governors and heads. The concept of 'filter' is intended to refer not to an impermeable barrier but to a tendency, a predisposition, a bias towards certain outcomes rather than others, which may be more or less determining. These filters operated in conjunction, often at a series of levels, such that even when issues of 'race' passed through one filter they were likely to be screened out by another. Thus, though there were countervailing factors at work, the overall *cumulative* thrust of the combination of these filters was to marginalise or exclude issues of 'race' and to sustain and reproduce racial inequalities.

I now want to bring together in summary form this complex of filters.

### The local education authority

The LEA was a 'moderate' Labour authority with a traditionally relatively non-interventionist stance. The fear of provoking schools to opt out had led it to minimise any contentious policies or practices on its part, including those concerning racial equality.

## The schools

Policies on 'race' tended to be conceived in very cautious terms, focusing on meeting what were perceived as the language and cultural needs of ethnic minority pupils. There was an avoidance of explicitly addressing racism through the curriculum. In addition, the impact of the National Curriculum tended to marginalise the issue of 'race'. Cuts in the budget, as a result of a reduction in the LEA's spending on education, were also having an adverse effect on their racial equality policies.

## Governing body agendas

Governing body agendas were constructed principally by the LEA and the head, often of course in response to DfE initiatives, in which the issue of racial equality was often not prominent. The factors that served to marginalise the issue of 'race' in the schools, and on the LEA's agenda, also served virtually to exclude it from governing body agendas. This was compounded by another factor: the conceptions that the heads had of the role of the governing body, which were shaped by the distinction they asserted was between lay and 'professional' concerns. Professional matters were often not placed on governing body agendas, or were done so for information and formal endorsement rather than debate.

## School governors and 'race'

In theory, of course, the lay governors themselves had the right to raise issues of 'race', either as an agenda item or in the context of other topics. Yet they virtually never did so. They were inhibited from doing so by a series of 'filters' which operated cumulatively.

### *The ethnic composition of governing bodies*

Ethnic minority governors, who might have had a particular interest in issues of 'race', were under-represented on the governing bodies of the four schools we studied, which corresponds to the national pattern.

### *Lay governors' knowledge of school*

In general, governors had little direct knowledge of their school, particularly of the teaching and learning process. They had very rarely spoken to teachers about educational issues, or to pupils about their concerns. They were often unaware of the school's policy and practice on issues of 'race'.

### *Lay governors' perceptions of 'race'*

Some believed that racism was not an issue in the locality. Some of the governors in white schools felt that the issue of 'race' was irrelevant to their school situation. They were largely unaware of the educational debate that has taken place in recent years on this issue, and they had not taken part in governor training which dealt with racial equality. The views of some governors appeared to be coloured by their own racial prejudices.

### *Lay governors' conceptions of their role*

Many lay governors were, however, interested in issues of racial equality in education. In some cases governors were worried about developments in their school. Furthermore, some were aware that there were issues of concern in their 'constituencies', among parents, the school staff, local employers and the local community. Yet even these governors virtually never raised these issues and concerns, even if they themselves were members of ethnic minorities. Why was this? Three factors served to filter them out.

The first affected ethnic minority governors. Their isolation on predominantly white governing bodies, perhaps perceived as likely to be unsympathetic to their particular concerns, discouraged the raising of issues of 'race'.

The second factor was the attitude that lay governors in general had towards 'educational' issues. They regarded them as the province of the 'professionals' and deferred to their expertise. If the head didn't think 'race' was sufficiently important to put on the agenda, who were they to disagree?

The lay/professional divide received powerful reinforcement from another attitude widely held by lay governors. They tended to be very supportive of their school (perhaps contrasting it favourably with their own schooldays) and were reluctant to criticise it, particularly as to do so might seem to associate them with those (government politicians, the popular press) who they regarded as hostile to what schools like theirs were trying to do. Here, the evidence strongly supports Thody's expectations that governors will protect and support the professional staff of their schools. This climate militates against raising an issue as potentially controversial as 'race'.

## The dynamics of meetings

In some governing bodies the most powerful members — the chair and the head — 'managed' the meetings in ways that pre-empted or suppressed dissent. At other schools, however, the governing body meetings were managed with a great deal of concern for democratic participation. Despite this formal equality of access to participation in their discussions, many lay governors, who might have had concerns about racial equality, seldom made any significant contributions to meetings. One factor deterring them was the formal procedures of meetings. Another was the mode of discussion and decision-making, the 'climate', which tended to be consensual. Governors' awareness of this could inhibit them from raising or pursuing issues, such as 'race', which they knew could be contentious.

## School-based management as a hegemonic process

In our research, the multiple social processes that were set in motion by or transmitted through the operation of local management of schools (LMS) had the cumulative effect of maintaining and reproducing racial inequalities, in spite of the impact of those countervailing processes which promoted education for racial equality. This conclusion supports the more general critique of school-based management in this country and others, that it serves to reinforce existing patterns of power and inequality in society, through a potent combination of structural and cultural elements: of coercion and consent.

Jill Blackmore (1990), writing of School-Based Management (SBM) in Australia, stresses the coercive character of centralised state control (see also Robertson 1993).

> In the 1980s government reports throughout Australia have also focused upon the school as the unit of decision-making, but within a framework of corporate management. [They] utilise the language of collaborative decision-making whilst effectively rendering school-based decision-making outside the control of teacher unions, local bodies and the majority of parents by other centralising tendencies (National Curriculum, assessment procedures, funding). School-based decision-making in this form ultimately serves particular managerial and class interests (p.246).

Malen, Ogawa and Kranz (1990), in an American study, summarise the research literature on SBM and 'influence relationships'.

> The dominant theme is that site participants, notably teachers and parents, rarely exerted influence in the core domains of budget, personnel and program through community school

> boards, . . . through advisory councils . . . or through other participatory decision-making arrangements. In some cases, these structural adjustments operated to diffuse conflict, restore confidence, calm the system and garner support for the schools (p.310).

They stress the role of consent:

> . . . informal norms dictate that district officials and school administrators set policies, teachers deliver instruction, and parents provide support. Although school-based management grants participants the formal right to change this presumption, informal norms nullify that option. Thus, deeply engrained norms tend to keep agendas confined to marginal matters and leaves conventional influence relationships intact (p.308).

One of the merits of the concept of hegemony is that it focuses our attention on the ideological and cultural processes through which social reproduction is accomplished. It is from that perspective that I want to develop the notion of 'informal norms' by exploring the cultural and ideological formation of governors. In our research, the marginalisation of 'race' was achieved through the combination and interaction of state policy and the commonsense understandings that headteachers, teachers and different categories of governors brought to their roles.[2] In the case of teachers and headteachers, those common sense understandings were rooted in an elaborated educational ideology of 'professionalism' and the lay/professional divide that it entailed. But my concern here is with lay governors. I will take as illustrative examples governors at one school in our study who came from very different social locations. Two were co-opted as representatives of the business community. The third is a parent governor, a woman who in many ways was typical of a number of women from working-class backgrounds on the governing body, as parent governors or as LEA governors nominated by the Labour Party.

## Business governors

The two business governors saw their role as being explicitly interventionist. They saw this as the result of their business training. In addition, they saw themselves as not only being able to contribute business expertise but also as representing a business perspective. The combination of these two gave them a distinct stance and role in governors' meetings. The main elements of their 'business perspective' were the following.

### *The relationship of school to work*

The question of the standards of school-leavers was important to both business governors. This is not surprising, but they differed from other governors in tending to see this much more explicitly from the standpoint of the needs of the labour market.

### *School management procedures*

They strongly believed that many of the management procedures in use in school could be improved by learning from those in the business world.

### *The culture of the school*

They questioned the culture of school from a business standpoint. The key concepts they used concerned responsiveness to change and 'value for money'. Both were grounded in the market as the 'real world', the authentic arbiter of social life.

### *Teachers as employees*

Both expressed positive attitudes towards the teachers, but their 'educational protectiveness' (Thody, Chapter 2) was qualified by criticisms based on the business model of employee relations. They argued that some teachers didn't work hard enough and didn't realise how well off they were compared to workers in industry. Teachers lacked financial realism: they were not 'worldly-wise' (a key term in the business governors' vocabulary). In their view, the root of the problem was that teachers were shielded from the realities of the market.

### *Attitudes to the LEA and the Labour Party*

The reality of the market was again used as the criterion against which the culture of the LEA was judged and criticised. It was seen as resistant to 'technically rational' ways of working because of an inflexible adherence to political principles. The world of business had a distinctive set of values and ways of seeing things, as did the Labour Party, but while the Labour Party was political — defined as representing a sectoral interest — the business interest stood for the universal interest, above politics. The economic was non-political because it was simply 'how things are': in other words, market relations were *naturalised*. The business frame of reference therefore provided a taken-for-granted, not-to-be-questioned yardstick, apparently continuously validated by everyday life, with which to measure education, and beat it when necessary.

In the context of education, the 'system-maintaining' function of the business perspective that I have outlined is evident. This was true too of the specific issue of 'race'. In my interviews with them, both business governors expressed concern for racial equality from what might be called a liberal integrationist point of view. Both also stated that they had never discussed issues of 'race' on the governing body, apart from supporting calls for more Section 11 provision from the LEA for English as a Second Language teaching. Why had they themselves never raised the issue in governing body meetings? There were two reasons. The first concerned their conception of their role: in particular, their deference to the professional expertise of teachers and the headteacher on 'educational ' matters, including the omission of 'race' from the educational agenda they put before the governing body. The second concerned their conception of racial equality as an issue. It was not central to the business perspective on education. They had little knowledge of the reality of issues of 'race' in the school or in the local community (in which neither of them lived). As a consequence, they tended to idealise both relations between ethnic groups in the locality and the school's response (e.g. the extent to which multicultural education took place). In interview, both supported positive measures, such as the need for a bilingual home–school liaison teacher and for bilingual teaching staff, which were in advance of existing practice in the school. However, the dominance of business values, educational and financial, meant that in practice such measures were low on their agenda of priorities.

### Working-class women governors

Mrs Smith, a parent governor, illustrates how social processes of class, gender and ethnicity shape biography and ideology. Her story is unique to her, but it is also typical of some other working-class women governors in our study. She was the daughter of a miner, and her working life had been spent as a production worker in local industry. She had lived within a few hundred yards of the school all her life, in a stable and parochial working-class community. She had failed the 11+ and had had to leave school at the earliest opportunity. The negative self-concept that her own school experience had left her with was reinforced by her experience as a governor, and as a result she rarely spoke at governing body meetings.

> Hearing what the other governors . . . hearing the answers that I miss because they're looking for different things, I'm listening for different things. As I say, being thick it's awful, it really is.

Her past experiences, as a pupil, of authoritarian teachers and low academic achievement led her to compare and strongly approve of the teachers at her school.

> Mainly it is the amount of time they put in, other than school hours. But the amount of time they spend on individual children. I don't mean the better achievers, the under-achievers mainly. I've realised how much they want for all children. The cameraderie sometimes between teachers and pupils. . . . The different methods of teaching. This is all comparing me own teaching and the children's.

The question of social class equality in education, rooted in her own life-history, was central to Mrs Smith's perspective as a governor. What were the implications for how she saw the issue of racial equality?

Mrs Smith's views on 'race' arose out of her experience of the changed ethnic composition of the neighbourhood. She evoked a strong historical sense of the white community bound together by a network of social relationships, exemplified by mothers chatting in the street and children playing out together. The Asian families remained separate from this web of relationships, principally because the mothers did not speak English. She shared the wish of many white parents in the area that the Pakistani families didn't live there.

But she also accepted the reality that, in her words, 'they are here to stay'. From that followed the need for mutual accommodation. In her view the Pakistanis had got to integrate, which above all meant the women learning English, but she also recognised that 'we've got to change our ideas'. She supported measures to tackle children's lack of English, which she saw as an obstacle to integration and a threat to white children's progress, but she also supported a multicultural curriculum as being in the interests of all children. She saw face-to-face discussion as the only way to satisfy the interests of the two ethnic groups: 'until you can get them to sit down and bash it out I don't know'.

That discussion never took place. One possible forum was the school governing body, but she herself had never raised these concerns there, partly because of her general inhibitions about speaking, but partly because she felt that 'race' was not a legitimate issue for governors' agendas. She explained the reason why.

> Well when I brought it up at a PTA it had to go off the record, yes, because I was bringing up racial prejudice problems. So it went off the record. . . . What I've said today I voiced then, and the answers couldn't be met properly, because the headmaster

> is between two fires. He cannot be racial prejudiced. So we were still at stalemate.
>
> Do you think that the governing body is a place where it could be talked about and 'bashed out' or . . . ?
>
> Yes but there again, the questions we're raising are racial prejudice.

The case of Mrs Smith illustrates how a complex of factors can interact to filter out concerns about 'race' from governors' meetings. The failure of the LEA and the headteacher to place the issue on their agendas reinforced her belief that to talk about racial issues was illegitimate because it was 'racial prejudice'. Consequently, the real concerns of white parents were never discussed, while the possibilities inherent in the positive elements in Mrs Smith's thinking were never taken advantage of by the school and the LEA because of their fear of a 'white backlash'.

Mrs Smith exemplifies the way in which the education-related ideologies and cultures of working-class governors are rooted in their life-situations and can serve to maintain rather than challenge existing patterns of unequal social reproduction by the school. A similar conclusion is reached by Phil Carspecken (1991) in his analysis of the community campaign at Croxteth comprehensive school in Liverpool. The school was closed in 1981 because of falling rolls. A campaign in the local working-class community to keep the school open led to the school being occupied in July 1982 and opening in September, with volunteer teachers and 260 pupils, under the control of an action committee of people from the local working-class community. It ran for that whole school year, and was then reinstated as a state-run school.

The community activists who led the campaign during that year operated with an ideology of 'community rights', which Carspecken defines as accepting the nature and form of services, and only questioning the amount and the 'quality'. As a result, they favoured a traditional school regime: a traditional curriculum, the grouping of pupils by ability and the centrality of examination success. Carspecken sees this popular educational ideology as rooted in the social locations of those who held it. He speaks of 'deep-seated and largely unquestioned attitudes to politics and schooling, all of which are related to social routines common to the daily lives and social positions of the people drawing upon them' (1991, pp.238–9). Local residents felt unqualified to comment on or criticise educational matters. Their attitudes were influenced by their own largely negative experiences of schooling, but these led to a reaffirmation, rather than a questioning, of that traditional model of education.

Carspecken identifies two reasons. One was their acceptance of a reified notion of school knowledge, divorced from practical concerns. The other was their approval of authoritarian pupil–teacher relations, which they derived from the cultural norms of adult-child relationships that predominated in the community.

The distinctive characteristic of LMS and other versions of school-based management that I want to emphasise here is their ability to co-opt and construct consent (a feature also noted by Thody in Chapter 2). The combination of state coercion and market relationships acts to select, shape and sponsor elements of the ideologies of school governors in ways which maintain patterns of dominance and inequality. I have sketched in two illustrations of this process: the business governors and Mrs Smith. Further research is needed to gain a fuller picture of the repertoire of modes of assimilation and accommodation — and contestation — entailed in SBM. The power of the process of incorporating the aspirations of governors and subordinating them to state imperatives and market logic is demonstrated in Liz Gordon's (1993) study of SBM in New Zealand, and in Cusack's chapter in this book. New Zealand schools are governed by boards of trustees, similar to English governing bodies but comprising a majority of parents (as in Scotland). The state 'although acting at a distance, needed to ensure that trustees . . . did the work of the state' (p.8). It had a range of coercive means at its disposal, such as the 'school charter' (a contract defining the trustees' role), 'effectiveness reviews', and funding arrangements. But Gordon suggests that 'It may not be these coercive factors, but more informal ones, which define board compliance with state goals' (p.10). In particular, trustees are highly motivated to maintain and improve their schools. However, in a market context, that commitment to a 'public service' notion of schooling is assimilated into a 'business logic' of competition between schools which leads to a conformity to state goals, which has as one consequence a reinforcing of social inequalities, as women and Maori people are marginalised from school governance.

## Governors' ideologies

Rosemary Deem and Kevin Brehony, in a number of publications drawing on their research, have discussed the ideologies of lay governors. Deem (1992. See also Deem, 1994) argues that there are two ideologies of 'lay participation in educational administration'. A 'collective concern' ideology is based on democracy and public accountability, while a 'consumer interest' ideology is based on markets, competition, consumer rights, and private interests. She found no special affinity of co-opted governors for the 'consumer interest' ideology, but few of the co-opted governors in the schools she studied were from business or industry (1992, p.15). Deem and her co-authors rightly point out that governor's ideologies cannot simply be read off from their social locations (Deem, 1992; Deem, Brehony and Hemmings, 1992). But it would be equally wrong to assume that the relationship was wholly indeterminate. As Terry Eagleton (1991) puts it:

> ideology is never the mere expressive effect of objective social interests, but neither are all ideological signifiers 'free-floating' in respect of such signifiers (p.223).

Our analysis shows how the ideologies of the business governors and of Mrs Smith, as a working-class woman, are shaped by their social locations and the interests that arise from them — in the case of Mrs Smith, stretching back to her childhood — in more complex ways than can be accommodated in Deem's bipolar model. While Mrs Smith clearly expresses an ideology of 'collective concern', the 'business perspective' in our research does not conform to Deem's *counterposition* of private and public, of consumer and collective, interests. Her concept of 'collective concern' conflates two distinct political ideologies. The notion of education provision driven by social values rather than market choice can be harnessed to very different, and fundamentally conflicting, educational programmes: from one of radical emancipation to one of conservative cultural restoration. In our study the 'business perspective' is a public, collectivist, ideology of education. What distinguishes it from other collectivist perspectives, such as that of Mrs Smith, is that it articulates aspects of education in crucial ways to the market. But it is also more complex than that. It is an ideological ensemble which contains at least two elements that are not directly subordinated to the market. One is an integrative concept of 'community'; the other is a concept of the integrity of teachers' expertise and professionalism.

## Participation and resistance

The institutionalised hegemonic process represented by the role of governing bodies in school-based management is not unique to education. There is a long history of experiences of, and debates around, popular participation, control and incorporation in relation both to the state and to enterprises in the private sector. I want to draw on this wider debate both to understand school-based management as a hegemonic process and to think about the possibilities of resistance.

Le Panitch uses the concept of *corporatism* to analyse developments in the private sector (1986). He defines it as follows (p.161):

> The corporatist political structure is *specific* in the sense that it involves: a linkage between the state and functional groups constituted by institutionalised representation in public policy making; interaction among the groups themselves in this process (in contrast with the one-to-one relationship between interest groups and the state normally constitutive of pressure group politics); and an element of state control over the groups whereby their autonomy is limited and they are employed as agencies of mobilisation or administration for state policy. . . . On the basis of this kind of approach, corporatism in the modern context can be seen as a specific form of state-induced class collaboration.

The Conservative goal at a national level has been to defeat organised opposition, not incorporate it. This has, however, prepared the ground for the introduction of forms of corporatism at the 'local' level. In the workplace it has taken the form of participation schemes — 'teamwork', 'quality circles' and other 'new management techniques'. In some areas of the public sector, however, including the schools, we are also seeing the emergence of another form of corporatism, aimed at integrating the users of services into the administration of provision. In this way consumers are to become 'active citizens', displacing and substituting for state bureaucracies.

The balance-sheet that critics have drawn of experiences of 'participation' in the public sector is that 'participatory movements function to reproduce the system of domination rather than to challenge it' (Saunders, 1986, p.288. See also Croft and Beresford, 1992; for education, see Vincent, 1993). Saunders, in a survey of recent British experiences, concludes that:

> While participation may carry within it the seeds of a more radical movement, it nevertheless seems to be the case that the social control function is usually paramount . . . by establishing formal links with a group such as a tenants' association, a local authority can 'educate' its public, inducing trust in decision-makers, the institutions in which they operate and the political culture which they take for granted. . . . It can, furthermore, explain what is possible and what is not, thereby avoiding any future potentially awkward demands (1986, p.290).

Saunders' view of the hegemonic process by which subordinate groups come to tailor their view of the world, or at least what they conceive as realistically possible, and therefore their aspirations and demands, to the dominant agenda, is congruent with my own analysis of governing bodies. But it would be a pessimistically partial and one-sided analysis that ignored the possibility of resistance. It should be stressed that Panitch does not use 'corporatism' to mean an absence of contestation. On the contrary, criticising liberal theories of corporatism, he says 'there has been a tendency to ignore the high degree of instability that marks corporatist structures within liberal democracies' (1986, pp.138–9). There is a history of participatory movements that have successfully, even if only temporarily, broken the bounds of incorporation. (A classic instance is Cockburn's (1977) account of the tenants' movement in Lambeth.) In education, there are some important international experiences of 'community control' of schools (see for example Rubinstein, 1970; Levin, 1970; Anderson and Dixon, 1993). But what is the picture in Britain since the introduction of LMS in the 1988 Education Act?

In the last few years there has been an increasing number of local disputes between school heads and teachers and their governors. A typical example, taking place in Birmingham as I write, is the dispute between the governors and staff at a primary school, where the governors overturned an exclusion order made against a pupil for assaulting a teacher. Such disputes are evidence of an increasing degree of autonomy of school governing bodies from headteachers and their staff, but conflicts over their relative powers and responsibilities do not in themselves represent any real challenge to the dominant order in education. Deem and Brehony (1993), following Orton and Weick (1990), have discussed the degree of independence of governing bodies from their schools in terms of the concept of 'loose-coupling'. But, as Lawton (1992) points out, the origins of the concept lie in new management thinking in industry and business, which argues that control which is tight on objectives but loose on procedures is more efficient than traditional bureaucratic control (Caldwell, 1990). So, in the education context, the key question is not the degree of loose-coupling but the objectives that the participants are pursuing. Loose-coupling offers the possibility of governing bodies exercising their independence from the headteacher in order to challenge the state's objectives, but it can also represent a flexible hegemonic process in which the headteacher and the governing body mutually regulate each other within the framework of state policy.

Brehony (1992) discusses the role of school governors in terms of the notion of 'active citizenship'. He notes the wide differences in effectiveness among governors and identifies three causal factors: motivation, time and knowledge about education, which differentiate governors as a result of the lay/professional divide, class, gender and 'race' factors, and the amount of political experience they have. These are all true, but on their own they provide no means of distinguishing between an effective governor in terms of the

Conservatives' version of active citizenship and a governor effective at defending very different interests. While Brehony rejects the Conservative concept of active citizenship, he is sceptical about the possibility of a radical alternative: 'the unequal distribution of resources both material and cultural together with pervasive sexual and racial inequalities mean that active citizens can only ever be a miniscule proportion of all citizens' (p.215). Furthermore, participation means incorporation, even of the tiny minority of 'active citizen' chairs of governors. In his case-study he found few signs that governor dissatisfaction was being translated into political dissent, and 'Where dissent has arisen moreover the governors are generally powerless to alter the situation due to their atomisation as governors of schools competing for pupils' (p.214).

What conditions might permit governors to challenge the subordination and atomisation that Brehony describes? In his study of urban social movements, Peter Saunders (1986) proposes two conditions for a successful resistance to incorporation. The first is *widespread popular support and mobilisation*. In the school context this raises the question of the relationship between governors and their various social bases, especially among parents and the community. Resistance to incorporation is only possible on the basis of *external* pressure that can be brought to bear on the state. The question therefore of how governors build those links of accountability and campaign around issues is crucial.

The second condition is *political organisation*. Saunders says it is important for four reasons: it aids mobilisation of the social base; it enables links with other struggles; it provides a coherent political programme; and it provides a means whereby the protest can articulate with the political system (1986, p.293). He suggests that its source might lie in the radicalisation of state professional employees making alliances with service users.

In education in Britain recently we have two very important practical experiences of precisely the two conditions Saunders stipulates: the alliance between school governors, parents and teachers in Scotland in support of the boycott of national testing in 1991 and 1992 (Munn, 1993), and the widespread support among school governors for the teachers' boycott of national testing in England and Wales in 1993. This is the most important indicator so far that the possibility exists of governors offering a challenge to their incorporation, and the conditions that make it effective.

## Notes

1. This research project was funded by the Commission for Racial Equality and I would like to acknowledge their support. I would like to thank Barry Troyna and

Deborah Gewirtz for their help. Neither they nor the CRE necessarily share the views expressed in this chapter.

2. School governing bodies in England are composed of parents (who are elected by the parent body), teachers (who are elected by the school teaching staff), nominees of the local education authority (who may be from any of the political parties represented on the local council), and co-opted governors, who are usually figures in the local community and generally include 'business interests'. In addition, the headteacher may choose to be a governor or to attend meetings in an *ex-officio* capacity.

## Bibliography

Anderson, G. L. and Dixon, A. (1993) 'Paradigm shifts and site-based management in the United States: toward a paradigm of social empowerment' in Smyth, J. (Ed) *A Socially Critical View of the Self-Managing School*, London: Falmer.

Blackmore, J. (1990) 'School-based decision-making and teacher unions: the appropriation of a discourse' in Chapman, J. D. (Ed) *School-based Decision-making and Management*, London: Falmer.

Brehony, K. J. (1992) 'Active citizens: the case of school governors'. *International Studies in Sociology of Education*, **2**, 2, pp.199–217.

Caldwell, B. (1990) 'School-based decision-making and management: international developments' in Chapman, J. D. (Ed) *School-based Decision-making and Management*, London: Falmer.

Carspecken, P. (1991) 'Parental choice, participation and working-class culture' in Education Group II (Ed) *Education Limited*, London: Unwin Hyman.

Cockburn, C. (1977) *The Local State*, London: Pluto.

Croft, S. and Beresford, P. (1992) 'The politics of participation'. *Critical Social Policy*, **35**, Autumn, pp.20–44.

Deem, R. (1992) *School Governing Bodies — Public Concerns and Private Interests?* Paper presented to the International Conference on 'Accountability and control in educational settings', Centre for Educational Development, Appraisal and Research, University of Warwick, April.

Deem, R. (1994) 'School governing bodies — public concerns or private interests?' in Scott, D. (Ed) *Accountability and Control in Educational Settings*, London: Cassell.

Deem, R. and Brehony, K. J. (1993) *Watching education policy happen: studying the policy process through multiple-site case studies*. Paper presented to the British Sociological Association Conference 'Research Imaginations', University of Essex, 5–8 April.

Deem, R. Brehony, K. and Hemmings, S. (1992) 'Social justice, social divisions and the governing of schools' in Gill, D. and Mayor, B. (Eds) *Racism and Education: Structures and Strategies*, London: Sage.

Eagleton, T. (1991) *Ideology*, London: Verso.

Gordon, L. (1993) *Who controls New Zealand schools? Decentralised management and the problem of agency*. Paper presented to the annual conference of the British Educational Research Association, Liverpool, September.

Lawton, S. B. (1992) *Restructuring educational systems and school-based management*. Paper presented at the conference 'Restructuring Education: Choices and Challenges', Toronto, Canada, 5–7 March.

Levin, H. (Ed) (1970) *Community Control of Schools*, Washington DC: The Brookings Institution.

Malen, B., Ogawa, R. T. and Kranz, J. (1990) 'What do we know about school-based management? a case study of the literature — a call for research' in Clune, W. H.

and Witte, J. F. (Eds) *Choice and Control in American Education* Volume 2: The Practice of Choice, Decentralisation and School Restructuring, Lewes: Falmer.
Munn, P. (1993) 'Parents as school board members: school managers and friends?', in Munn, P. (Ed) *Parents and Schools: Customers, Managers or Partners?*, London: Routledge.
Orton, J. D. and Weick, K. E. (1990) 'Loosely coupled systems: a reconceptualisation'. *Academy of Management Review*, **15**, 2, pp.203–223.
Panitch, L. (1986) *Working Class Politics in Crisis: Essays on Labour and the State* London: Verso.
Robertson, S. L. (1993) 'The politics of devolution, self-management and post-Fordism in schools' in Smyth, J. (Ed) *A Socially Critical View of the Self-Managing School*, London: Falmer.
Rubinstein, A. T. (Ed) (1970) *Schools Against Children: The Case for Community Control*, New York: Monthly Review Press.
Saunders, P. (1986) *Urban Politics*, Harmondsworth: Penguin.
Troyna, B., Hatcher, R. and Gewirtz, D. (1993) *The Local Management of Schools and Racial Equality: Final Report to the Commission for Racial Equality*.
Vincent, C. (1993) 'Community participation? the establishment of 'City's' Parents' Centre'. *British Educational Research Journal*, **19**, 3, pp.227–241.

# 10 Developing roles and relationships in primary school governance

Lynda Huckman

This chapter will review briefly the models of school governance developed in the 1980s to see if they are applicable in the 1990s. Using concepts introduced by Thody in Chapter 2 above it will be argued that these models incorporate features of overt managerial approaches that are often adapted by headteachers to disguise strategies aimed at influencing decision-making and maintaining authority. An illusion of democracy is thus created by heads which is legitimated by the covert responses of governors defined in terms of consent and protectionism. The chapter will conclude by suggesting that unresolved problems preventing fuller governor participation indicate that there is a need for a review of the roles that governors are expected to perform, and that these roles are not adequately explained in terms of current management theory.

Management models have been specifically selected because the focus of the research on which this chapter is based was on the new management responsibilities of governors rather than considering their democratic place. To support these arguments, examples have been taken from a two year study (1990–1992) of the processes of decision-making at five financially autonomous primary schools under what is referred to by the heads and governors as local management of schools (LMS). Material is drawn from informal interviews with headteachers which took place throughout the course of the study, and from formal interviews with heads and selected governors at the end of the study. These interviews were used to obtain perspectives and to verify data collected from non-participant observation of governor and finance sub-committee meetings. For the purposes of respecting confidentiality, pseudonyms have been given to the two Infant schools and three Junior schools which took part in the study. Eastlyn Infants was situated on an adjacent site to Eastlyn Juniors in what both heads described as a leafy suburb of the city in a catchment area described as being predominantly middle class. Unlike the head of Eastlyn Juniors who described himself as being democratic but a very bad account keeper, the head of Eastlyn Infants prided herself on being a competent manager, always able to balance the books satisfactorily but she admitted to adopting an autocratic style. Budlyn Infants and Juniors were situated on a joint site. The heads described the catchment area as being inhabited by mainly working-class and semi-skilled people. Both heads reported that they would have liked more participation from their governors but that they were forced to adopt autocratic approaches since their governors were reluctant to become more involved. Oakley Juniors was situated in an outer suburb about twelve miles from the city in what was described by the head as a 'commuter village' inhabited by mainly professional families. Like the head of Budlyn Infants he was new to headship and admitted to having had no training and very little experience in financial management. Like both the Budlyn heads he hoped to be able to foster democratic approaches and to share management responsibilities.

It is not surprising that the majority of heads professed to wanting to encourage participation from their governors since the Education Reform Act had considerably widened the decision-making arena for schools giving new responsibilities to governing bodies in key areas such as finance and the curriculum. Heads and governors of financially autonomous schools manage over 90 per cent of the schools' budget. As well as the day-to-day running costs, repair and maintenance of the schools' premises, governors can decide how many staff work at a school; they have the power to hire and fire staff and decide what extra incentive allowances are paid to them. Selected governors also have the right to 'virement', that is the right to transfer sums of money from one heading to another as they see fit, or they may delegate budget management to the headteacher. Governors are now required to appraise the work of members of staff, to oversee the school's delivery of the National Curriculum, to monitor standards in terms of pupil assessment and to report to parents at a Parents' Annual General Meeting.

## Models of governing body performance

The model of school governance which underlies this piece of legislation is borrowed from the world of business. The governing body is the board of directors, the head is the managing director and the parents are the shareholders (Coopers and Lybrand, 1988; Haviland, 1988). Each year the board of directors must issue its annual report to the shareholders and hold a shareholders' annual meeting to which the board is answerable for the way it has run the company during the preceding twelve months. In this role as a board of directors, school governors could be compared to that of overseers' with a monitoring role, as the Audit Commission implied in 1993:

> Governors should reconsider their decision to delegate to headteachers authority to spend money without limit. They should set a limit at which they expect to approve, not only the decisions to make a purchase but also the decision about the supplier of goods and services, as it is this latter decision that has the greatest need for openness.

Governors' power as potential overseers is not, however, untrammelled. First they are restricted by governments and secondly they appear to be restricted by their own attitudes and capabilities. In relation to government powers, governors' decision-making takes place within parameters which have been laid down by central and local government with the added requirement that performance should be self-monitored as well as externally monitored. Governors' autonomy is further circumscribed by restrictions imposed by budgets which can often prove to be inflexible (Huckman, 1994).

Secondly, previous research indicates the limiting features of governors' attitudes and capabilities. Governors are more ready to advise and support than to monitor the performance of headteachers (Packwood, 1984; Pascal, 1987). Their chances of being effective monitors are affected by the potential conflict which exists on governing bodies between the 'professional' members (heads, teachers and local education authority representatives) and the 'lay' members (parents, governors and co-opted members). This can arise because of the unequal distribution of power between the 'laity' and the 'professionals' (Kogan, 1984; Pascal, 1987); it becomes very difficult for part-time amateurs to question decisions made by full-time professionals. Tension on governing bodies can be caused by the need for governors to be supportive of a school's efforts while maintaining the objectivity required by their monitoring role. Unless carefully handled the monitoring of performance can also lead to a deterioration in the relationships between governors and heads and members of staff (Pascal, 1987, p.199).

These relationships seem unlikely to change, according to

recent research. Deem (1989) investigated the issue of how representative governing bodies are of the general population, and the extent to which classism, sexism and racism contribute to the unequal involvement of individual members of governing bodies. She observes:

> There is a tendency in some governing bodies in our study to treat parent governors differently, appealing to them only on particular issues and apparently not expecting them to contribute on other matters; this is especially marked where there are female and black or Asian governors (p.255).

Deem and Brehony (1991) suggest that the level of educational knowledge of many lay governors is fragmentary and not sufficient to enable them to discharge their responsibilities; that as a result their power to act with confidence or to change established modes of operating is affected:

> as a consequence, most lay governors appear relatively powerless to reshape education (p.25).

The board of directors' model has elements of the overt managerial approaches described by Thody in Chapter 2 and of the monitoring aspects of the overt democracy of governing bodies (ibid.). The reluctance of governors to utilise the potential monitoring role appears to indicate their move to covert protection and consent (ibid.). Similar trends seem to be apparent in other managerial approaches developed in Thody's (1992) study and which have been implied by both the Office for Standards in Education (OFSTED) and the Audit Commission. Thody's (1992) study for example, sees school governors adopting the roles of director, consultant or representative.

Responses to managerial roles for governors indicate possible complications, again postulating the covert results outlined in Chapter 2 above. David Hart of the National Association of Headteachers (NAHT) observes that the adoption of a management model can lead to a blurring of the line of responsibility which results in confusion of roles and responsibilities.

> Governors, armed with their new powers are seeking to manage rather than govern ... with the result that the question of who should take management decisions is becoming obscured (*Independent* 25 October 1990).

A similar caution is contained in the OFSTED 1993 report 'Keeping Your Balance' but emphasis here is placed on the need to apportion accountability for decision-making:

> Schools should define the responsibilities of each person involved in the administration of the school's finances to avoid the duplication or omission of functions and to provide a framework of accountability for governors and staff (p.4).

The Audit Commission's report (1993) comments on the reluctance of some heads to share authority and the unwillingness of some governors to assume their full powers:

- No governors with an interest in financial management
- Heads are nervous about the governing body involving themselves in the day to day running of the school
- Governors have surrendered the formal controls which would act as safeguards — they have delegated to the head unlimited authority to spend and to move money from one budget area to another (p.26).

The reluctance of primary school headteachers in particular to relinquish their management role and their control over decision-making, is also recognised by the 1993 Audit Commission's report:

> Primary school heads involved in the routine tasks of financial administration should consider how they can delegate these. Many headteachers have not done this for fear of weakening financial control (p.31).

The introduction of collegiality into a school is very dependent on the headteacher and is not always compatible with notions of leadership because of the expectations held by heads and others about the role of the head. Research in this area has suggested that primary heads display a feeling of ownership of their schools which can impede the progress of collegiality and which drives heads to protect their schools from what they see as outside interference, (Coulson in Peters, 1976; Coulson, 1985; Southworth, 1987). Coulson's (1990) overview of research into primary headship suggests that this situation has not altered with the extension of responsibilities which accompanied the 1988 Education Reform Act:

> Research confirms the heads' dominance in primary schools . . . paternalism remains in many schools but many heads favour a management style which combines direction with consultation (Coulson, 1990, p.106).

These views on the operation of managerial inter-relationships of heads and governors seem to indicate that the ideal partnership model of school governance described by Beckett, Bell and

Rhodes (1991), which is based on equal 'open' partnership between head, staff, governors, and Local Education Authority (LEA), will not easily be achieved by all schools. Yet it is the partnership model that is reflected in the inspection guidelines contained in OFSTED (1992). A criterion given for the assessment of the performance of governors is whether heads and governors work together to provide 'a clear sense of purpose for the school' assuming that efficient working at governor level will be translated into efficiency in the classroom and result in improved outcomes for pupils.

The partnership model seems predicated on assumptions of power sharing although the above research indicates this is not happening. This apparent conflict of expectations and reality focuses attention on the strategies which headteachers employ to maintain the balance of power in their favour and to avoid or resolve conflict within their governing bodies which can be viewed as lying within the domain of what Hoyle (1986) and Ball (1987) calls micropolitical processes. Evetts (1993) has noted the growth of the micropolitical dimension since the advent of LMS which she views as a consequence of the expanded role of headteachers as decision-makers, advisers and negotiators. The extended arena for their decision-making results in the redirection of micropolitical activity towards LEAs. According to Thody, (above pp.21–22), governors as yet lack micropolitical skills because of their political immaturity. Headteachers may, therefore, be able to hide micropolitical activity under the guise of legitimate practice so that lip-service can be paid to orthodox procedures while the day-to-day realities are managed. It is to an examination of these processes of interaction that we now turn.

## Primary school experience: the research evidence, 1990–1992

### Headteachers' control of information

The day-to-day running of the school and the operation of financial autonomy (LMS) was undertaken by heads and through correspondence with the LEA. Much of the information necessary for decision-making at the schools was possessed solely by headteachers. Not even chairs of finance were allowed access to the LEA Management Information System. Control of information provided heads with a considerable degree of power. Items for agendas were invariably drawn up by the heads themselves; issues which were presented for discussion, and the definition of issues could be selective. Heads could control the direction of governors' meetings, presenting only those issues on which they needed or required their governors' support, opinions and action.

Heads put forward practical reasons why governors could not be involved in every detail of the vast amount of correspondence that entered the school. Lack of governors' time, interest and understanding of educational issues were viewed as presenting problems for fuller participation. These explanations also meant that as far as heads were concerned, issues that were presented needed to be summarised and focused on points to be discussed. The clarification of educational issues and their possible effects on the school were felt to be necessary for lay members to be able to form considered judgements.

The power to select and present their analyses of issues was viewed by heads as being essential for the maintenance of their authority and for the avoidance of confusion. The head of Eastlyn Infants was concerned over the growing powers of governors and the effect this could have on her control of the management of the school. She had noted that an increasing amount of correspondence from the LEA was now being sent solely to her chair of governors. As manager of the school, she felt that she had the right to be informed on all pertinent issues, and she objected strongly to any attempt to circumvent her role.

Heads were also aware of the possibility that governors could misinterpret or misreport information given to them by agencies outside the school and that it would be the head's task to resolve any confusion that resulted. An example of this occurred at Budlyn Infants when a governor who had attended a training session on equal opportunities that had included some discussion on the formulation of staff pay policies, reported back to the full governing body with important information about which the headteacher was completely unaware. The head had felt she had been placed in a difficult situation, since she had not known how to respond to her governor, or whether the information was correct or had been correctly interpreted:

> I can only say, we were all open-mouthed and horrified. I didn't know anything about it. Was it correct the way it was presented to us?

## Headteachers' micropolitical techniques

As Handy (1976) observes, the presentation as well as the control of information can be an effective means of achieving objectives.

As he suggests, it was difficult for other participants to argue with facts that were presented by an accepted specialist. Headteachers are obviously the accepted specialists. They all appeared to use the basic strategy of dominance through use of their specialism but there were considerable variations in the degree of discussion and debate that ensued. Much depended on the management style adopted by the head. The ways in which information was presented was considered to be essential to the achievement of consensus.

The head of Eastlyn Juniors, for example, who professed to adopting democratic approaches to decision-making saw it as meaning arguing and counter arguing until members gradually came round to seeing his point of view:

> I decide what I think is the best idea and I go on talking until they agree with me — I'm very rarely overruled.

The new head of Oakley Juniors had used a similar strategy to mediate between the Parent Teacher Association (PTA) and governors over the use of money the PTA had raised as a fund in honour of the previous headteacher:

> I kept sowing seeds and sowing seeds, although I could see both sides. The PTA thought I was going ahead and doing what we had agreed.

'Sowing seeds' had involved him in persuading the governing body to reconsider the original objective for the Fund which was to provide resources for children with special needs, and the head used this as a means of furthering his argument by extending the meaning of 'special needs' beyond what was usually accepted by governors:

> I put it to them — you can't have more of a need than a child wishing to play an instrument who hasn't got a stand to put his music on, or someone who needs to develop library skills who hasn't got a reference book.

Further progress was made through a reiteration of this argument at the joint meeting held between the governors and the PTA. Although the head's and PTA's more general interpretation of special needs was not shared by the governors who had thought the money should be spent helping children who were experiencing greater handicaps, a decision was finally taken to accept the PTA's proposals.

At all the schools, influence was brought to bear by the presentation of a rationale or acceptable 'vocabulary of motive' (Wright-Mills, 1940), aimed at getting governors' acceptance of heads' decisions, which entailed a considerable amount of preparation for meetings on the part of heads.

Budget presentations took on the form of a ritual (Olsen, 1970) in which heads demonstrated, often with the aid of a flipchart, the budget situations that existed and the possible options for allocating funds, providing their governors with overwhelming evidence in support of their favoured option. The logic of the arguments which were used could not easily be disputed by governors who were not in full possession of the facts and information that lay behind their construction.

As non-professionals, governors were not in a position to disagree with their heads' objectives which underpinned many of the decisions that had been made. Money that was spent often represented the heads' visions for their schools — spending on particular resources, increasing or reducing staff could be viewed as enactments of those visions. The simple need to balance the budget could conceal other objectives. Governors could not always discern less obvious motivation. In the case of Budlyn Infants, the decision to place two new teachers on fixed term contract had been taken ostensibly to increase budget flexibility. Not to make them permanent at the end of their first year had involved other considerations. They had been the first new appointments the head had made, and she had been pleased with their performance and wanted to keep them. After two years they would become permanent members of staff anyway. Having got them into the school on fixed term contract, she did not want to go through the formal interview procedure and risk the possibility that her governors would prefer other candidates. It would also have incurred unnecessary stress for other candidates who would be called for interview without any real likelihood that they would be accepted for the posts.

Decisions could be presented so that they accorded with the perceived ideology that financial decisions should not direct educational decision-making. Thus decisions to appoint 'cheaper' staff, the use of fixed-term contracts and part-time assistance, the maintenance of incentive allowances were all viewed in terms of educational as well as financial considerations (Huckman and Hill, 1994).

## Headteachers and covert democracy

Control of information and micropolitical techniques relate directly to managerial approaches but evidence from the research also indicated headteacher's influence on helping to create the illusion of democracy discussed on pp.17–22. This occurred through processes of co-option and of networking. Teacher governors at all the schools were observed to support their heads' arguments but at Eastlyn Infants an increase in the educationalist perspective considerably reduced the need for the head to defend her position and rationalise her objectives. An educationalist perspective at the school was increased by the co-option of the deputy head who joined the teacher governor and a link governor who was a lecturer at the local polytechnic. The co-option of a former teacher was made later in the study. Although the head had elected to be a member of all the sub-committees, the larger teacher representation at Eastlyn afforded an extra opportunity for an educationalist perspective to be represented on what all the heads considered to be the key subcommittees, that is, finance, staffing and curriculum. All appointments had been made after a consideration of the expertise that an individual could contribute and of the likelihood that the potential governor would show commitment to the school but since headteachers' views of possible appointees generally took precedence over those held by other participants, their selection could be directed. Governors at both the Eastlyn schools had noted with some reservations the growing power of an educationalist perspective at the schools and were aware of the dangers of such an imbalanced view on decision-making:

> I'm sure the academics prefer to have people around them that they can recognise. If we're not careful we could have a governing body which is short of a commercial view. We have twelve governors and only two or three commercial governors with an interest in education *per se* (a co-opted governor, Eastlyn Juniors).

All governors were given the opportunity to give their opinion of the suitability of prospective nominees, and therefore such decisions were ostensibly made collectively. But many of the governors were not always aware that a position on the governing body was vacant until they received their agendas or when a candidate was proposed at a meeting. These governors were often not in a position to suggest alternative candidates who would gain acceptance by the majority of participants. A similar attempt at promoting collaboration was made by the head of Budlyn Infants in her choice of subcommittee members:

> As for the finance and curriculum one, I won't say it was hand picked, but it was 'carefully guided'. I was looking for a parent who liked or who was ready for change, who saw greater depths to change than just change for change sake,

> who could see the value of the National Curriculum and that sort of thing. I knew that anything that involved change would have their support, and I wasn't actually going to 'battle' with them, and that seemed beneficial, and they've been very useful.

Instances of paired collaboration could occur between participants based on the influence they could exert over the general governing body. The fact that chairs of governing bodies and chairs of finance gained closer access than other participants to the font of decision-making could be accounted for by the special roles which they performed within governing bodies. 'Bargaining coalitions' (March and Olsen, 1976), or 'bargaining zones' (Abell, 1975), were formed between participants who were privy to information and to an understanding of the inner dynamics of decision-making at the schools from which other participants were excluded. Teacher governors and chairs of governing bodies were often observed to support the views of headteachers who had consulted them in advance of their intentions. Heads consulted with chairs of finance to gain their support and to provide a rationale for the recommendations which would be accepted by the full governing body. The fact that the majority of the headteachers had elected to be members of what they regarded as being the key subcommittees (staffing, curriculum and finance), had ensured that an educationalist perspective, and a continuity of perspective was maintained throughout the process.

The influence of headteachers could be extended through informal networks of communication. The head of Budlyn Infant school was able to use informal communication links with parent governors to obtain views and support for her decisions. The operation of subcommittees at both the Budlyn schools could be subverted and used as a means of achieving speedy approval for decisions which could then be presented to the full governing body as a virtual *fait accompli*. In the case of Budlyn Infants and Juniors the support of subcommittee members was used to circumvent the lengthy process of decision-making which involving the full governing body entailed.

## Governors and the experience of covert management: the exercise of power

Governors were aware of their potential powers conferred on them by the 1988 Education Reform Act; that decisions sanctioned by the heads could be overruled by governors if they so wished, but they refrained from exercising their full powers. No decision at the schools which the head supported was rejected. Governors were aware of the need to preserve relationships within the relatively small, close-knit communities which they governed, and of the dangers of interfering with the professional autonomy of members of staff.

Governors acknowledged the need to proceed warily in exercising their powers since before the advent of financial autonomy the heads were viewed as having managed virtually alone, and the majority had been regarded as being competent and successful managers of their schools. The chair of Eastlyn Infants was of the opinion that:

> Local management of schools is an enormous intrusion to competent heads. Governors are, after all, mostly lay people, learning on the job. She's having to refer to us when she must have known all along that we have no views to express.

The chair of governors at Eastlyn Juniors held a similar view:

> The relationship with the head is potentially difficult. I think the head is ambivalent — partly glad to have these people interested in his school, and partly, 'Well, these nosy-people-parkers telling me how I should run the school — they're not professionals.'

The governor's consent to, and protection of, the authority invested in their headteachers' professional and managerial role, tipped the balance of power in favour of their headteachers, and resulted in their acceptance of what Dunlap and Goldman (1991) describe as 'facilitative power', in which their supportive role (Kogan, 1984) was emphasised and used by headteachers as a means whereby accountability was shared and decisions sanctioned.

Governors were mindful that whatever decisions were made at governor level it would be left to the head to implement them at the 'chalk face'; they were also aware of the implications for other members of staff of decisions that were made which could affect their working lives. As the chair of finance at Eastlyn Juniors explained:

> Teachers have to work within the constraints that are made if we get rid of teachers.

Governors also acknowledged the fact that the involvement of even the most committed member of the governing body was at best, spasmodic and the implications of decisions that were made could well outlast their four-year term of office. Their intermittment involvement in decision-making meant that governors lacked the opportunities which were available to headteachers to exercise their power by using both formal authority and informal influence.

Governors' perceptions of the levels of micropolitical activity depended on their degree of satisfaction with their involvement. Highly satisfied governors viewed continuity of involvement as being a crucial factor which influenced the development of a culture within governing bodies which emphasised the needs and objectives of the school rather than individual perspective or interest. These governors reported that they had observed a reduction over time of the political dimension within governor meetings, so that in situations in which views on issues differed, governors were more willing to concede to what they had come to believe to be the interests of the whole-school organisation which were embodied in definitions provided by the headteachers.

## Governors and covert democracy: political immaturity

Observations and interviews revealed that governors had not yet achieved political skills to participate fully in policy making and monitoring. In Budlyn Infants and Juniors, for example, the heads assumed an overriding control over proceedings which limited debate and which left governors with little to do except 'rubber stamp' decisions that had already been made. The governors who were interviewed were not happy with this dominance. While acknowledging that the head should be in control of his school, the Budlyn governors resented the fact that the head gave them only information that he felt governors needed, and that decisions had been made before the meeting. They viewed autocratic leadership as being dysfunctional and the source of micropolitical activity:

> An autocratic style can make everyone tense at a governor meeting. You're not sure what's going to happen next, whether you're going to say something awkward. The other thing is lack of confidence in the other governors. If you meet afterwards and have a quiet word, you think, how did that go? What's going to happen? What is happening? All sorts of rumours, often false rumours spread and they can perhaps build up into issues.

In contrast, where the governors perceived themselves to have been involved, their interest in influencing proceedings was considerably reduced. This supports the views of Homans (1961), Blau (1964) and Thibaut and Kelley (1959) that the dynamics of decision-making interactions were influenced by the relative values governors placed on the degrees to which they felt they had been informed and consulted during the process. Thus the desire to exercise their powers to influence proceedings could be considerably reduced in situations in which an individual's contribution to decision-making was perceived to be at a level which was acceptable, and perceptions of acceptability took account of the circumstances which placed limitations on involvement.

In taking part in policy making, governors perceived that changing established patterns would be problematic and dependent on an individual's personality and 'how far you're prepared to step in'. This fact was perceived to affect the nature of consensus that could be achieved within a governing body, as one governor observed:

> with an autocratic head people take things as read and don't have the courage to make a stand. I'm not sure that's consensus, that's rule by fear — abject consensus.

Another governor felt that:

> consensus is easily achieved when governors do not understand or involve themselves with issues.

This appears to support Thody's views of how difficult it is to 'break the habits of consent' (p.25 above).

## Governors and professional knowledge

Governors' confidence in their ability to assume managerial responsibility can be dependent on their own views of the competencies needed to perform the tasks which confront them. Thody suggests above (pp.24) that this confidence can be reduced by the head's power as gatekeeper and by the very strong feelings of governors that they should be supportive of the professionals' views of the curriculum and of pedagogy. As Deem and Brehony (1991) suggest, governors may have only partial knowledge of the processes of education and of educating, but the majority of governors in the study did not have any previous experience of management either. The ambiguity inherent in the role of governor was highlighted by a parent governor at Eastlyn Juniors. Non-professionals had been placed in a position of power to monitor educational outcomes, precisely because they were not experts but because they could as she described 'convey the precious light of ordinariness'. However, she viewed the skills needed by governors as being anything but ordinary:

> Nobody has thought through the implications of these things.

> We are not professionals, but to say we are ordinary people? You need a fair bit of knowledge for a lot of what we have to do. You need the ability to think logically, to analyse issues and decide what you're going to do and why and how.

The use of educational jargon added to governors' feelings of exclusion from the educational issues under discussion. Whether intentional or not, at schools where the head and chair or head and teacher governor entered into professional dialogue, it had the effect of marginalising the involvement of the laity. Governors on curriculum subcommittees reported having some involvement in the writing of policy statements on individual subjects, but this had only entailed making linguistic changes to convert the terminology used by the professionals who had written the original document into lay persons' language. A governor describes his involvement in writing the school's policy on special educational needs:

> It was a case of, 'let's find a form of words that mean that to everyone.' Debates were on the turn of words sometimes. Some of us got a bit pedantic, I think, but to us it made things clearer and it tilted the whole essence of what they were doing.

## Reflections

In moving towards the assumption of a board of directorship role, the evidence from this research is that governors appear to be able to operate more the illusion than the reality of management. They do not yet match the professional knowledge of headteachers so that the term 'partnership' for the head/governor relationship seems inappropriate, at least as far as policy making is concerned. The expectation that governors might monitor headteachers, appears to be restricted by the support and protection governors display for educationalists. Even when they disagreed with their headteachers, governors were reluctant to make this evident. Definitions of situations presented by headteachers in the form of rational arguments could hide motivations which were not readily discernible to participants who had restricted understanding and involvement of the day-to-day running of the school and of the micropolitical activity that existed at other levels of the organisation. Such hidden agendas could involve the overriding need to preserve good relationships amongst members of staff, as in the case of the dispensation of incentive and discretionary allowances, or of the need to recruit staff who were considered to hold perspectives that accorded with the views of existing members of staff, or if these were regarded as being unsatisfactory, to appoint staff who were likely to support the heads' objectives for the school. Heads were glad to have the support of their governors and to be able to share accountability with them, but they were often placed in the position of having to balance their ultimate responsibility for the management of their schools with the expectations of collegiality and these were not always compatible.

Governors, on the other hand, understood this dilemma and were sympathetic. In the majority of cases they recognised that heads should have the leading role in decision-making and be allowed to manage their schools. Governors were aware of the difficulties which prevented their fuller involvement, the limitations placed on their time, energies available and understanding of educational issues. They were more willing to devolve responsibility to the head in situations in which they felt they had been adequately consulted or when they had confidence in the head's ability to manage or when they shared his/her vision for the school. But even in circumstances in which the 'legitimacy' of exchange and power (Blau, 1964) was questioned, the unpleasantness associated with confrontation was a powerful deterrent to those who sought change, especially when participant involvement in the process was perceived to be transient.

The findings of research suggest that extending governors' responsibilities in the areas of curriculum, finance and staffing has not provided lay governors with a clearer base of authority. It would seem that these additional responsibilities have made them more reliant than before on information and guidance from the headteacher and professional members. The balance of power on governing bodies and levels of participation remain unequal therefore which supports the views expressed in Chapter 2 above.

## The future?

Uncertainties continue to exist over the role of governors in the school; messages are often contradictory. Are they supposed to support, advise or control school activities? Since they are not often involved in the implementation of decisions which are taken, governors are often viewed as being peripheral rather than central to school life. What effect then does their performance have on the educational effectiveness of the schools they govern, and to what extent can they realistically be made accountable for it? Recent government legislation is intended to encourage schools to opt out of LEA control, but unlike governors of LMS schools who cannot be held responsible for decisions taken in good faith, the governing bodies of grant maintained schools have corporate status and can be sued (Davies and Andersen, 1992, p.18). If governing bodies are to be made accountable in this way, then a clear and realistic definition of their role and responsibilities is required, one that takes full account of the idiosyncratic nature of participation on governing bodies and one that acknowledges the managerial as well as professional expertise of the majority of headteachers who have been appointed by their governors to the task of management, as well as the considerable commitment and goodwill of the majority of governors who give their time and energies freely.

## Bibliography


Abell, P. (1975) *Organisations as bargaining and influence systems*, London: Heinemann.

Audit Commission (1993) *Adding up the Sums: School Management of their Finances*, London: HMSO.

Ball, S. (1987) *The Micropolitics of the School: Towards Theory of School Organisation*, London: Methuen.

Beckett, C., Bell, L., Rhodes, C. (1992) *Working with Governors in Schools*, Milton Keynes: Open University Press.

Blau, P. M. (1964) *Exchange and Power in Social Life*, New York: Wiley.

Coopers and Lybrand Associates (1988) *Local Management of Schools: a Report to the DES*, London: HMSO.

Coulson, A. A. (1976) 'The role of the primary head' in Peters, R. S. (Ed) (1976) *The role of the Head*, London: Routledge and Kegan Paul.

Coulson, A. A. (1985) *The Management Behaviour of Primary School Heads*, NE Wales Institute of Higher Education, Educational Management Centre.

Coulson, A. A. (1990) 'Primary school headship: a review of research' in Saran, R. and Trafford, V. (Eds) *Research in education management and policy: retrospect and prospect*, London: The Falmer Press.

Davies, R. and Anderson, L. (1992) *Opting for Self Management*, London: Routledge.

Deem, R. (1989) 'The new school governing bodies — are gender and race on the agenda?' *Gender and Education* **1**, 3, pp.247–261.

Deem, R. and Brehony, K. (1991) *School governing bodies: reshaping education in their own image?* Paper presented at the Symposium on school governorship at the British Educational Research Association Conference, 'Creating Education Through Research', Nottingham Polytechnic August 1991.

Dunlap, D. M. and Goldman, P. (1991) 'Rethinking power in schools'. *Educational Administration Quarterly*, **xxvii**, 1, pp.5–29.

Evetts, J. (1993) 'LMS and headship: changing the contexts for micropolitics'. *Educational Review* Vol 45 No. 1, pp.53–65.

Handy, C. (1976) *Taken for Granted? Understanding Schools as Organisations*, Schools Council, Harlow: Longman.

Havilland, J. (1988) *Take Care Mr Baker*, London: 4th Estate.

Hoyle, E. (1986) *The Politics of School Management*, London: Hodder and Stoughton.

Homans, G. C. (1961) *Social Behaviour in Elementary Forms*, London: Routledge and Kegan Paul.

Huckman, L. and Hill, T. (1994) 'Local management of schools: rationality and decision-making in the employment of teachers'. *Oxford Review of Education*, **20**, 2, June.

Huckman, L. (1994) 'LMS in the primary school: winners and losers'. *Education Management*, June 1994.

Kogan, M. (1984) (Ed) *School Governing Bodies*, London: Heinemann.

March, J. G. and Olsen, J. P. (Eds) (1976) *Ambiguity and Choice in Organisations*, Oslo: Universitetsforlaget, Bergen.

OFSTED (1992) *Handbook of the Office for Standards in Education*, London: HMSO.

OFSTED (1993) *Keeping your Balance: Standards for Financial Administration in Schools*. London: HMSO.

Olsen, J. P. (1970) 'Local budgeting — decision-making or ritual act?' in J. G. March and J. P. Olsen (Eds) (1976) *Ambiguity and Choice in Organisations*, Oslo: Universitetsforlaget, Bergen.

Packwood, T. (1984) 'Models of governing bodies' in Glatter, R. (Eds) (1984) *Understanding School Management*, Milton Keynes: Open University Press.

Pascal, C. (1987) 'Democratised primary school government: conflicts and dichotomies', *Educational Management and Administration* **15**, pp.193–202.

Southworth, G. (1987) 'Primary leadership and collegiality' in Southworth, G. (Ed) *Readings in Primary School Management*, Lewes: Falmer Press.

Thibaut, J. W. and Kelley, H. H. (1959) *The Social Psychology of Groups*, New York: Wiley.

Thody, A. M. (1992) *Moving to Management: School Governors in the 1990s*, London: David Fulton.

Wright-Mills, C. W. (1940) 'Situated actions and vocabularies of motive in school and society' *American Sociological Review*, 5, 6, pp.439–452.

# 11 Has England got it right? Alternatives to governing bodies

Alastair Macbeth

In assessing the contributions being made by governing bodies to the democracy and management of schools, it may be helpful to put the English experience into a wider European context. Does evidence from other countries reinforce or weaken Thody's suggestion that governors are making hidden bequests of illusory democracy and protective legitimation? Do models of school governance elsewhere in Western Europe, especially Scotland, offer experiences and thinking that could help to put English assumptions into a wider perspective and even lead to a questioning of some elements? In considering these questions, this chapter is in three parts.

1. Diverse school boards in Europe
2. The Scottish model
3. Accountability or control? Speculations about the future.

## Diverse school boards in Europe

The impression which an intelligent being from outer space would get on looking at European education systems would be one of similarity across Europe. He would see children from about five or six years of age taken away from their families for fixed hours and placed in institutions largely cut off from society and taught in groups by ages. He would see teaching provided by specialists and would observe this process as compulsory for most children for about ten years at the end of which there are written examinations in which understanding is 'packaged' in subjects. He would note some national direction, especially through law-making, financial control and curricular guidelines. Yet he might also detect an incipient tension between national identity in education systems and aspirations for cross-European influence through the Treaty on European Union (known as the Maastricht Treaty) and European Commission programmes. He would note that resolution of this tension is attempted through the concept of 'subsidiarity', but he might have difficulty in understanding Article 3b which sets out to clarify the term. He would see intermediate regional and municipal levels of administration within national systems and a trend to devolve decision-making to the school. He would usually encounter a school board for each school.

Within that breadth of similarity we may consider the diversity of school board provisions in Europe. In this chapter I shall use 'school board' as the generic term to describe all bodies of participatory administration at school level. When discussing particular systems I shall use national titles such as school council, school conference, governing body, board of governors, council of administration, board of management, etc.

Although there were pre-war examples, and although new schemes of participation emerged in some countries immediately after the second world war (e.g. in England and Germany), the main recent growth of neighbourhood influence on school governance throughout Europe was in the 1970s. Laws, for example, were passed in Norway (1969), Italy (1974), Denmark (1970 and 1974) and France (1976, 1977 and 1978). Ireland introduced a less prescriptive system in 1975. German provinces passed local laws. Commentators on these early European schemes tended to doubt their efficacy. Baron (1981, p.280) refers to 'hopes frustrated' and Beattie (1985, p.230) to 'pseudo-participation', though both also espied potential benefits. A report by Boppel and Kollenberg (1981) criticised German school conferences for being over-formal and legalistic and the Glasgow University study (Macbeth et al., 1984) in nine European countries noted complaints about poor communications between boards and education authorities, expectations unfulfilled, trivial but time-consuming functions, community apathy, the 'pooling of ignorance', professional dominance of boards and rubber stamping.

Yet advantages such as the potential for accountability and neighbourhood democracy, increased responsiveness of schools and better information for those involved as well as enhanced partnership between parents and teachers for the benefit of children were cited. Perhaps in part because (as Beattie, 1985, p.228 pointed out) boards are 'relatively cheap and capable of rapid implementation', the trend has continued and the 1980s and early 1990s saw the Netherlands (1982), Spain (1985), Portugal (1991) and parts of Belgium (1990) introduced boards and some countries modify pre-existing schemes, giving more influence to boards.

Participatory councils need not just be at school level. Germany, France and Italy commonly have class councils as parts of their formal systems and sometimes even a pyramid of councils from class level to regional level. Yet the school is generally seen as the prime managerial unit and in Britain the move away from the grouping of schools under one board to a system of one board per school followed the recommendations of British territorial reports: for England and Wales, the Taylor Report (1977, pp.17–18); for Northern Ireland, the Astin Report (1979) (pp.14–15); for Scotland the Glasgow University Report (1980, p.104). A board per school has now become the normal arrangement in the UK and is found in most European Community countries.

**Membership**

To describe European school board membership briefly demands over-simplification. Whereas parents and teachers are commonly regarded as stakeholders, diversity among others can be bewildering. They include senior secondary school pupils, church representatives (especially, of course, for church-run schools), nominees of the municipal council (e.g. Spain, England), the social, economic and cultural interests of the region (Portugal) and a variety of officials (e.g. French secondary schools) or co-optees (e.g. England and Scotland). There may be differences in composition between primary and secondary schools or between types of secondary school. Then there is the distinction between voting and non-voting members. The headteacher may be a voting member (e.g. France, Ireland, Spain) a non-voting member (e.g. Denmark), or an optional member (e.g. England according to the headteacher's choice). It is difficult to generalise about some countries such as Germany because of regional differences. Finally, numbers of members may vary according to size of school.

If we simplify by concentrating on parents and school staff (who always appear), while lumping the rest into an 'others' category we may identify the following variants.

- School staff outnumber all other members combined (e.g. Portugal)
- Parents outnumber all other members combined (e.g. Denmark; Scotland)

- Others outnumber parents and teachers combined (e.g. England and Wales; some Irish post-primary schools)
- Balance between parents and teachers, irrespective of numbers of others (e.g. Italy; parts of Germany; Dutch primary schools; Irish post-primary schools)
- Balance between teachers and home (i.e. parents + senior pupils) (e.g. Dutch secondary schools)

If we were to adopt a stakeholder perspective, primacy might be given to parents and teachers. Abrahamsson (1977, pp.117–18) defined stakeholders as 'those individuals or groups who are dependent on the enterprise for the implementation of their own personal needs, and upon whom the enterprise is dependent for its continued existence'. Pupils would also come into that category, but since, throughout Europe, national laws make parents responsible for their child's education, parents are pupils' agents until the end of compulsory education at which point senior pupils are direct stakeholders. French, Spanish and Dutch laws, for example, include senior pupils as a group to be represented on secondary school boards. Otherwise, equal parent and teacher membership (as in Dutch primary boards) might be defended.

However, if a purpose of school boards is to make a public service accountable to its legal clients, then a majority of parents (as in Denmark and Scotland) might be justified. If accountability is owed to a wider range of citizens, the problems arise of where and how to draw the line. The word 'community' includes connotations of both territory and shared interests. Who can represent the area and who the interests? Do local employers, ethnic minorities, recreational interests, churches, environmental groups, the police have stakeholder interests?

Does local government have a stake such that it should nominate members? That would seem difficult to justify in terms of stakeholder theory just as we do not justify the nomination of members of local councils by Parliament. Perhaps the territorial argument mentioned in the previous paragraph might justify an education authority nominee, but scarcely several. With regard to arguments for accountability, school staff are already accountable to the education authority which is their employer. So is there a distinction to be drawn between a council of neighbourhood democracy, implying *election*, and a locality quasi-autonomous non-government organisation (a LO-QUANGO?), implying *nomination*? Are English governing bodies a cross between the two? It seems to be less common for European school boards to have municipal nominees as voting members, though some (Denmark, Scotland) allow them to attend but not vote. Further, for church-run schools, the church is commonly represented. For example, in Ireland the nominees of the Patron, trustees or owners (often the church) control half the places on boards of management and the 1992 Irish Green Paper (p.144) proposes to reduce that to just under half, but still leaving such nominees as the largest block. One may argue that much depends on whether the school board has decision-making powers of substance or not. Most European school boards are largely advisory, but with some (often minor) powers. In such a circumstance a local council might feel less inclined to have nominees. Where real or potential power is delegated to a board (and that seems to be increasingly the case) then the LO-QUANGO model may be attractive to municipalities which may want to ensure consistency.

Elected or nominated, the member is likely to be regarded as a representative. Representation may be viewed either as a status or as a process. When a member is castigated as being 'unrepresentative' because she/he is middle class or white or whatever, the complaint is really one of being untypical. That may matter if it is assumed that representation is *trustee* in nature: that is, that the representative functions without reference back to those who elected or nominated the representative. A member of parliament, for example, is generally a trustee. If English school governors are defined as operating within the trustee tradition, then Thody's worries about limited representation creating illusory democracy may be of less concern.

Whether or not members are seen as having a mandated role, a school board is so local that consultation with constituents is not difficult and representation may be seen as a process; typicality is presumably irrelevant if the board member is conscientious in ascertaining the concerns of the electors. Structures may assist. Some German provincial systems elect parent board members from a separate, but legally-established, parents' council. Class councils also offer a network of contact. The 1991 law in Portugal envisages parental representatives to the school council being elected through the school's parent association, thereby providing a channel of communication and representation. The British paucity of formal links between parent board-members and fellow parents, combined with the tendency to have peripheral parent-teacher associations concerned predominantly with social and fund-raising events rather than interest-group parent associations, make representation as a process more difficult but not impossible.

## Functions

If membership of school boards across Europe is difficult to portray, functions are more so. Yet some analyses are possible. Working within the area of overt democracy and its particular objective of influencing policy, it may be helpful to distinguish between deciding, having the power of veto, advising and supervising (checking upon). A Danish school board (Bach, 1990):

Decides on
(a) The school's educational structure (number of lessons, special education, etc.)
(b) Policy on co-operation between home and school
(c) Information to be sent to parents
(d) Arrangements for special events and school projects
(e) Allocation of workload to teachers
(f) The school rules
(g) Aspects of general school policy

Approves (i.e. power of veto)
(a) The school budget
(b) Teaching materials (including text books) to be used

Makes proposals to the Municipal Council about
(a) The curriculum
(b) Experimental education
(c) Employment of headteacher and teachers
(d) Any other aspects of the school

Supervises (checks upon)
Any aspects of daily management of the school.

Such graded delegation is more common in other European countries than is the sort of block responsibility accorded to English governing bodies. The relative vagueness of that block responsibility would appear to compound the English problem of deciding how to divide responsibilities between governors and headteachers (see Chapter 2 above). Graded delegation also makes it easier to free the school board from the dominance of nominees. Membership of Danish school boards usually consists of seven parents, two teachers and two senior pupils, with the headteacher as a non-voting member plus, if the board so wishes, a non-voting member from the municipal council.

In other countries school boards are commonly involved less in academic and more in 'domestic' decisions such as school discipline (French secondary schools having discipline sub-committees), the school's daily routine, school rules, use of school buildings, transport, school excursions, homework, extra-curricular activities, counselling services and relations with parents. Such involvement is often advisory, but there is too much diversity of practice to summarise here. There is a tendency to leave decisions about curricular matters to teachers (hints of Thody's educational protectiveness here?), though often with the right for the board to discuss them or sometimes to approve aspects of them.

We may discern some recent trends. Several countries changed their systems to increase the powers of such bodies (Netherlands in 1982 and 1992, England in 1986 and 1988, Scotland in 1988, France and Denmark in 1990) and others such as Ireland and Scotland are debating further changes now. In part this has coincided with a move to greater decentralisation. Economic pressures have been mounting and decentralisation may appear to some to be the delegation of misery, the passing downwards of uncomfortable decision-making necessitated by diminished resources. However, it also accords with increasing interest in local accountability whether accompanied by simulated market forces through parental choice or not. An enhanced role for school boards is integral to that trend.

The central message from European experience would seem to be that there is no consensus about the most appropriate logic or format for school boards.

## The Scottish model

Scottish school boards are currently more similar in spirit to some of those in Continental Europe than to the English model of delegated power, but the School Boards (Scotland) Act of 1988 contained a unique feature: the facility for any individual school board to seek greater powers when it feels willing and able to take them on.

Historically, Scotland first introduced bodies called 'school boards' in 1872, but these were, in effect, in excess of 900 education authorities for groups of schools which in stages (1918, 1929 and 1973) were whittled down to the twelve education authorities which exist today and are soon likely to be replaced by a scheme of unitary local government. As local government changed, so did neighbourhood representation with regard to schools. In 1918 school management committees were introduced and given minor and menial tasks related to groups of schools. These were replaced in 1947 by area education subcommittees and in 1973 by school councils. The Glasgow University study of the latter (Macbeth et al., 1980) pointed to the problem that these councils, dealing with groups of schools, had no point of focus. The report also demonstrated the peripheral nature of their functions and the need for change. We contested some of the English Taylor Report's recommendations, especially arguing that there was little justification for LEA nominees and that, if accountability of a public service is a central purpose, boards should have unfettered right to make inquiries, to give advice and to have influence, but little power. We argued that the headteacher should have main delegated authority and be *responsible* to the education authority but *accountable* to the school council. However, we agreed with the Taylor Report that there should be a council for each school.

What emerged in the 1988 Act followed these general points, but with important differences concerning both membership and functions. Whereas we had suggested equal parent and teacher representation, membership now is as follows:

| School roll | Parents | Staff | Co-opted |
|---|---|---|---|
| 1–500 pupils | 4 | 1 | 2 |
| 501–1000 pupils | 5 | 2 | 2 |
| 1001–1500 pupils | 6 | 2 | 3 |
| 1500+ pupils | 7 | 3 | 3 |

As the table shows, parents have an overall voting majority, but in some senses this is more symbolic than effective since few issues go to the vote and it is the voices around the table which tend to matter more. Those voices include the headteacher who is not a voting member but has the right to attend and to be heard (and usually is present), and the regional (or islands) councillor. Further, the director of education may attend or send a nominee. Thus parents are often in an *attending* minority. Co-opted members are chosen by the elected members and are not permitted to be staff or parents of the school. Where a school is denominational, one of the co-optee places is reserved for the nominee of the church in question. Otherwise the board may co-opt as it pleases, though there has been government encouragement to include members of the business community, a task which has sometimes proved difficult to fulfil (Soltysek, 1990). Some secondary schools have co-opted senior pupils, and local church personnel have commonly been selected at both primary and secondary levels. Co-optees are sometimes teachers living in the catchment areas of other schools, so that the teacher voice may be greater than formal representation suggests.

With regard to functions, the legislation specifically mentions managing school buildings after school hours (though the board may leave that to the education authority), dates for occasional holidays and reporting to parents with children at the school at least once a year: scarcely stirring stuff. More importantly, the board is represented in the process of appointing senior staff for the school and has the legal duty to promote relations between the school, its parents and the community.

However, greater potential power resides in something which at first seemed quite minor. The headteacher must get the board's approval before spending money on books and equipment. The sums involved are, of course, small. Scotland had no counterpart to the English 1988 Education Reform Act and it is only now that devolved school management (similar to English local management of schools) is being proposed and in March 1993 the Scottish Office guidelines (p.3) stated, with regard to delegation of at least 80 per cent of a school's funding to the level of the school:

> . . . responsibility for decision-making should be devolved to the headteacher, with a consultative role for the School Board. This arrangement would be comparable, though not identical, to the provisions of Section 9 of the School Boards (Scotland) Act 1988 in respect of expenditure on books and teaching material.

Thus, delegation will not be to the school board but to the headteacher; but the school board, it seems, might have the power of veto over most of the school's expenditure. However, each education authority is (at the time of writing) being permitted to develop its own interpretation of the concept and the emerging schemes seem to range from bare consultation to veto.

The potential for school board influence was enhanced by two other features of the school boards legislation. A board has the right to request information on any topic related to the school and to make recommendations to the headteacher or to the education authority who are required to reply. Most boards would probably not link such requests to high profile publicity, but a school board dissatisfied about an issue could do so and if the board had a good case, it would be difficult for the professionals to resist. If the normal mode of school board operations is watchful acquiescence coupled with support for what is beneficial and a preparedness to pursue what is not, then the watchfulness element can be enhanced by the information and response rights laid down by law.

Further, a board may request 'delegation orders' (Section 15 and Schedule 3 of the Act). Decision-making powers may be sought from the education authority with regard to any aspect of the running of the school other than curriculum, employment and dismissal of staff and certain other functions. If the education authority refuses, the board may appeal to the Secretary of State for Scotland. It is not yet clear whether a board in an area which merely permits consultation over the budget could seek a veto over it through a delegation order. Such a facility would seem to be in keeping with government policies.

If a board decides to go further in the pursuit of executive control, it may, by legislation of 1989, initiate steps to make the school self-governing, the Scottish counterpart to English grant-maintained status. It may be added that very little interest in the last step has so far been shown in Scotland.

Thus the basic duties of Scottish school boards are few but the potential for making schools accountable is considerable. I have argued elsewhere (Macbeth, 1990) that if purposes are to be converted into practice, then the law as it stands provides the tools. In particular it:

1. Enables the board to make the school accountable for all aspects of its functioning, including curricular and staffing matters.
2. Enables the board to provide support and publicity for those aspects of the school which deserve praise and encouragement.
3. Enables active representations (i.e. influence) with regard to matters about which the board has reservations or adverse criticisms.
4. Enables the board to take initiatives in generating a sense of educational partnership between parents and teachers.

It is my impression that most boards have tended to operate somewhat minimally and, if so, have reflected tendencies similar to the covert inaction alluded to in Chapter 2 above with regard to English governing bodies. It is my judgement that both the official school board training materials and the advisory documents from the School Boards Support Unit have insufficiently emphasised purposes for school boards and the possibilities boards have to influence events. In an analysis of the Scottish Office training materials, O'Brien (1990) shows that relatively little attention is given to purposes for school boards (p.106), to representation, to accountability or to autonomy for the board's self-development (p.113). Public statements from politicians at the inception of school boards put stress on the importance of parents and the intention 'to give parents a greater say in the running of schools' (Scottish Office, 1989), but O'Brien concludes, with regard to the training materials, 'The centrality of the parental role is rarely suggested, and there is minimal reference to schooling being a service to parents' (p.111). There seems to me to have been some difference of emphasis between politicians who initiated the law and public servants who are now advising boards. Whether that is the case or not, the potential for any board to acquire greater influence and even power is built into the legislation.

## Accountability or control? Speculation about the future

Perhaps school boards or governing bodies will always under-perform. They are composed of busy people for whom time is at a premium and who are generally giving their services without pay. These volunteers usually do not see themselves as experts, or perhaps only as specialists with regard to specific facets of the governing tasks. They usually have, or want to have, respect for the professionalism of the teaching staff. I referred above to 'watchful acquiescence' and there could be a tendency for board members to operate within a zone of tolerance: to support the headteacher and staff unless things go badly wrong in their estimation. (That could be a version of Thody's consent, protection and legitimation.) One could advocate such a philosophy as long as the board has sufficient criteria, information and sensitivity to know when to move from acquiescence to intervention. It gives rise to the question of whether boards should have controlling power or just the facility to influence.

Governors of independent schools have traditionally had power. It might be argued that the best talent will only be attracted to governorship if there is control, but one may question whether that is the appropriate model for state schools, not just because there are insufficient bishops and barristers to go round, but because influence may be more appropriate than executive control. In England there has long been an assumption that governors should govern. The 1945 model articles of management and government envisaged that governors 'shall have the general direction of the conduct and curriculum of the school'. By 1977 the Taylor Report could aver (para. 2.11) 'In short, the extent to which managing and governing bodies carried out the functions assigned to them was slight'. The Taylor Report was written at a time when it was generally assumed that the state should both fund and run schools. The 1988 Education Reform Act (ERA) somewhat altered that perspective by introducing simulated market forces and competition, with the intention that each school could adjust its provisions (within the limits of a National Curriculum) to attract clients. While the state would fund schools, it would lessen its detailed control.

Three elements of the ERA are especially seen as inter-dependent: open enrolment, devolved finance and governor control. The question which I am posing is whether governor *influence* would not have been sufficient. In Scotland we introduced a thorough system of parental choice of school in 1981, departing markedly from the somewhat unsatisfactory English 1980 Act. In broad thrust, if not in detail, the English open enrolment provisions of the 1988 ERA (chapter II) appear to be following the Scottish example. Yet Scotland introduced its choice legislation as much on grounds of liberty and equity (i.e. giving to all families what had previously been the prerogative of families who could buy houses in the areas of favoured schools) as of consumerism; it was not linked to devolved funding and powerful governors. The Scottish arrangement for parental choice of school settled down well and there was evidence that it has been used proportionately by all social classes (Glasgow University, 1986; Adler, et al., 1989). The system has had its critics (e.g. Jonathan, 1993), but administratively it has bedded down independently of devolved school management.

However, Devolved School Management (DSM), the Scottish equivalent to LMS, will delegate power to the *headteacher* who will be held accountable to her/his school board. The system does not require the full burden of responsibility to be placed on those not paid to bear it. Headteachers in England may, as Thody reports in Chapter 2 of this book, sleep better at night because they share decision-making with governors, but could that just be a blurring of responsibility, a buffer against criticism? In our 1980 report on the old Scottish school councils we warned (p.18) that such bodies could be used cynically as shock absorbers, as diversionary tactics and as the means to acquire the appearance of public support without the reality. The more that power is nominally vested in people who have insufficient time or remuneration to exercise it, the greater these dangers would appear to be.

I am non-party-political and I believe that much educational policy could be a matter for inter-party consensus. We may note that the first parental choice Bill to be placed before parliament (in 1979) came from a Labour administration and that James Callaghan envisaged a National (core) Curriculum in his 1976 Ruskin College speech. The Taylor Commission was set up by and reported to a Labour government. In Scotland it has been Labour-controlled Strathclyde Region which first started to devolve financial power to the level of the school in a scheme which it calls delegated management of schools (DMR), the Scottish Office DSM following after. Although there appear to be inter-party differences about the role of education authorities and the extent of state intervention as distinct from free market competition, the model of an advisory rather than a controlling board for each school would seem compatible with either philosophy.

I suggested above that school boards/governing bodies may have a tendency to 'under-perform' because they are composed of unpaid, generally non-specialist volunteers with limited time available. If that is so, then one argument in favour of the English system of nominal power to a governing body could be that such control puts extra psychological pressure on governors to take their job seriously and to tackle central issues. On the other hand, if the logic for influence rather than power is accepted, then there would seem to be a need to increase understanding among board members about purposes for boards and about what constitute key aspects of school management; also a need to increase awareness about accountability, monitoring, establishing real contact with constituents and making representations to those who are in authority. If an attitude is a preparedness to act, then in part this would seem to be a problem of attitude change. That, in turn, requires clear statements not only in training manuals but in all routine pronouncements from central and local governments that boards are a mechanism of representation.

If the tasks of board members are to represent stakeholders, to be supportive of the school when appropriate and constructively critical when appropriate, there would appear to be only limited arguments for giving them full authority. The Scottish approach of influence rather than power does not challenge the essential features of simulated market forces or of devolved decision-making to the level of the school. However, if it is to be made to work more effectively, then I suggest that there needs to be a new emphasis on process. I consider that, since their time is limited, boards should eschew trivial and menial tasks which are at times wished upon them. This they can do by delegating them to sub-committees or to paid personnel or by simply designating them as irrelevant to the board's purposes. They should avoid case-work (e.g. concerned with truancy, indiscipline and social problems of individual children); steer clear of most 'community' issues which may distract from the school's central, that is curricular, provisions; insist on systematic monitoring of the school; ensure that there is an active parents' association (or a PTA) through which there can be two-way communication with parents; and ensure that representatives are encouraged to carry out their task of representing.

Would such a prescription apply to governing bodies in England also? Indeed, would the switch from boards with power to boards with influence be an adaptation appropriate to England? Further, are the grounds for having nominated LEA governors dependent upon the scale of delegated power and, if so, would a shift in the proportion of nominated members be appropriate if governing bodies were more advisory than controlling? My perspective derives more from having examined other systems than from familiarity with the English arrangements in detailed operation and it must be for those in England who are more conversant than I am with those practices to answer my questions. Yet I would argue that they may be appropriate questions to ask.

## References


Abrahamsson, B. (1977) *Bureaucracy or Participation*, Beverly Hills: Sage.

Adler, M., Petch, A. and Tweedie, J. (1989) *Parental Choice and Educational Policy*, Edinburgh University Press.

Astin Report (1979) Department of Education for Northern Ireland, *Report of the Working Party on the Management of Schools in Northern Ireland*, London: HMSO.

Bach, P. (1990) Private communication: translation of Danish documentation for Macbeth, A. M. (1991) *Danish Case Study: Parents, Schools and Skole og Samfund*, Baron, G. (Ed.), EPA: Brussels. *The Politics of School Government*, London: Pergamon.

Beattie, N. (1985) *Professional Parents: Parent Participation in Four Western European Countries*, Lewes: Falmer Press.

Boppel, W. and Kollenberg, U. (1981) *Mitbestimmung in der Schule*, Deutscher Instituts-Verlag.

Council of the European Communities and Commission of the European Communities (1992, ratified 1994) *Treaty on European Union*, ECSC — EEC — EAEC, Brussels: Luxembourg.

Education Reform Act (1988) Ch. 40, London: HMSO.

Education (Scotland) Act (1980) Ch. 44, London: HMSO.

Glasgow University report on Scottish school councils (1980): *see Macbeth, Mackenzie and Breckenridge (1980), below.*

Glasgow University report on parental choice of school (1986): *see University of Glasgow (1986), below.*

Irish Green Paper (1992) *Education for a Changing World*, Dublin: The Stationery Office.

Jonathan, R. (1993) 'Parental rights in schooling', Ch. 2 in Munn, P. (Ed) (1993) *Parents and Schools: Customers, Managers or Partners?*, London: Routledge.

Macbeth, A. M. (1989) *Involving Parents: Effective Parent-Teacher Relations*, London: Heinemann Educational.

Macbeth, A. M. (1990) *School Boards: from Purpose to Practice*, Scottish Academic Press.

Macbeth, A. M., Corner, T., Nisbet, S., Nisbet, A., Ryan, D. and Strachan, D. (1984) *The Child Between: a report on school-family relations in the countries of the European Community*, EEC.

Macbeth, A. M., MacKenzie, M. L. and Breckenridge, I. (1980) *Scottish School Councils: Policy-Making, Participation or Irrelevance?* Scottish Education Department, HMSO.

Macbeth, A. M.: *see also University of Glasgow (1986), below.*

O'Brien, J. P. (1990) *A Study of the Scottish Office Training Programme for School Boards*, M.Ed. thesis, University of Glasgow.

School Boards (Scotland) Act (1988) London: HMSO.

Scottish Office (1989) *School Boards Information Pack*, Scottish Office.

Soltysek, R. F. (1990) *A Study of the Policy and Practice of Co-opting on to Scottish School Boards and the Contribution made by Co-opted Members to the Work of those Boards*, M.Ed. thesis, University of Glasgow.

Taylor Report (1977) *A New Partnership for our Schools*, Department of Education and Science and Welsh Office, London: HMSO.

University of Glasgow (1986) *Parental Choice of School in Scotland*, Parental Choice Project, Department of Education, University of Glasgow.

# 12 A little learning is a dangerous thing: governor training

Terry Mahoney

> Education can no longer be led by the producers — the academic theorists, the administrators and even the teachers' unions. Education must be shaped by the users — by what is good for the individual child and what hopes are held by parents (K. Baker, M.P., at the Autumn Conservative Party Conference 1986).

In making this statement, Kenneth Baker clearly envisaged education as needing to become responsive. Such responsiveness could come through governors exercising their overt democratic role. Their management role was also presaged by Kenneth Baker in the same speech when he likened the education system to a wheel, saying that the intention of this and subsequent legislation was to remove power from the hub, along the spokes to the rim, where the users were. If power is to be moved, then it has to be managed; by implication, this management is to be by the users, represented by the governors.

In order to be effective democratically and managerially, the need for training was recognised.

> The responsibilities . . . for governing bodies are so important and complex that a governor cannot be expected to discharge them effectively without some training going beyond the normal process of picking up the job by doing it. That process is by itself relatively slow to act and could in this case serve to perpetuate unsatisfactory practice (DOE, 1984, para. 93).

> More needs to be done, nationally and locally, to raise the

> competence of school governors individually and collectively. More and better training will be of crucial importance: too little will happen by chance (1994 Teachers' Pay Review Body Report).

In response to views like these there were initiatives from individual local education authorities (LEAs) and other agencies like the Workers' Educational Association (WEA) in the 1970s (Sheffield LEA) and early 1980s (Leicestershire LEA in partnership with the WEA). Such initiatives owed much to the Taylor Report's recommendations which included just eight short but highly pertinent paragraphs on governor training (See 'A New Partnership for our Schools', 1977 — known as the Taylor Report, quoted in Mahoney, 1988, p.208). In 1977 Joan Sallis, a lay member of the Taylor Committee and considered by most, rightly, to be the governors' guru, had called governor training, which hardly existed at the time, the most ambitious venture in adult and community education ever. Local developments expanded but every national review of governor training in the mid 1980s showed provision to be patchy, cursory and failing to meet needs. However, a vast untapped reservoir of some 300,000+ school governors, many of them clamouring for training, was identified (Mahoney, 1988, Chapter 11). Requirements for governor training were formalised in the 1986 Education (No. 2) Act, section 57 of which requires every LEA to secure free information and training for its governors. In response to this and with the assistance of central government funding most LEAs established a post for governor training co-ordination and in the period 1986–1990, and beyond, governors' information centres were established in many LEAs and very varied programmes of training events were organised. However, in 1994 LEA governor training budgets have been cut, in one case by 22 per cent; LEAs, struggling to give schools even more control of their delegated budgets, have less to encourage county-wide initiatives; and one of the national organisations for governor training, Action for Governors' Information and Training (AGIT), founded in 1986 to give a stimulus to governor training developments, has had to retrench in order to survive. The original cohort of Governor Training Co-ordinators — most had contracts from 1989–1992 — have been made redundant, moved to pastures new, or have had even more jobs thrust upon them so that governor training is now, even to them, a marginal activity.

Throughout these developments, key arguments have centred around what form such training should take, who should control it, how it should be funded, and, more recently, how its impact should be measured. These arguments have been set in the context of the various twists, turns and tensions which have surrounded the relatively short history of governor training since the 1980s. Whilst this chapter acknowledges some considerable achievements and comments on the public sloganising by government ministers about active citizenship, parent power, governor empowerment, *local* management and 'choice', to what extent, one wonders, do these signify real goals, shared by the consumers of the system as well as mouthed by the politicians? Does government really want governors as active citizens to be empowered through training? If so, what forms should this training take?[1]

In Chapter 2 above, Thody suggested that governors have not taken the power, anticipated by government, to manage schools and that governing bodies have failed to operate on expected democratic pathways. The provision of training suggests, however, the possibility of disagreement with this view since training, by its very nature, is empowering. The radical adult educator, Paulo Freire, coined the term 'conscientisation' to describe the transforming power of education, its potentially political force. His starting point was the use of politically relevant ideas for the education of whole communities. Freire wrote:

> The more active an attitude men take in regard to the exploration of their thematics, the more they deepen their critical awareness of reality, and in spelling out these thematics, take possession of that reality (Freire, 1972 p.29).
>
> ('Thematics' put simply here could signify governors' exploration of just what is meant by education sloganising such as 'choice', 'freedom', 'self-governing', 'open enrolment', 'standards').

On the other hand, the evidence could be taken to indicate that governors are becoming empowered within the polity as a whole but not within the schools where training may be helping to encourage Thody's covert managerialism of legitimation, consent and protectionism.

How real the government's commitment to move power along the spokes to the rim through training school governors; how governor trainers exploiting adult education strategies may have become victims of their own success; and how governor training may develop into the next century — these are themes dealt with in the rest of this chapter.

## Government commitment to governor training

In 1985, central government grants for governor training were only £100,000 nationally. In contrast, the period 1989–1992 (a period of frantic growth in governors' responsibilities and duties following the 1988 Education Act) saw an annual governor training budget of some £5 million rising to £6.8 million in 1994. Whilst this seems a lot of money, it only amounts to some £20 per governor per year rising to about £30–40 in those LEAs where governor training is more highly regarded and hence more generously funded since they are willing to commit more of their own resources to it. The outcome of this financial commitment was that, in the late 1980s and early 1990s two DES surveys of governor training (DES, 1989 and 1990) pointed out many positive aspects. Some 80 per cent of the provision was described as displaying good practice or having good features. The bulk of LEA provision was deemed to have been helpful, if insufficient. It was estimated that some 60 per cent of governors had attended some form of training.[2]

Impressive as the outcomes may be from such small investment, the likelihood of training enabling governors to gain parity with teachers (and hence avoid Thody's covert supportiveness of educators) seems small. It has been estimated that such funding equals about 1/40th of that available for the in-service needs of already trained teachers. Money is, however, only one of the vital ingredients. What also seems lacking in 1994 is any national commitment to the training needs of governors, a point strongly made in the 1994 Teachers' Pay Review Body report (HMSO, 1994) which mentioned 'insufficient priority' (*Education*, 1994, p.99) given to governor training in the government's programme of education reforms.

More recently, the declining powers of LEAs could be undermining training provision. Frequent Education Acts, increasing attacks on the powers and responsibilities of LEAs, the possibility of local government reorganisation, political manoeuvring to encourage more and more schools to 'opt out' of LEA control into Department for Education (DFE) control — all these have had a massively unsettling influence on all aspects of the education system, including governor training. Training provision has never been generous and is becoming less so. In such circumstances it is unlikely to empower governors to apply the overt, effective management roles which Thody considers the government expected of governors.

This is compounded when one adds to the inadequate extent of training, the differential needs of governors and the vastly increased powers they have acquired in the last ten years. What the education legislators seem to have overlooked is that new arrangements for making governing bodies more overtly democratic have meant that there is constantly a new supply of governors with very little or no background in how to perform their ever lengthening list of duties. This currently stands at over 100 legally defined (although few can recount them all!). Indeed, the general feeling in the early 1990s is that legislation — not all of it educational — has built up cumulatively an unworkable load for unpaid volunteers who now have to take on, in the guise of *local* management, what thousands of paid professional LEA 'bureaucrats' previously did with considerable expertise. Hence, many governors are reputedly leaving thus creating even more needs for induction training for those who fill their place. Although there is a strong sense of commitment from this new cohort of governors, there is still a feeling of frustration, disillusionment and uncertainty. Recruitment campaigns have succeeded in attracting new governors, but these feel uncertain about what the job actually entails. In 1991 the Senior Chief HMI reported that:

> Many governors remain uncertain about the nature of their responsibilities for the curriculum and for the standards of work achieved in their schools. Demands on governors' time are increasing. The time they have needs to be used to best advantage in addressing broad policy issues rather than the minutiae of day to day management (*Education* 21 January 1994, p.42).

## Meeting the needs — the response of adult education

The environment for governor training appears, from the above, to offer little opportunity for governors to develop beyond the covert behaviours described by Thody in Chapter 2. The *contents* and *methods* of governor training, in contrast, have offered the possibilities of a different role model emerging. The governor trainer's complicated task, given the limited resources outlined above, has been to cope with the learning needs of a diverse group of adult learners and how to steer them through the many competing demands on their time and non-gubernatorial life.

Some of this training has been provided by adult educators who would identify governors as having the key characteristics of all adult learners. These have been identified by Knowles' (1978) seminal descriptors thus:

1. As people grow and mature their self concept moves from one of dependency to one of increasing self directedness.

2. As people mature they become an increasing reservoir of experience, and thus a rich source of learning.

3. As people mature their readiness to learn is the product of the developmental tasks required for the performance of their evolving social roles.

4. Adults have a problem-centred as opposed to a subject-centred approach to learning.

Adult education tutors therefore tend to ask themselves not 'How do I train governors?', rather 'What do governors need to learn, and how can I help them to learn it?'. The outcome of this appears to have been highly regarded training since the DES surveys mentioned above revealed that the best training sessions were led by tutors with an adult education background.

The training provided has been categorised into five models of delivery (Liddington, 1990).

(a) *Didactic*. This includes mass lectures by various educational professionals which can be viewed as a kind of 'receiving of the wisdom'.

(b) *Distance learning*. This comprises a range of self-help study packages which have the benefit of offering learning where and when each governor can best access it, but in isolation.

(c) *Collective self-help*. In this approach governors train other governors, often in school-based groups. Such a model of self-help, 'is surely vulnerable to the problem often associated with voluntaryism, of unrepresentative take-up' (p.71).

(d) Liberal adult education. This involves governors self-choosing from a varied menu of centrally-arranged courses usually, but not always, led by an experienced adult education tutor, and meeting with other governors and sharing views, experiences, frustrations. Governors often say that meeting other governors is one of the greatest benefits of such courses.

(e) School-based training — led by the head, chair or link governor for training.

Liddington argues that financial pressures are pushing governor training away from an open-ended liberal adult education approach (cf Knowles above) to a more vocational model largely within the cheaper categories of training (a), (b) and (c) above.

## Types of training: the debate

The DES surveys cited above picked out the most effective training evaluated as whole governing body training in their school: management training *in situ*. Such a finding on relatively small samples

(1989 survey: 13 LEAs; 1990 survey: 24 LEAs) overlooks a key feature of governing bodies: *all* are at different stages; governors come and go, bringing with them different biographies, skills and knowledge; governing bodies have their own history and culture, some of which is not fertile to training; heads and other teachers have a range of views about governors and their abilities; governors have a similar range, on the whole more positive. Consequently, no one particular training method can ever satisfy all needs. A coherent, progressive strategy, over time — say the life of a governing body (whatever that may be since individual four-year terms of office generally result in governors being at different stations on their four year journey) — will entail a variety of Liddington's five models outlined above; e.g. a distance learning package can be very valuable for an induction programme for a shift worker; mass lectures can impart useful information in a cost-effective way. What is needed is systematic research into the lasting impact of such training styles.

If we accept the varied biographies of governors, and consequently within a governing body anything between 9–19 varied biographies, expectations and needs, a useful concept to adopt is that of recurrent education (Houghton and Richardson, 1974; Mahoney, 1978). Key features of the recurrent education philosophy are availability, access and relevance, and key aspects of these features are choice, diminution of bureaucratic control, and the encouragement of autonomous learners and groups of learners. The appeal of recurrent education philosophy is that governors have, indeed, recurrent learning needs. A central feature of recurrent education is that control of learning be vested in the learner. There are echoes of this in the 1989 DES survey, 'The Quality of School Governor Training' which stated:

> Governors . . . have an important part to play in the development and delivery of governor training provision and have a valid claim to be part of any consultation process (para. 89).

Features of recurrent education can be found in the link governor system, pioneered in Hertfordshire from 1989. Link governors take a lead on training issues within a governing body. The link system recognises that governors are central in identifying their own training needs, influencing the shape of training programmes, supporting the training needs of new governors, acting as the governors' motivator to make use of such training as is available, and, in those few cases in which link governors have appropriate technical skills acquired through those other aspects of their biographies, actually leading training. Controlling a training budget could also be part of the 'job description' of a link governor (Calibre Training, 1990).

Controlling a training budget would, however, give governors power which not all professionals might welcome. There are some heads and senior management teams who resent the influence and powers of governors as some governors cease to adopt the protective roles described by Thody in Chapter 2. Sometimes, professionals have good reasons to dislike governors as a result of previous, or existing, maverick governors and a detrimental mix of personalities, motivations and biographies which can result in:

> combat zones, dominated by destructive headteachers, obstructive chairpersons, political hack governors, unsympathetic LEA officers, and internecine warfare on the governing body (George, quoted in Mahoney, 1988, p.228).

In response to this, it is possible that the legitimate training needs of governors have been frustrated by the diversion by the professionals in the schools, and in some LEAs, of the appropriate GEST funding for governor training. It is also important to point out that there is anecdotal evidence that devolving training funds to schools occasionally leads to misappropriation, inappropriate use and/or underspending. Schools can be very cautious about how to spend on priorities: marginal areas (governor training?) tend to be avoided, as do individual development needs of less senior staff. Such strategies illustrate nicely a point this writer made long before governor training became, relatively, big business:

> Whilst from a governor's point of view knowledge is power, from some heads' points of view a little knowledge is a dangerous thing (Mahoney, 1988, p.218).

The cumulative effect of governments' low levels of training funding and the extension of governors' duties combined with professional manipulation of training appears to be producing Thody's emasculated governors despite adult educators' efforts.

These efforts are likely to be increasingly frustrated if governor training moves more into schools with governors being taught by their headteachers in their own schools with colleagues of the same governing body. Governor training will then be more within the control of teachers who have demonstrated their suspicion of, and hostility to, governing bodies. Their many public pronouncements include statements such as:

> governors, armed with their new powers, are seeking to manage rather than govern . . . with the result that the question of who should take management decisions is becoming obscured (Hart, NAHT leader, 1990, p.19).

The Taylor Report itself was termed by the NUT a 'busybody's charter'. The NASUWT warned that:

> we must register our complete opposition to what is nothing less than an attempt to give lay people the right to dictate to professionally trained and experienced teachers how the teachers should carry out their tasks (Mahoney, 1988, p.9).

Such is not the best of settings into which to engage in partnership and is why writers such as Liddington rightly warn against in-school governor training, often led by the head:

> since so many of the real problems governors initially face are rooted in the practices of their own governing body, *starting* training here is less likely to have the necessary liberating effect on these relations (op. cit. p.72).

Thus, whilst accepting that whole governing body training with the attendance of the professionals, can be clearly an effective way to train governors, one must ask, for whom is it effective? Is it more effective for governors trying to enter the management of the school, or is it more effective for headteachers, the gatekeepers who can prevent entry?

Boundary issues, as Hart elucidates above, underlie this tension: to what extent are governors managers? What do the actual words of the legislation mean? Such expressions as 'exercising oversight' actually erect a semantic professional/lay barrier: Joan Sallis, for example, suggests that 'insight' is a more appropriate word if the aim is to encourage professional/lay partnership. Headteachers are, rightly, territorial and can give examples of governors stepping over the line into day-to-day management issues — the head's province.

It was the management of this province which was the focus of the 1990 Report by the School Management Task Force (SMTF). This was a DES body established in 1989 consisting of a group of mainly heads, charged with developing school-management training for the needs of the 90s. Their report, 'Developing School Management: the Way Forward' (DES, 1990) was largely silent on governors, repeating the conventional wisdom of the time:

> All LEAs were involved in some form of governor training but most experienced unease at its over-general, unfocused quality . . . (Para. 30, p.11).

This was a statement of dubious accuracy (which was challenged by this writer at the time and no subsequent 'proof' was forthcoming). Soon after their report was published, however, it dawned on the SMTF that there were implications for governors and governor trainers. Consequently, the SMTF hosted a national conference in

January 1991, in collaboration with the National Association of Governors and Managers (NAGM) and AGIT at which over 150 governor trainers, LEA officials, heads and others attended. The line the task force wanted to adopt was cogently presented in their report:

> In the Education Service as a whole, there are pressing problems of scale and access to training. It is necessary to increase the relevance, scale and accessibility of training at realistic unit costs. Time should be made available for teachers to undertake training, but programmes must be organised to create the minimum disruption to the work of the school. This will require a radical review of the general balance of provision. There should be a shift of priority along the following lines:

| **current emphasis** | | **redirected emphasis** |
|---|---|---|
| tutor-directed courses | → | support for self-directed study by individuals, school teams, peer groups |
| off-site training | → | in-school and near-to-the school training |
| predetermined times | → | flexitime study |
| oral presentations | → | distance learning materials, information packs and projects |
| provider determined syllabus | → | school determined agenda |
| knowledge acquisition | → | performance enhancement |

[ibid. para. 56, pp.20–21]

Leaving aside the irony of trying to induce change by staying in the left-hand column of their taxonomy, the task force organisers had seriously under-estimated their audience, especially the governor trainers who were critical of the notion that such a model could be translated to governors and their training needs. It was felt there was a danger of marginalising governors in the thrust to school-based development (cf. Liddington's approach above). Involving governors as an add-on was not appropriate, nor was extrapolation from professional needs to the needs of governors. It was argued that devolving power to governors and their schools, far from empowering governing bodies, might reinforce existing unsatisfactory power relationships between governors and staff. LEAs still had an important co-ordinating and support role; the many and varied training and support needs of governors could not be met through in-school training. Rather, the mood of this conference (and shared by the writer who was a workshop leader) was that instead of shifting the training emphasis from one side (the left) to the other (the right), the vertical dividing line should be withdrawn from the diagram to produce a training model which is multi-layered and three dimensional; à la carte rather than table d'hôte. It needs to recognise that governors and governing bodies have individual training needs which change over time. At some time these are best met on the left of the model, at others on the right, or a combination of the two, or more.

Such training menus could help ensure that governors move from covert to overt management roles and could also assist with the same movement in the democratic roles of governors.

## Governors and democracy

Central government appears to be centralising more and more power to itself, i.e. moving back from the rim and down the spokes to the hub described in Kenneth Baker's comments reported in the opening of this chapter. The 1990s moves to encourage more schools to 'opt out'[3] for example, appear unlikely to increase the democracy the government is claiming to enhance by permitting more schools to become fully self-governing. The 'opted-out' schools could be said to have less democratic control since their previous controllers, the locally elected and accountable local education authorities, are being replaced with a non-elected, non-accountable 'quango', the Funding Agency for Schools (FAS). This itself is dominated by central government. This decline in local democratic control of schools is also evidenced in the 1992 Education Act which abolished the requirement for LEAs to have an elected education committee (a statutory requirement since 1902). In addition opted out schools will not have to have LEA governors amongst their members. These new arrangements were termed 'profoundly undemocratic' by the National Union of Teachers (*TES* 2 October 1992, p.6).

All these features seem to illustrate the illusive democracy reported by Thody in Chapter 2. It seems to be further encouraged by the allowance that several small 'opted-out' schools can cluster under one governing body (1993 Education Act, sections 117–126, pp.78–84) thus removing something like 100 governors of all categories from direct participation in their local schools' affairs and complicating the type of training provision which might be offered. The encouragement to group schools under one governing body is curious when one considers that the Taylor Report highlighted the failures of the hitherto grouped system of governing bodies, and the 1980 Education Act — reinforced by the 1986 Education Act — made it illegal, for partnership and democratic reasons, to group more than two schools into one governing body.

The chances of such clustered governing bodies exercising effective management control appear to be, like their democratic features, limited. Since school management teams, including governors, complain that they are overwhelmed by paperwork, the volume of individual school business caused by the constant torrent of legislation, regulation and 'reforms', it is difficult to see how any yet-to-be-formed opted-out cluster schools will cope any better. They might have to follow the example of USA school boards some of which meet at least fortnightly to manage the workload. Will volunteer governors come forward for this workload and, if they do, will they have any *time* for training?

Despite the rather gloomy predictions here that school democracy will not operate other than in an illusory sense, there is a feeling that democracy is becoming more of a reality through governors, though in a different way to that envisaged in the legislation. Talking with governors at training sessions reveals that many are incensed at some of the government's recent educational changes. In their protective roles as supporters and legitimators of schools, they have seen the lowering of teachers' morale, the increased stress of heads, the inadequacies of funding, the problems caused by league tables and an overladen National Curriculum. Governors are starting to speak out against Tory policy as witnessed by governors' support of the teachers' boycott of National Curriculum testing in 1993. There were protest letters in the press and governors wrote to their MPs. As yet, such protests cannot be claimed to be overwhelmingly influential, but the signs are there. Is it possible that training has encouraged an empowered active citizenry? If so, the prospect of 25,000 dynamic governing bodies is either impressive or daunting depending on whether one favours illusory or real democracy. If governor training has encouraged such a response from governors (or at least, if it could be said to have enhanced the citizenship learning that has come simply from the act of being governors) then its radicalism might be seen as a threat by the government. Is it likely that money currently earmarked by government for governor training will cease to be so delineated? If so, governors will have to make a case for their training funding in competition with any other group in our locally-managed schools. In these circumstances governors might defer their own training needs to what may be seen to be more pressing management needs of professional staff.

One must hope that the 'Iron Law of Education' will operate (McGivney, 1990, p.12): the more education people have had, the more likely they are to want more and the more competent they will be at getting it. This is where the link governor system can be so important. Effective link governors champion the training needs of governors who are so burdened with other priorities on their time, and keep training on the governing body's agenda.

The above discussion has focused on governors within the democratic polity, showing the possibilities of a more active citizenry emerging with help from their training. What the educational legislators have ignored/overlooked is that being a school governor is, for many, a political activity as well as an educational or community-motivated one. Governors want to make their views known about what many see as educational change inimical to their educational motives and ideals. Generally, they did not make their unwritten psychological contract to become school governors in order to collude with the demise of LEAs nor to be the Secretary of State's lap-dog.

## Governors and management

What of governors' contribution to the management of the school? Training has assisted with this role but governors are still, on the whole, seen not to have a management role. Their contribution is covert rather than overt. Governors have been advised to keep their side of the boundary, as specified in the DFE 'School Governors: a Guide to the Law' thus:

> The governing body has a general responsibility for managing the school effectively . . . it is not expected to take detailed decisions about the day-to-day running of the school — this is a function for the head. A good governing body will delegate enough powers to the head to allow the head to perform his or her management duties (DFE, 1993, p.15).

Governors' advice books reiterate such suggestions. Thody (1992) for example, suggests that governors are best involved at the planning and reviewing stages and should not try to do every task of school management:

> Making choices should help us to cope with the large number of duties we have and should help create a sense of 'usness' rather than of 'them and us' in the management of the school (Thody, 1992, p.19).

If these suggestions are to be adopted, governor training must move on from the information, skills based induction type training which is prevalent, to exploring key management functions of governing bodies and the associated boundary issues. This is the challenge for governors, heads and governor trainers from now on.

## Future training

If governors are to emerge from the covert democratic and managerial roles which they currently appear most to operate within schools and to utilise some of the democratic strength that has begun to emerge in national representations, then what is needed is a variety of training strategies which link training to roles, to exploring boundary issues, to legal requirements, to polity, to management. What is required is not the kind of shift envisaged by the School Management Task Force but a mixed economy. There must be an acknowledgement that there are a number of training and support strategies which meet governors where they are, take them forward, developing individual, group and whole school needs. Governor trainers must avoid putting all their eggs into one basket. Moreover, there is a strong argument that central (LEA?) co-ordination is essential if efficient and effective use of resources is to be made. This may sound like a standard LEA argument, but the evidence suggests that 'the market' is no regulator in such cases.

Alternatively, it can be argued that an increase in the low level of funding available for governor training and a radical shift in control, from LEAs to governors themselves may be required if governing bodies are not to lose out. The time may come when we take the bold step to deschool governor training so that, within a system of self-governing schools, Illich's (1971, p.75) three purposes of education are fulfilled:

> It should provide all who want to learn with access to available resources at any time in their lives, empower all who want to share what they know to find those who want to learn it from them; and, finally, furnish all who want to present an issue to the public with the opportunity to make their challenge known.

The challenge for governors, heads, LEAs, governor trainers is to have the courage to let this happen. The signs are there. Governors are trying to find a national voice — through the formation early in 1994 of a National Governors' Council. Curiously, this is funded by the DFE in its early stages and led by individuals whose background is headship, management consultancy and LEA administration: which causes one to wonder whether this is really a grass roots movement from 'ordinary governors', and to question its political motivation.

Technology is available to encourage networking (cf Illich above): an article in the *Times Educational Supplement* (1994, p.6) outlined an emerging national electronic mailbase linked to the UK Joint Academic Network — JANET — which enables governors with the appropriate IT technology at home or work, and with the necessary knowledge, to join computer mail discussion groups enabling information and ideas to be rapidly transmitted and responded to. Moreover, an internal DES (as was) working paper (1990) talked about bypassing LEAs through an electronic mailbox system:

> Looking ahead to possible high-technology solutions . . . we are exploring . . . CD/ROM technology to get up-to-date technology into schools. This approach might also be extended to other materials of use to governors . . . More importantly, we shall have established a toe-hold for governors in a technology which may in due course become the new standard for information flows within the education service (DES, 1990, para. 5).

Exploring the potential of such a technological network was one way of facilitating information flow which could be top-down (in DES paper above), bottom-up or truly networked amongst governors and governing bodies.

The same DES paper also explored the generation of self-help training packages:

> addressed explicitly to the senior management team in a school, including the governing body (ibid., para. 13).

The challenges for the year 2000 and beyond are how to make the illusion of democracy a reality. How can governors be involved as active citizens in the management of schools? How can there be protection and extension of the many varied and excellent governor training initiatives undertaken so far? For, as Alan George (quoted in Mahoney, 1988, p.219) wrote of school governors over a decade ago when a national scheme of governor training was only a twinkle in someone's eye:

> . . . the quality of their voluntary service provides some measure of the health of our communities. Good experience in school governing can release energy for contributions in other areas of civic and rural life. Ignoring the training needs of this substantial body of volunteers leads at best to a moribund

system and at worst to alienation. Surely the nation's governors deserve something better.

A little learning could truly be a dangerous thing.

## Notes

1. An interesting philosophical treatise could be developed as to whether training can empower anyone. However, since 'governor training' is what is recognised in the legislation, the reader should take this to include support, education, development, empowerment.
2. This healthy estimate was challenged in 1990 by the teachers' union NASUWT which reported that most LEAs had trained fewer than 30 per cent of their governors: a more realistic estimate.
3. The Tory government's policy since 1986 has been to encourage diversity in the education system, and to remove the power/control of LEAs. Thus it legislated to allow schools to seek grant-maintained status (GM schools) and to 'opt out' of local authority control. In 1994 about 4 per cent of schools, mainly secondary schools, have so far 'opted out' or become grant-maintained. Such schools are also being called by the DFE 'self-governing schools', as if LEA locally managed schools were not also self-governing.

## Bibliography

Calibre Training (1990) 'Developing Governing Bodies'. Hertfordshire County Council.

DES (1989) *The Quality of School Governor Training*. INS 56/12/357 316/89. London: HMSO.

DES (1990) *Developing School Management: The Way Forward*, London: HMSO.

DES (1990) *Options for the Future*. Paper 8/4. London: HMSO.

DES (1990) *School Governor Information and Training*. Paper 8/3. London: HMSO.

DFE (1993) *School Governors: a Guide to the Law*. London: HMSO.

DOE (1984) 'Parental influence at school'. March, para. 93. London: HMSO.

Freire, P. (1972) 'Cultural action for freedom', Harmondsworth: Penguin.

Hart, D.(1990) 'More power to the head'. The *Independent* 25 October, p.19.

Houghton, V. and Richardson, K. (1974) *Recurrent Education*, London: Ward Lock.

HMSO (1977) *A New Partnership for our Schools*, London.

HMSO (1993) *Education Act 1993*, London.

HMSO (1994) *School Teachers' Review Body*, London.

Illich, I. (1971) *Deschooling Society*, London: Calder and Boyars.

Knowles, M. (1978) *The Adult Learner — a Neglected Species*, Houston, Texas: Gulf.

Liddington, J. (1990) 'Window on the Future: the School Governor Training Revolution'. *Adults Learning*, 2, 3, pp.71–73.

Mahoney, T. (1978) 'Recurrent Education: Theoretical Antecedents and Some Implications', Unpublished M Ed University of Nottingham.

Mahoney, T. (1988) *Governing Schools: Powers, Issues and Practice*, Basingstoke: Macmillan.

McGivney, V. (1990) *Education's for Other People: Access to Education for Non-Participating Adults*, Leicester: National Institute of Adult Continuing Education.

National Union of Teachers (1992) quoted in *Times Educational Supplement*, 2 October, p.6.
Rogers, R. (1992) 'Power to the People — in Whitehall'. *Times Educational Supplement* 2 October p.6.
Senior Chief HMI (1994) quoted in *Education*, 21 January, p.42.
Teachers' Pay Review Body Report (1994) 'New Pay Award is a Job for Governors', quoted in *Education*, 11 February, p.99.
Thody, A. (1992) *Moving to Management: School Governors in the 1990s*, London: David Fulton Publishers.
*Times Educational Supplement* 11 February 1994.
*Times Educational Supplement* (1994) 'Janet and the big E', 18 February, p.6.

# 13 An opportunity for partnership: annual parents' meetings

Jane Martin and Stewart Ranson

The questions of overt and illusory democracy in school governance are nowhere more pertinent than in relation to the Annual Parents' Meeting.[1] Since 1981 school governance in England and Wales has undergone a transformation which central government rhetoric would have us believe has been borne out of a desire to increase lay participation in education.[2] The legal requirement for schools to hold an Annual Parents' Meeting placed a very significant cog within a school governance reform wheel moving into top gear. Indeed, such an accountability mechanism was the only formal braking mechanism (operated by parents as consumers) preventing governing bodies with much increased responsibilities from careering out of control. Research findings related below not only explore the issue of effective accountability, but also the possibilities for the meeting to involve parents, as a collective body, in school policy-making and ultimately school management. In unravelling some of the ends which presently exist around the bundle of issues connecting parents, governors and professionals, and their beliefs about the Annual Parents' Meeting, the findings from the study raise our awareness about the potential for parents as partners in schools and the notion of local participative democracy: a reality or an illusion?

The research in Birmingham (Hinds, et al., 1992) set out to investigate the current state of the Annual Parents' Meeting, which was conventionally understood to be a barren exercise greeted with much apathy, and to investigate its potential for positive dialogue between parents and schools.

## The Annual Parents' Meeting: just an accountability exercise?

> It has to be formal: all meetings have to be (A Chair of governors).

Annual Parents' Meetings have usually been conceived in legalistic terms: a statutory duty. Governing bodies and headteachers have been preoccupied with making the Governors' Annual Report a success and have perceived the Annual Parents' Meeting as simply providing an occasion for parents to acknowledge the information given. Focusing only on the annual report would appear to be an inappropriate constraint: some parents may feel if they have read the report that there would be no need to attend the meeting. But more seriously, the report is by its nature retrospective and a more open meeting can enable lively discussion about the future development of the school. The study has revealed other concepts of purpose which focus more on the children's learning and achievement: 'When the child is the centre of the occasion, they come in droves. The obstacle is that the Annual Parents' Meeting is not perceived by parents as connecting with their interest in their child'.

In our observation of meetings, virtually all the Chairs were comfortable with the Annual Parents' Meeting as an occasion to satisfy statutory requirements for discussion of the governors' annual report. Some believed strongly that the meeting should not probe issues outside the report. For some the legal duty defined the style and organisation of the meeting: 'It's a business meeting'. There are signs of recognition that: 'a report can be written defensively'; 'the report alone is not enough for a good Annual Parents' Meeting'; 'it does not break down the barrier, parents won't come just for the report'. Many understand that while the law establishes a basic duty it should not stifle the possibilities of the forum.

However, too many Chairs made the annual report the single focus for their agenda. Often this entailed tedious reading point by point. Questions were usually invited but the tone of responses, though sympathetic and conciliatory when required, was in a number of cases defensive: while questions were listened to politely they were inclined not to disturb the Chair's intended direction and control of the meeting. There was little interaction between the Chair and other governors: indeed, in many meetings the Chair was the only governor to speak. Most Chairs of governors, moreover, agreed that their responsibility was to explain and justify their stewardship of the school. Sometimes this was expressed as, 'to speak and to be seen'; and occasionally, 'to be accountable in some sense' (usually, 'as being held to account' in order to 'confirm support for going on governing').

Governors appeared more willing to explain and justify their actions in response to questions rather than to engage openly in discussion with parents, though a few worked hard to create a dialogue, with the Chair's open and relaxed style striving to encourage communication: 'We seek your views'. One Chair tried even to act for and mobilise the voice of parents and clearly wanted the power of a resolution. However, more frequently we observed meetings where the resolutions item was passed over, where questions were usually referred to the headteacher and where responses were sometimes adversarial. One meeting assumed that no comments from parents was an expression of satisfaction: 'We must have done a good job!'

Headteachers and Chairs have felt that simply because the Annual Parents' Meeting was required by statute, that the meeting had to be a formal occasion. Formality has stifled much discussion while the word 'annual' has inhibited more imaginative approaches. Even the word 'meeting' is seen as requiring formal behaviour and language that is untypical of how teachers and parents and governors usually behave and talk together. Lecture style seating arrangements predominated with a headteacher table and parents in rowed seats. There is a misunderstanding here about the need for formal conventions in conducting discussions, for furniture and its location is one key to the dynamics of a meeting. (In only one case was discussion in small groups used to encourage participation by the parents.) The mood and style of relationships which are as important for a meeting as its administrative trappings, require qualities other than formality. If headteachers and staff can apply the skills they have in arranging contexts of learning for children, this might facilitate the dynamics of the meeting.

At a practical level the issue of formality is a very real obstacle to the development of a useful meeting. Obstacles to meaningful participation, or interaction between parents and governors, were primarily caused by the formality of the 'shareholders' business-like AGM model which most schools had tended to adopt. As we shall explain later, such a tradition creates misunderstanding which needs clarification and explanation in order to foster a new democratic culture.

## The Annual Parents' Meeting: do parents have a voice?

> I do not feel it is worthwhile voicing an opinion on school issues when it won't have any effect whatsoever on the way things are done (A parent).

The Annual Parents' Meeting provides a forum within which local democracy may be exercised. Indeed, as a forum for functional representation and purposeful participation it suggests a model appropriate for other locally provided public services (see Wright, 1994, and Clarke, 1994). That this opportunity is not being vigorously taken up begs the question why.

Governors tended to blame the parents for the failure of the meetings: they are indifferent to the Annual Parents' Meeting, it was proposed, because of their general satisfaction with the school; they are already well-informed about the school and the information in the governors' report is familiar to them; they are only interested in their own child; the school has an open door policy to sort out problems as and when they arise. A few governors saw the 'blame' as lying with themselves, in the way they wrote the report and planned and conducted the meeting. They were also willing to acknowledge that parents were often reluctant to attend because they lack confidence; fear of being volunteered; lack of understanding of the legislation and the purposes of the Annual Parents' Meeting, and other more pressing personal commitments.

The attendance of parents was indeed generally poor. Only two of the meetings we observed were quorate (i.e. had a number of parents attending equal to or more than 20 per cent of the number of pupils on roll which is the required number in order for the meeting to pass resolutions by a simple majority). The majority of meetings (69 per cent) had less than 9 per cent of parents at the meeting. The school we observed with the highest attendance was a small village primary school and the second highest attendance was a Special school.

Most parents wished to be helpful, expressing commitment to the development of the school as well as to the education of their children. The issues they raised for discussion were generally practical: traffic arrangements outside or near the school; a request for hand dryers; laying some pavement in a muddy area of the school grounds; a request for school uniform; the state of repair of buildings. It was unusual for parents to introduce curriculum issues, although discipline and bullying were raised for discussion, as was testing. Nevertheless, a number of question were asked on significant issues of school management including LMS, open enrolment and the budgetary implications of formula funding (in particular for a small school with falling rolls). Moreover, it was clear that parents were often willing to make helpful suggestions, and become involved, in support of the school: to help with reading schemes; and to help explore transport options.

In most meetings the parents appeared as a collection of individuals rather than as a parent body, although there was a real sense of such on a few occasions. Often only one or two parents would raise questions at the meeting. Indeed at one meeting the same parent raised six out of the seven issues discussed. Generally, the manner in which the annual report was presented and the meeting conducted gave parents few openings for real discussion. We saw no instances of parents wishing to raise an individual case during the meeting but in one meeting parents had mobilised themselves to speak against the governors' proposal to change the time of the school day, including the presentation of a petition at the meeting.

In the main, parents who attended the Annual Parents' Meeting expressed satisfaction with the organisation of the meeting despite adopting a passive role. It is apparent that parents who attend the meeting are those who usually attend other events at school. They value the opportunity to take part in an annual meeting and believe the purposes of such meetings have been clearly explained in the invitations received. Nevertheless, a quarter of these parents believe that the publicity for the meeting could have been improved and, more seriously, a significant minority feel that their involvement will have no influence upon the work of the school. A sense of futility is clearly not fertile ground for enthusiastic participation.

Parents were clear about their reasons for attending the annual meeting. These can be grouped into four categories of purpose:

- To receive information about the governing body, the decision-making process and the business of the school. 'To find out what is happening in school and to find out what they do.' 'To ensure the school is running well and that there are no problems.'

- To support the school out of interest of a sense of duty. 'It is important for parents to be seen to be taking interest.' 'I am very interested in my children's education.'

- To express views and participate in the meeting. 'To offer input to improve the school.' 'To use my right to vote on any matters arising.'

- To contribute out of interest in a particular issue on the agenda.

While parents were concerned to acquire information about the governing body and the running of the school none, however, referred to the purposes of accountability invested in the meeting.

Understanding of the purpose of the meeting by parents reveals much about the culture of parental involvement in schools (See Figure 13.1).

Parents appear to be defining their role in terms of reinforcing a deferential political culture whilst hinting at a growing understanding of the purposes of accountability embodied in the meeting. Both the head and (less certainly) the LEA also are expected to contribute 'accounts' to the meeting. A few parents however remain uncertain about their capacity to have a say how the school is run which suggests that further clarification of the reciprocal roles in the meeting can only enhance the emerging sense of partnership.

Indeed the evidence is that the parent voice is having little effect so far. Of those schools who had reviewed the latest Annual Parents' Meeting, the positive outcomes appeared to be very few: changing the date of the Annual Parents' Meeting; or reviewing a school policy such as equal opportunities. However there were a number of expressions to the effect that the meeting had been useful and that further efforts were needed to be made to gain the interest of the parents.

In two thirds of the cases no changes in school policies and practices followed discussions at the latest Annual Parents' Meeting. But taking the previous years' meetings into account the changes seem more numerous and substantial: a number of changes in the management of the school and attempts to inform parents about the curriculum, as well as the other opportunities to take part in the life of a school were reported.

## The Annual Parents' Meeting: illusory democracy?

> Would the Annual Parents' Meeting realise its full potential only if parents all act together as a responsible collective body, and not just as a collection of individuals? (A headteacher).

The concept of democracy in terms of the Annual Parents' Meeting struck many as unfamiliar, but some Chairs and headteachers were willing to acknowledge it as a democratic forum — 'some decision-making and parental ownership'. Most, though, wished to retain control. They were often relieved that meetings were not quorate and were apprehensive about the subject and tone of resolutions that might emerge from meetings that were quorate. Moreover, Chairs and headteachers were divided about the existence and relevance of the concept of a parent body. Yet a few do grasp its place. While the sentiments of 'Parents aren't experts on education, you mustn't displace the professionalism of education' can still be heard, a new perspective is beginning to be articulated: 'There is a parent body.

**Figure 13.1 Perception of purposes, the views of parents who attended the annual parents' meeting.***

| | % Strongly Disagree | % Disagree | % Agree | % Strongly Agree |
|---|---|---|---|---|
| The governors present their annual report (96)† | 1 | 2 | 71 | 26 |
| The governors explain and justify to parents what they have been doing through the year. (96) | 1 | 4 | 68 | 27 |
| The headteacher explains and justifies to parents what the school has been doing through the year. (95) | 6 | 6 | 57 | 31 |
| The LEA explains and justifies to parents what it has been doing in relation to the school through the year. (92) | 18 | 17 | 45 | 20 |
| Parents can have a say in how the school is run. (95) | 3 | 14 | 60 | 23 |
| I'm not sure what the meeting is about. (92) | 33 | 57 | 7 | 2 |

*Figure rounded to nearest whole number.
†Total number of responses to each statement in brackets.

How you organise it as a force, I don't know'; 'I've been conscious of bringing the parent body with me since the mid 70s'. 'You need the two channels, parents as individuals, parents as a body'. Too much reliance on the notion of a collective body as a precursor to effective parental participation, however, would be just as mistaken as dismissing the contribution of individuals. The significance of a meeting of all parents, with governors and school staff, allows individuals to represent themselves in association with others. In such a way, the meeting may become one of the 'institutional arrangements which develop and involve an active citizenship' (Clarke, 1994). Yet it seems that such an arrangement may still be no more than an illusion.

The issue of sharing power is manifested in how the meeting is controlled. Where governors and headteachers seek to retain ownership, and want to resist conceding control then this is an obstacle to the Annual Parents' Meeting as a democratic arena. The contribution of school staff was generally minimal, often because there were none or few present, on some occasions teacher governors were able to contribute to particular issues where they had experience or expertise. Parental deference will reinforce traditional professional-parent relationships — 'parents see their place at the school gate' and don't see the power of the quorum and the scope of the Annual

Parents' Meeting. Parents can be daunted by the exercise of authority; the Chair's position is powerful — 'shouting down a parent'; 'talking down to parents'. There was, perhaps understandably, a genuine feeling of apprehension amongst headteachers about the meeting: the sense of 'being on trial in public' was real. In only a few cases could this be articulated as opposition to the purpose and working of the Annual Parents' Meeting although the anxiety about 'the power of resolution' was manifest. Yet the experience of cautious progress should reassure headteachers about the prospect of future development.

In many cases the headteacher played the leading role in the meeting both in presenting the report and in answering questions. Most Chairs believed that the headteacher, as well as the governors, had a responsibility to explain and to justify what the school had been doing during the year. When interviewed, Chairs and headteachers agreed that the role of the headteacher was advisory, supportive, and to answer questions. Yet only a few referred to the accountability of the headteacher: and in only some of the interviews did the headteachers articulate their role as 'a facilitator in the community', or as 'a link with the parents'. This networking and enabling role is probably a key to the success of these meetings and not appreciated by all headteachers.

Many individual governors, however, played a very small part in the meeting: they were present to demonstrate their support for the school. They saw a minimal role for themselves in the Annual Parents' Meeting which was perceived as the business of the Chair and the headteacher. They have chosen to be silent rather than being excluded by the Chair and the headteacher. The absence of a particular role for parent governors was significantly interesting given the potential for these governors to develop interaction. Such predominance by the leaders of the meeting, however, is likely to preclude the contribution of parents engaging in the business and discussion of the Annual Parents' Meeting.

Analysis of 'traditions' begins to reveal the deeper structures that work to constrain the development not only of the Annual Parents' Meeting but other initiatives in the reform of public institutions, and indicates the scale of the challenge. Change is necessarily more difficult when it confronts traditions — those patterns of value and practice which have become institutionalised over time and are deeply embedded in experience.

## The traditions of education

Two traditions have interacted to shape the style with which schools and the service more generally have been managed. Professionalism has emphasised the authoritative knowledge of teachers in their practice and the deference of parents as clients. This tradition has been complemented and reinforced by the individualism of parents who invariably have been preoccupied with their child and have been content to leave the business of schools and education to teachers.

This tradition of education therefore has been 'created' by all the parties to it, parents as much as teachers, even though its effect is to distribute power and control unevenly over the process of education.

This study of Annual Parents' Meetings has illuminated much of this tradition: the reservations of parents about a 'parent body' and their enduring concern for the interests of their child. Governors and headteachers, alike, have typically been reluctant to dissolve professional control of 'curriculum and examinations'. Professionalism and individualism are, therefore, mutually reinforcing practices resisting the Annual Parents' Meeting as a rather alien idea. These traditions suggest many professionals as well as parents may have embraced the encroaching Annual Parents' Meeting with limited enthusiasm. Yet the parental sense of futility in participating is telling: the individual interest and the right to influence may not be incompatible as we shall argue. The professional tradition may be the more resistant to change.

## The civic traditions of our society

Our society has lacked 'a public culture'; it has valued a style of civic virtue which expresses private and voluntary service to the community. Public services are the domain of professionals and political representatives. Individuals do not get involved in public affairs. The individualism and privatism of our civic life reflects and reinforces the traditions set out above describing the management of education (and of public services generally).

Policies which seek to reform such traditions and encourage participation in the life of our public institutions not only go against the grain of post-war public life but find a public in large part bereft of the capacities required: for public discourse and persuasion. Or, more accurately, the skills often reflect characteristics of social class: Bernstein's 'elaborate' and 'restricted codes'. Yet, one of the distinctive findings of this study is not the expected evidence, that many ordinary people lack confidence and skill in the public arena, but that many governors and headteachers do as well. The professional world has also been a private world and often lacks skills in working closely and openly with parents and the community.

## The Annual Parents' Meeting: from illusion to reality?

> How meetings are conducted and arranged sends messages to the parents about what the school puts value into and what it values (A headteacher).

The distinctive values which can bring life to democratic processes build upon the evidence of the study that the meetings stand far more chance of flourishing when they are part of a continuing tradition of partnership between the school, parents and the community.

There is sufficient evidence, if such were sought, to warrant abandoning the project of the Annual Parents' Meeting. Yet it is clear that in places the meeting is working, or beginning to work. If the Annual Parents' Meeting was established partly in order to promulgate nationwide the best practice of Parents' Associations, it seems to have begun to work. The flow of information to all parents, through the governors' annual report associated with the Annual Parents' Meeting, is an improvement, while in a number of schools there is the practice of involving and encouraging parents to discuss the development of the school. Despite low attendance at the Annual Parents' Meeting, discussion in partnership is now beginning to take place in more schools through and around the Annual Parents' Meeting than was the case before 1986 in the eight thousand schools nationally which had an Association. This study suggests there is value in deferring retreat. We argue against abandoning Annual Parents' Meetings, but for abandoning the concept which too often informs the Annual Parents' Meeting project — a traditional business-meeting AGM, narrowly briefed to present information. This model is better replaced with a design more suited to the educational tasks of the school and closer, moreover, to the purposes of parents, teachers and governors as they presently define them. It proposes a vision of the learning institution in which the partners understand the benefits of working together to enhance the education of young people.

The business meeting format and its accompanying formalities are, arguably, responsible for much of the limited enthusiasm and even disenchantment parents are expressing in relation to the Annual Parents' Meeting. The proper sense of futility lies with the parents. They want an opportunity to participate freely yet this is largely denied them. The format is stifling the contribution which parents might wish to make: the dominance of 'the Report' forces retrospection when parents will wish to consider the implications of the many current changes for the future well-being of their child's education, while the preoccupation with formal information reinforces parents into a quiescent role in the meeting. If it is the case, that parents do wish to have a say in the development of the school, then 'a meeting' is appropriate but requires a very different perspective if it is to enable parents to make their appropriate contribution to the well-being of the school.

It is clear from this study that the Annual Parents' Meeting works, or begins to work, where there is a tradition of the school working in partnership with parents, valuing the contribution which they can make to the processes of learning and thus the life of the school. This suggests that some schools have chosen to make the concept of the Annual Parents' Meeting work. The relative success of their meetings (sometimes in the disadvantaged inner city) cannot be put down to social (middle-class children) or geographic factors (rural contexts) beyond their control. The success reflects their agency and imagination, working on factors within their power. It has worked because they have wanted it to work: the potential of the meeting has been shaped by their values and belief that the quality of education can only be enhanced by the active participation of parents working with teachers and governors to the same ends.

Implementing a revitalised Annual Parents' Meeting will take time. Altering, what Braudel has termed, the 'long duree' of cultural and political traditions is not something that can be accomplished even in a year or two. The timespan is long. But then the agenda, begun a decade ago of altering the culture of the polity — encouraging the active participation of the public, passive for a generation and more — could never have been conceived as being realised in a matter of years.

The barriers to the involvement of parents have been breaking down over time as understanding of their value and contribution has grown (see Atkin et al., 1988). What Sallis (1988) describes as the 'decade of progress' (p.48) from the Plowden Report to the Taylor Committee hailed the development of parental involvement in schools as part of the learning process for children. Plowden recommended much closer contact between parents and teachers for the benefit of the individual child, including the opportunity for informal and formal consultations in school, open days and reports on children's work. The development of parents as a 'para-professional aide' (Meighan, 1989, p.108) encouraged parents to be increasingly used as a resource in schools — providing assistance and support for teachers in the classroom — as fund raisers through PTA activity — and significantly through a close partnership with teachers for example in primary school reading schemes. Projects such as the Haringey Reading Project (Tizard et al., 1982) and the Belfield Community Primary School Project in Rochdale (Hannon and Jackson 1987) clearly demonstrated the benefits for the children when parents became involved in their learning.

A patchwork of development has ensued, however, which usually reflects the domination of the professionals (see Bell and Macbeth, 1989). As Meighan (1989) points out, too often 'the school and its teachers take the initiative and encourage parents to assist, largely on the school's terms, for school defined ends and to become aids to the enterprise of the professionals' (p.108). If parents, however, are to enter into a true partnership with schools then they need to be involved as a parent body in the policy process as well as with matters of individual progress in learning. The quality of school management, as Caldwell and Spinks (1988) argue, requires the involvement of parents as much as teachers in the management process. Success will require a change of culture from both.

If parents are to develop a constructive policy-making partnership with professionals in schools, then the onus may be upon the professionals initially to create the climate of welcome. This will require a fundamental acknowledgement by professionals that sharing power with parents is beneficial for pupils in schools. Many parent governors have found their commitment and enthusiasm diminished by 'initial feelings of being out of their depth and blighted by jargon' (Golby and Brigley, 1989). Indeed Golby and Brigley's study highlights the difference in effectiveness between parent governors operating in an 'enabling environment' (p.17) with enlightened professionals and those struggling against 'tokenist attitudes' (p.21) which impose 'crucial limitations on the conception and practice of governorship' (p.22).

Parents themselves, however, will also need to change how they perceive their role, if they are to play a greater part in formulating policy in schools. Parent groups in Britain appear to have failed to achieve the degree of influence on policy that some continental organisations have gained (see Beattie, 1985) and remain, as Shipman (1984) describes, 'outsider groups'. Interestingly, recent research (Hughes, et al., 1990) suggests that notions such as 'consumerism' and 'parental choice' have only limited relevance, yet parents are intensely interested and concerned about their child's education. Parents will need to understand the need to become involved collectively at the level of policy formation if they are to influence the quality of education as experienced by their individual children. The challenge for parents is to grasp the educational value for the learning process of working together with the school to manage change. The Annual Parents' Meeting provides an opportunity for parents with teachers to define a new way of working together.

Three models of the Annual Parents' Meeting can be presented building upon the language used by schools. The models are informed by different values and perspectives about the function of the Annual Parents' Meeting, its organisation and the role of the participants within it. The models we propose reflect stages of development in the meeting.

## 1. Validation

The study indicates that most Annual Parents' Meetings are still at the first stage of validation: a model preoccupied with information-giving within a formal business meeting at the end of the year. It empowers the Chair and the headteacher and requires the parents to be passive listeners, merely validating or confirming what is presented to them. It implies a one way conception of accountability and an outmoded didactic transmission model of learning. It is clear from Circular 8/86 that while the Government expected the Annual Parents' Meeting to adhere to conventions of conducting a meeting it expressed a much larger vision of involving parents.

## 2. Interaction

Such a model is set out, we believe, in the second stage of interaction. This model expects and encourages the active participation of parents in the life of the school: valuing them as 'complementary educators', recognising the contribution they can make to the learning process and the well-being of the school, willing to listen and to learn from them. The model is one of a learning workshop in which the participants are valued as equal partners in discussion and work together to develop a shared understanding of a particular policy or dimension of school practice.

## 3. Partnership

The third stage of partnership takes a step further the emphasis within the previous model of shared understanding and collaborative working. Here governors, parents and teachers enter into a public partnership which holds them jointly responsible for the governance and development of the school. Adversarial relationships are eschewed, but it is acknowledged that understanding needs to be reinforced by shared ownership and commitment. This requires a degree of formal organisation in which rights and responsibilities are defined, roles, procedures and joint accountabilities clarified and policies negotiated.

The study suggests that most Annual Parents' Meetings are stuck at stage one and that many of the participants express anxieties about the third stage: that it will become adversarial rather than collaborative; that there will be loss of control; that unrepresentative groups will gain undue influence. Some of this unease is unnecessary and reflects the limited development of partnership in many schools. Our concluding analysis proposes the advantages of moving quickly to the second stage of interactive partnership with parents. There are three aspects to the argument. First, that unless the partners agree about school policies the learning process will be disadvantaged for many. The interactive model emphasises the unique opportunities provided by the meeting for the partners to develop a shared understanding and agreement about the educational environment that will best provide the conditions for learning and achievement of all the young people within the school.

It is the model which helps the partners to grasp the connection between the needs of the institution and those of the pupil: the individual interest in the child requires a parent to develop understanding and agreement about the whole. The quality of the whole is understood as a condition for the development of each individual. This is the key lesson to be learned by all the partners. Unless parents and teachers agree about homework, or uniform, or behaviour and language, or many key areas of the curriculum, then the divergences in practice are likely to impede the learning of pupils severally. (Unless homework, for example, is an agreed practice, then the commitment of young people can slip easily through the crevices of adult disagreement or the inequity of 'rules' applied differently). Only a shared understanding between teachers, parents and governors, as well as pupils, can provide the necessary climate required for all to learn effectively.

Secondly, the need for agreement provides the rationale for the participation of parents in a number of ways including a meeting of the parent body. Beginning with the need of the parents to develop understanding about the progress their child is making, provides the rationale of the meeting and the involvement of parents. The meeting recognises the indispensable role which parents play in the education of the child and thus the success of the school. This is the argument for a partnership between governors, the teachers and parents as well as the pupils. The opportunity is presented to focus the meeting on workshops and activities which allow all involved to develop a shared understanding of the learning process. Rather than an isolated occasion this purpose should happen more frequently, with the school creating opportunities throughout the year to welcome and value the contribution of parents.

Thirdly, the need for partnership suggests the importance of all learning a language which supports these processes: communication, accountability, negotiation. The model ties the pedagogy of the meeting to the best practices of education within a school: engaging rather than instructing, enabling rather than directing, learning rather than teaching. The purposes of partnership as conceived here, present a challenge for the diversity of groups involved to develop understanding of the different 'languages' that might exist within each of the different 'bodies' (parent, teacher and governor) as much as between them. A capacity to listen, to understand, and to seek the common ground will be invaluable in overcoming the barriers. The authority of the Annual Parents' Meeting will derive from the value accorded to these purposes, and the success of the processes, in harnessing the partners to enhance the quality of the school as a learning institution.

The model of joint responsibility can provide the framework of organisation, support and accountability which relatively autonomous schools may need in the future, for it is our belief that they will be more effective where they are underwritten by the public agreement and collaborative working of the partners.

## Acknowledgement

This is an expanded version of a paper in press: Martin et al. (1995) 'The Annual Parents' Meeting: Potential for Partnership' *Research Papers in Education*, London: Routledge.

## Notes

1. The 1986 Education Act set out the statutory requirements for schools thus: 'It shall be the duty of the governing body to hold a meeting once every school year ('the Annual Parents' Meeting') which is open to: (a) all parents of registered pupils at the school (b) the headteacher and (c) such persons as the governing body may invite. The purpose of the meeting shall be to provide an opportunity for discussion of: (a) the governors' report and (b) the discharge by the governing body, the headteacher and the local education authority of their function in relation to the school.' Section 31(1) and (2).
2. A circular (8/86) from the Department for Education and Science (DES) elaborated upon statutory duties and made it clear that the Annual Parents' Meeting was to provide an opportunity for parents to become more closely involved in the life of the school. The Parent's Charter reinforced the significance of the meeting for parents. 'The Annual Meeting allows parents to have their say about the standards they want from the school. If enough parents — at least 10 per cent — attend, they can vote on resolutions put forward by individual parents. The governors must consider and respond to any resolution which is supported by the majority at the meeting. Governors will welcome your views and the chance to talk about their plans in more detail.'

## Bibliography

Atkin, J., Bastiani, J. with Goode, J. (1988) *Listening to Parents*, Beckenham: Croom Helm.
Beattie, N. (1985) *Professional Parents*, Lewes: The Falmer Press.
Bell, R. and Macbeth, A. (1989) Unit 6 Parent–School Relationships in The Open University, *E208 Exploring Educational Issues*, Milton Keynes: Open University Press.
Caldwell, B. J. and Spinks, J. M. (1988) *The Self-Managing School*, Lewes: The Falmer Press.
Clarke, M. (1994) *The New Local Governance*, London: European Policy Forum.
DES (1986) *Circular 8/86*, London: DES.
DES (1991) *The Parent's Charter: You and Your Child's Education*, London: HMSO.
Golby, M. and Brigley, S. (1989) *Parents as School Governors*, Tiverton: Fair Way Publications.
Hannon, P. and Jackson, A. (1987) *The Belfield Reading Project*, London: National Children's Bureau.
Hinds, T., Martin, J., Ranson, S. and Rutherford, D. (1992) *The Annual Parents' Meeting: Towards a Shared Understanding*, School of Education: University of Birmingham.
Hughes, M., Wikeley, F. and Nash, T. (1990) *Parents and the National Curriculum*, School of Education: University of Exeter.
Martin, J., Ranson, S. and Rutherford, D. (1995) 'The Annual Parents Meeting: potential for partnership', *Research Paper in Education*, London: Routledge.
Meighan, R. (1989) 'The parents and the schools — alternative role definitions' in *Educational Review*, **41**, 2.
Sallis, J. (1988) *Schools, Parents and Governors*, London: Routledge.
Shipman, M. (1984) *Education as a Public Service*, London: Harper and Row.
Tizard, B., Schofield, W. and Hewison, J. (1982) 'Collaboration between teachers and parents in assisting children's reading'. *British Journal of Educational Psychology*, **52**.
Wright, T. (1994) *Citizens and Subjects*, London: Routledge.

# 14 The finishing point. Where to now?

Angela Thody

## The 1995 finishing point

A swift and simplistic summation of all the research evidence presented in the preceding chapters appears to show that in England, governors are not performing effectively their overt functions of democratic representation and the direction of managerial effectiveness and efficiency. The covert functions of providing illusory democracy and managerial legitimation, predicted in Chapter 2, are being performed. The evidence from outside of England shows a somewhat different picture with governors moving more towards providing the overt functions of democratic accountability and managerial direction and oversight.

These statements are massive generalisations and the researchers reporting here have all offered some indications that English governing bodies are moving slightly away from covert functioning alone. But the movement is slight.

Charles Batteson's and Denise Syndercombe-Court's account of the events at Culloden School demonstrated that governors provided support and protection for a school under attack from OFSTED and from the media. Once having thereby 'gone native', governors become incorporated with ... other strands of a discredited educational system — as integral parts of an 'enemy within' (p.47). Kevin Brehony described the uneasy position of English governing bodies caught between the contradictions inherent in the rhetoric of local decision-making and the reality of expanded state power. Governors were uncertain about their roles and responsibilities. Governors wanting a more managerial control contrasted with those envisaging governors as democratically functional and these were dissatisfied with the under-representation of certain groups of citizens.

Confusions in the current position of governing bodies were also highlighted by Stephen Brigley's account of a school opting out (Chapter 5). There are, he reported, confusions of goals and values amongst different groups of governors. He demonstrated that these groups are becoming active politically within their governing bodies and this provided evidence of the development of political activity which I anticipated in Chapter 2 as the necessary next step in the maturing of governing bodies. Growing political activity was also reported by Richard Hatcher (Chapter 9) but he pointed out that it was activity in which governors and school principals regulated each other, leaving state hegemony untouched thus raising the question whether or not such activity demonstrates political maturity.

The development of political maturity and of managerial effectiveness might both be assisted by the clearer delineation of governors' functions, proposed Anne Curtis (Chapter 6). She made this suggestion in response to discovering governors' uncertainty and confusions, exacerbated by the extensive demands made on them since the mid 1980s. Lynda Huckman (Chapter 10) reiterated the confusion theme which, she felt, left governors in a peripheral role in school politics. The way out of the confusion, Lynda concluded, was to delineate governors' powers and duties more clearly. Terry Mahoney (Chapter 12) proposed the route of re-vamped governor training as a means of ameliorating inadequacies of governing body control and direction. There were indications, he considered, that governing body democracy was becoming more of a reality, though not perhaps in the way envisaged in the legislation. Terry reported that governors were speaking out against national policies, a development which may be further enhanced by the creation in 1994 of the National Council of Governing Bodies (colloquially known as the National Governors' Council). Alternative training, together with a national lobby association, may help to begin the political maturing process of governors within the state system of education governance which Hatcher reported as being lacking.

Political maturing within schools was the focus of Jane Martin's and Stewart Ranson's chapter (13) concerning Annual Parents' Meetings. Their evidence demonstrated that these meetings provided the illusion of democracy but that they were beginning to move towards real democracy where schools had earlier traditions of community–school partnership and where 'schools have chosen to make the concept of the Annual Parents' Meetings work (p.204). They suggested that such relationships could proceed towards creating 'a public partnership which holds (governors, parents and teachers) jointly responsible for the governance and development of the school' (p.206).

Such a suggestion is akin to New Zealand's establishment of

contacts between schools, their communities and the state. New Zealand's school governance developments were reported by Brian Cusack in Chapter 7. Extensive demands have been made of governors in New Zealand as his review made clear but they do not appear to be suffering confusions to the same extent as are English governing bodies. Governors in Australia likewise seemed happier with their lot than English governors appeared to be. David Gamage reported in Chapter 8, Australian feelings of empowerment, ownership, motivation and commitment and of satisfaction with the managerial and democratic composition of and functioning of governing bodies. Alastair Macbeth reflected on the under performance of Scottish school boards but indicated greater clarity in the delineation of board members' and school principals' powers than exists in England and Wales.

It is interesting to compare the differences between our situation and that elsewhere and to speculate upon the extent to which English and Welsh governance might be improved by adopting ideas developed in other countries. Elsewhere, governors' powers are less extensive than those accorded to English and Welsh governors and only a very few New Zealand schools have copied England and Wales' devolution of the full budget to schools. Elsewhere, governing bodies are smaller and have different composition and methods of election and selection compared with those of England and Wales. Elsewhere, there are stronger traditions of centralisation; English and Welsh governing bodies are having to adjust to a re-birth of central power. Elsewhere the middle tiers of administration (the equivalents of English and Welsh local educational authorities) have been *de facto* or *de jure* abolished; here, the LEAs remain in uneasy limbo with the inherent confusions that follow from this. Elsewhere there seems to be less confusion about the model to which governorship should tend.

## Role model confusion

The re-invention of powerful school governance in England and Wales has occurred in a context in which the political agendas offer differing models. Each of these arises from the various ways of interpreting late twentieth attitudes to the role of the state. These interpretations are accountability, a market economy, privatisation, effectiveness and efficiency, empowerment and transparency. Each of these results in a different interpretation of the roles of participants in the system and hence of school governors whose job is to reflect the needs of participants.

***Accountability*** responsiveness to what CITIZENS want through meeting the criteria laid down by the organs of state. Within accountability, governors operate at what might be defined as the state/citizen interface. Governors, as citizens, inform schools what citizens want; governors, as state representatives, check that schools are providing what the state thinks citizens want.

***Market economy*** ensuring that schools meet the needs of CUSTOMERS or go out of business. Governors themselves are customers if they buy school services for their children (or for themselves as adult learners in, e.g. community education), if they use the product of schools (educated people) or if they buy other services now being marketed by schools (e.g. printing, holiday courses, consultancy). Only the last of these is priced; the other two are not so that the usual working of a market through a price mechanism cannot operate. Governors, as customer representatives, can be seen as part of a substitute for a pricing mechanism. It can be governors' responsibility to inform schools if the product is right for the market. Is the type of educated person being created, the appropriate model?

***Privatisation*** removal of the ownership of education by the state. This is not yet seen as fully achievable nor acceptable, so it is substituted by CLIENTS being offered a choice of schools with different types of ownership and some differences in curriculum. The governing bodies of grant-maintained schools and of city technology colleges, for example, have fewer parents and more business representatives than those of local education authority maintained schools. All schools can co-opt governors so that there should be responsiveness to local variations. Establishing the concept of education's privatisation has also resulted in encouraging schools to compete with each other. Competition could be said to imply differentiation of products and hence schools are beginning to stress their distinctive features. This distinctiveness might be fostered by governors because of their incorporation into their schools' ethos which rapidly turns governors into a supporters' club convinced of their school's speciality.

***Effectiveness and efficiency*** getting value for money for the TAXPAYERS. The costs of state provision of public services are no longer considered to be supportable. Therefore, state subsidies have to be reduced and what is given has to be used as effectively, economically and efficiently as possible. Governors could be said to be part of the mechanism for ensuring this. Some will be from the business community and they are deemed to have the business expertise that schools are considered to lack. All will be taxpayers who might, therefore, be expected to want to keep taxes as low as possible. Their proximity to the point at which money is being spent should make them cognisant of where economies can be made; in this respect they might be seen as monitors for the government.

They might also have an additional use as 'whipping boys' for government; as the money for schooling has been reduced and parents become aware of how the reductions are affecting their children's' education, someone is likely to be marked out for blame. In the past, this has been the local education authorities. They have determined how much money schools receive and they have been perceived as those who have refused to give schools as much money as they wanted. Now it is governors who have the responsibility for the budgets of their schools. Is it possible that central government hoped that parents would transfer opprobrium to governors thus deflecting possible anger against national politicians?

Effectiveness and efficiency has a further meaning in that government wishes to see improved standards in education and strengthening external control is viewed as a way to ensure such improvement. In the USA, the alleged failure of this solution led to the idea of empowerment, which has also been incorporated in changes in the UK.

***Empowerment*** of NON-PROFESSIONALS in making decisions about education. It is this objective that has dominated the rhetoric of both central government and of education professionals during the 1980s. For professionals, the main stated rationale has been that the involvement of the community, particularly of parents, will better enable children to achieve well. For central government, the rationale for empowerment has been to move power away from the professionals. The extent to which empowerment of other stakeholders is the real aim of either teachers or government is debatable. Both groups may simply be seeking allies. Whatever the reasons, however, the result has been a shift of power from teachers to outsiders and this has taken varying forms of which governorship is one. School governing bodies could be described as the outward and visible sign of the inward and spiritual grace of empowerment of non-professionals.

Empowerment has also taken the form of devolving powers to schools from local education authorities so that the schools become self-managing units. Governors therefore could be said to gain a role, both as public servants operating the units and as public monitors. They offer the possibility of checking that government policies are carried out with some degree of uniformity in our 19,628 primary schools, 3,811 secondary schools and 64 tertiary colleges (1993 figures). In exercising their duty of checking that the National Curriculum is taught, that a daily act of mainly Christian worship is offered, that sex education and religious education are provided and that examination results are published and that action plans are drawn up for schools failing to meet the required standards of OFSTED.

The governors could be described as the eyes and ears of central government. There is no other way that central government policies could be checked on such a frequent and regular basis.

***Transparency*** citizens, customers, clients, tax payers and non-professionals can see what is happening in schools; there are to be no more 'secret gardens'. This transparency might be assisted through having, in each school, a governing body whose duty it is to ensure that full information is sent to parents, both about their own children and about the schools' achievements as a whole. Further transparency is required because governing bodies have legal duties to assure the national government that such matters as school attendance, examination results, health and safety and teachers' pay and conditions of service are being satisfactorily achieved.

## Where to now?

Citizen, customer, client, taxpayer or non-professional — the choice is unresolved as yet. The choice will vary as different governments, and administrations, hold office and school governance may need to retain the flexibility to accommodate the variations over time. Overt or covert democratic and management functions — the signs are that covert roles remain dominant but that there are possibilities that overt roles are developing. The possibilities emerge as governors and school staff take the actions reported by the researchers for this book. The possibilities can be enhanced or diminished according to whichever changes might be selected from the following range of proposals. These are ideas that might be imported from the other countries whose governance systems have been described by Gamage, Macbeth and Cusack (Chapters 7, 8 and 11) or ideas that arise in response to the conclusions from the English contributors to this book.

In considering these suggestions, readers might do well to reflect that my use of the word 'ideas' to describe the following proposals may be too effete. 'The current situation regarding school governing bodies is untenable', stated Kevin Brehony in Chapter 4 above (p.58) and it could, therefore, be time to propose far reaching and definitive changes.

The proposals discussed here are:

- Abolish governing bodies
- Wait and do nothing
- Reduce expectations
- Define, statutorily, the division of roles and functions between governors and school principals
- Alter governor training
- Reform structure and appointments
- Establish mechanisms for accountability

**Abolish governing bodies**

In this era of ideas of extending accountability, active citizenship and empowerment, and following the work done to extend governors' powers, the idea of abolition seems heretical. Proposing a revolution like this is uncomfortable for the author, but the possibility has to be considered. Apposite questions which must be answered if the existence of governing bodies is to be justified are:

- Is it possible to assert that the development of governing bodies (and of their equivalents in other countries) has resulted in more effective schooling? In countries without any form of governance, how do their students' achievements compare with those of English and Welsh students? Were students' results worse, their extra-curricular activities less extensive, their school days less happy or their pastoral care less devoted when our governors were less powerful? I recognise the difficulties of conducting research to ascertain correlations of effectiveness and governance but such research should, at least, be on the agenda for consideration.
- Is it any longer reasonable to accept that school businesses should be directed by those with no specialist knowledge of the business? What other public or private businesses, government quangos or non-profit organisations are legally dominated by lay people?
- Which school businesses can expect to thrive when the nature of education dictates that it requires long-term perspectives which the short term of governorship is not designed to accommodate and when many governors have

personal, and very individualistic, vested interests in ensuring the best for their own children?

- Is it time to accept that school governing bodies are anachronistic in an era which has accepted the objectives of creating a nationalised education system? Governors could be seen as supporters for each school's individualism which is now potentially a threat to the unity of a National Curriculum and of national outcomes at national standards. Is it not better to envisage schooling as a franchise operation, in which one central board of directors devises the menu and delivery procedures and the service managers in the individual outlets amend the produce for local conditions?

The franchise analogy first occurred to me after a visit to Australia in 1992 when I became a devotee of a franchised chain of ice-cream parlours and discovered that the 'Ned Kelly' special of New South Wales resurfaced in Tasmania as the 'Tasmanian Devil' and in Queensland as the 'Great Barrier Reef' with a slight variation in its accoutrements. I was thus able to feel secure in knowing exactly what I was getting, while feeling that there had been some recognition of my need for choice and diversity. The franchise analogy was further reinforced by a placement with a chain of restaurants in England (Thody, 1994). Site management was relieved of any necessity to select the menu, its ingredients, its mode of production or delivery. Site management could concentrate on ensuring the business outlet was financially viable, the staff were happy and motivated and that the customers all received exactly the same sized lettuce leaf in the same place on the plate. Site management did not have to spend time considering how best to placate the possibly idiosyncratic views of an on-site group of around 15 non-specialists in catering or business.

Such an on-site group creates the financial, political and managerial expense of an extra policy making layer. The existence of such a layer provides the possibility of dissonance between the views of school's part-time and full-time managers and between central government and the periphery. This dissonance can give rise to disputes when both central and peripheral layers of government can claim public mandate as can government and governors. Local Education Authorities have had their powers reduced since 1986 arguably because of their dissonance with central government. Leaving school governing bodies in existence and with growing political maturity appears to provide the possibility of reproducing that dissonance again.

## Wait and do nothing

For those, like myself, who have long accepted that local citizen involvement is 'a good thing', who have been governors or have worked with governors, who have watched the impressive maturing of governors as the years of training have proceeded, and who fear a system in which central government power is untrammelled, the idea of abolition is too extreme and it did not find favour amongst the contributors to this book. The revived school governance tradition of England and Wales is too young for abolition; it has not yet had time to prove itself.

Political and managerial maturity take time to grow and perhaps we are expecting too much too soon. The roles will emerge in time. Governors need to develop experience and to acquire training. Admittedly, the four-year life span of a governing body militates against the development of experience but many governors serve longer than their four years. Terry Mahoney detailed how training has changed since its inception in the early 1980s (Chapter 12) and adjustments are continually being made to address political and managerial needs. The experience which governors have gained and are gaining could be seen as a valuable resource in the development of government for the twenty-first century. School governors are a possible model for the administration of states that have become too expensive and too distant from the ordinary citizens. Such innovatory roles take time to develop.

## Reduce expectations

While the innovatory roles are developing it is, however, possible to consider whether or not governance might be able to grow more realistically if there were fewer duties which governors had to perform.

Governors 'have a task that in most respects is impossible to perform' (Brehony, Chapter 4, p.61) and, as I have argued elsewhere (Thody, 1992), governors should restrict themselves to setting and monitoring policy direction rather than attempting to become involved in every aspect of its detailed implementation (which the law allows, directs and encourages them to do).

Is it possible, for example, that, with respect to democracy, we are expecting more from governors than from any of our other democratic institutions? Open citizens' meetings are not a device we use elsewhere in our political system yet governors are hoping to make a success of the Annual Parents' Meetings. None of our other elected bodies are socially, racially, gender or age representative yet we criticise governing bodies for not achieving width of representation. We expect governors to represent diverse views but with no mechanisms for contacting their electorates, with no assumption of mandate, with many governors not even elected and with no party mechanism to formulate a 'line'. Elsewhere in our political system, there has been an enormous growth in the numbers of non-elected, non-accountable quangos largely composed of paid personnel. Volunteer governors are expected to accept greater inspection and criticism than these quango members and for no financial return.

In terms of management, governors are running organisations with larger budgets and responsibilities than most of them do, or have, operated in their other employments. They are 'directing' staff who, generally, have larger salaries, higher qualifications and wider responsibilities than themselves. Cusack's New Zealand evidence (Chapter 7) indicates that governors' training and experience are helping governors to learn to cope efficiently and that governor training and experience is proving to be a major input in adult education. It also has to be remembered that in England (and in most of the other countries discussed in this book) schools have all become self-managing during the period in which governors have been acquiring their new powers. Hence there has been double learning to be achieved, i.e. both school management and governor management, by both governors and by school staff. The staff have not been well positioned to help to guide governors in their new roles while staff themselves have been learning new responsibilities.

## Define, statutorily, the division of roles and functions between governors and school principals

Is it now possible to define what governors do and if it is, should we define it? The feelings of the 1980s could be characterised as suggesting that there should be flexibility for governors to choose how they interpret their roles. Definition would be antithetical to our traditions of governance in which there is, as Anne Curtis made clear, 'no single correct model of "the governing body"' (p.97) but the time for allowing such freedom may be past if governance is to develop strongly. If it is desired to keep it weak, then the current diversity can be allowed to continue.

The outcome of this lack of definition could have been the present uneasy position of school governance; Stephen Brigley, for example, concluded that the 'vague and ill defined' role 'may not translate easily into effective strategies in unusual and testing political decisions' (p.73).

Perhaps the time has come to stop this freedom of choice especially as it has to be remade every four years. The division needs to be made between what constitutes the proper sphere of school staff in the day-to-day running of the school and of the governors in the effective oversight of school activities. Policy direction and service delivery need to be distinguished from each other and the word 'direction' needs to be tightly defined.

For example, in staff selection, it should be made clear that appointments below the level of deputy head are not part of the governors' sphere of duties. Governors should select the head (and possibly there should be mechanisms for re-confirmation of this selection every five years) and one governor should be directly involved in the whole process for selecting deputies. The Head and the deputies should then be wholly responsible for all other appointments. Only the senior school staff are in a position to judge how potential staff will fit into the existing teams and, generally, it is the staff who will have the knowledge to determine the acceptability, the professional qualifications and experience of applicants. The governors' part in the proceedings should be to have discussed the overall staffing needs of their schools as part of the annual planning cycle. The staffing needs plan should be the responsibility of the staff to produce, as an advisory document for the governors. An appropriate subcommittee of governors should decide how status is to be distributed amongst staffing needs, again through consideration of a plan suggested by staff. Allocation of salary to particular staff is a matter for staff, not governors, to decide.

Readers may like to continue this exercise in delineation. The aim is to define governors' roles and responsibilities much more rigorously so that new governors can quickly assimilate precisely what is required. In the process of this delineation, it should be made clear that not every governor is expected to undertake every aspect of governance. Each governor should be encouraged (or even required) to select particular activities in which to specialise. They do not then participate in other areas of the job.

Overall, there must be a reduction in the legal requirements for governors' actions. There should be the move to governors with influence, rather than with power, as Alastair Macbeth proposed for Scottish school boards (Chapter 11). More must be formally devolved to headteachers unless governors are to be paid and required to devote as much time to school governance as is expected, for example, of the non-executive directors of health service trusts.

**Alter training**

A menu of ideas from which to select, includes:

1. Make training compulsory. It must be undertaken before governors begin their work as governors. While

acknowledging the practical difficulties of organising this, the availability of multiple delivery technologies should make it possible.

2. Introduce a standardised, national induction course. This should consist of delineating the governors' roles and how they share responsibilities with staff (see above). It should explain precisely what governors should do in planning for and monitoring their schools and should explain that governors are not to be involved in the organisation and implementation of tasks. It should include instruction on political techniques in negotiating, information on how the education system is governed and familiarisation with the aims and objectives of education.
3. The national course should be made available in various modes e.g. video, interactive media, programmed texts, school based courses, off site courses.
4. National training should be examined. Governors who 'fail' should have to re-sit the course or cease to be governors.
5. Each governing body should have to establish a training plan to be annually revised. Each member of a governing body should undertake short courses in particular specialisms so that each governing body has a member cognisant of each of the aspects for which the governors are responsible.
6. Abolish training. Joan Sallis long since effectively characterised governors as being valuable for their 'enhanced ordinariness'. It is arguable that training stops governors being ordinary. They then cease to ask the questions which those they represent might ask and the supportive legitimation which has characterised governing bodies will continue. There is no training for MPs or for local councillors. Why should there be training for school governors?

**Reform structure and appointments**

Possible, though conflicting, developments include:

1. Reduce the size of governing bodies (perhaps a maximum of ten per school).
2. Restrict membership to elected parents, teachers and students.

3. Restrict membership to elected governors only and have no reserved categories such as business community governors.
4. Have quotas for governing bodies to achieve in respect of ensuring equitable representation for gender, age, race and occupations.
5. Have no parental representatives, since their span of interest is likely to be restricted in time and because their personal interests might bias their judgements.
6. Include elected student representatives in both primary and secondary schools. It is students who experience the outcomes of school governance, it is students who need training in active citizenship for their future roles in society and it is students who can feed back to their peers the explanations of why everything desired by students is not possible.
7. Statutorily designate an elected governorship place for non-teaching staff.
8. Reduce the period of appointment to two years in order to reduce what is being asked of individual citizens.
9. Increase the period of appointment to six years so that experience can be built up.
10. Make a period of governor service a requirement for all citizens, as is jury service.
11. Payment, at least for expenses, should be mandatory and should not be simply another charge on schools' budgets without an addition to what is already received.
12. Allow governors to be designated — MGB (Member of a Governing Body). MPs and JPs have such nomenclature acknowledgement so why not permit similar treatment for school governors?

**Establish mechanisms for accountability**

Altering the representative base of governing bodies is the first phase of establishing more effective mechanisms for accountability. At the moment, governors could be said to have a sense of responsibility to their community but there is no effective way of their ascertaining what their communities want nor any way in which their communities can call governors to account. Stephen Brigley discovered that 'Stricter levels of accountability which would have obliged governors to consult, listen to advice and even to act upon it were clearly not entertained' (p.74). Governors' accountability is to central government through the OFSTED mechanism.

The vagueness of local accountability arrangements in England and Wales may be because there was no formal consideration given to the restructuring of the whole of our educational administration before the changes in governance began. Reforms at central, local, regional, school and quango levels have proceeded independently of each other in contrast with, for example, New Zealand and the Australian states. Both David Gamage (Chapter 8) and Brian Cusack (Chapter 7) detailed processes of systems restructuring for which there has been no English and Welsh equivalent. It would not be possible for us to substitute 'England' for New Zealand in Brian's conclusion that 'The future of New Zealand schooling is in no doubt' and 'that future is in the control of school trustees' (p.109). David's conclusions on the future of Australian governance were less definitive than this but still clearer on the success of accountability mechanisms than we are in England and Wales.

What governors are supposed to be achieving, and to which model of citizenship they should be aspiring, need to be clarified before amendments can be made to accountability mechanisms. Once this is done, then it should be possible to select from amongst the ideas below but selection is less simple than it may appear. The role clarification that must precede any changes is likely to reveal that school governance does not function now to challenge governments at any level, as Richard Hatcher's analysis showed in Chapter 9. If accountability mechanisms are altered, so also may be the direction of power. Is the system able to cope with an empowered, active citizenry? Are governors willing to take on a more dominant and demanding role?

Possibilities for the reform of accountability are:

- all governors elected by the whole community of local property tax payers (moving more towards the school board model of the USA)
- election meetings to be held; putative governors to produce policy manifestos; active canvassing by governors to be permitted
- mechanisms for the removal of governors to be established
- governors to develop methods of consulting the whole community (questionnaires, referenda)
- governors to cease to have any decision making powers and to become clearly the monitors of the implementation of

central government policy in schools. Current mechanisms of accountability then become adequate

- governors and parents to be in 'a public partnership which holds them jointly responsible for the governance and development of the school' (Martin and Ranson, p.206)

## Visions of the future

From the evidence presented in this book two scenarios present themselves. In the best tradition of late twentieth century interactive literature, readers will be left to make their personal choice between the two.

### Vision I

Governing bodies will effectively hide where power really lies in the English and Welsh system of educational administration. They will legitimate the power of school principals. Governors will continue to be incorporated into the state, providing an illusion of democracy. This will not change because those with power have a vested interest in maintaining the status quo as do governors themselves who would not want more responsibilities. The demands on governors will give them little time to act collectively and most will want to 'fire fight' at the school level only.

### Vision II

Governing bodies will gradually empower themselves, learning from experience and from training how to govern schools and through this, how to acquire expertise in political operation. Their national associations will become effective lobby groups, creating the balance with central government and teachers that has declined as the local education authorities have lost power. Governors will evolve a feasible division of powers with their school principals and the work load will become, thereby, manageable. They will be a new power, setting the example of how volunteer citizens can operate the state's functions in the twenty-first century.

School governance has become a new arena for educational politics. It may be obscuring the reality of where power lies in the system as a whole and within schools themselves. It may be the future model for the management of the state by empowered citizens.

## Bibliography

Thody, A. M. (1992) *Moving to Management*, London: Fulton.
Thody, A. M. (1994) 'Thank God it's Friday', *Management in Education*, **8**, 1, p.5.

# Index